Invisible Asians

Asian American Studies Today

This series publishes scholarship on cutting-edge themes and issues, including broadly based histories of both long-standing and more recent immigrant populations; focused investigations of ethnic enclaves and understudied subgroups; and examinations of relationships among various cultural, regional, and socioeconomic communities. Of particular interest are subject areas in need of further critical inquiry, including transnationalism, globalization, homeland polity, and other pertinent topics.

Series Editor: Huping Ling, Truman State University

Stephanie Hinnershitz, *Race, Religion, and Civil Rights: Asian Students on the West Coast, 1900–1968*
Jennifer Ann Ho, *Racial Ambiguity in Asian American Culture*
Haiming Liu, *From Canton Restaurant to Panda Express: A History of Chinese Food in the United States*
Jun Okada, *Making Asian American Film and Video: History, Institutions, Movements*
Kim Park Nelson, *Invisible Asians: Korean American Adoptees, Asian American Experiences, and Racial Exceptionalism*
David S. Roh, Betsy Huang, and Greta A. Niu, eds., *Techno-Orientalism: Imagining Asia in Speculative Fiction, History, and Media*

Invisible Asians

Korean American Adoptees,
Asian American Experiences,
and Racial Exceptionalism

KIM PARK NELSON

RUTGERS UNIVERSITY PRESS

NEW BRUNSWICK, NEW JERSEY, AND LONDON

LIBRARY OF CONGRESS CATALOGING-IN-PUBLICATION DATA

Park Nelson, Kim.
    Invisible Asians : Korean American adoptees, Asian American experiences, and racial exceptionalism / Kim Park Nelson.
       pages cm.—(Asian American studies today)
       Includes bibliographical references and index.
       ISBN 978–0–8135–7067–9 (hardcover : alk. paper)—ISBN 978–0–8135–7066–2 (pbk. : alk. paper)—ISBN 978–0–8135–7068–6 (e-book (epub))—
ISBN 978–0–8135–7373–1 (e-book (web pdf))
       1. Interracial adoption—United States. 2. Korean Americans—Ethnic identity. 3. Asian Americans—Ethnic identity. 4. Adoptees—United States. 5. Intercountry adoption—Korea (South) 6. Intercountry adoption—United States. 7. Cultural pluralism—United States. I. Title.
    HV875.64.P36 2016
    362.778957073—dc23   2015021886

A British Cataloging-in-Publication record for this book is available from the British Library.

Copyright © 2016 by Kim Park Nelson

All rights reserved

No part of this book may be reproduced or utilized in any form or by any means, electronic or mechanical, or by any information storage and retrieval system, without written permission from the publisher. Please contact Rutgers University Press, 106 Somerset Street, New Brunswick, NJ 08901. The only exception to this prohibition is "fair use" as defined by U.S. copyright law.

Visit our website: http://rutgerspress.rutgers.edu

Manufactured in the United States of America

For my husband, Peter, without whom none of this would have been possible

CONTENTS

Acknowledgments ix
Note on Text xiii

Introduction: A History of Korean American Adoption in Print ... 1

1 A Korean American Adoption Ethnography: Method, Theory, and Experience ... 17

2 "Eligible Alien Orphan": The Cold War Korean Adoptee ... 41

3 Adoption Research Discourse and the Rise of Transnational Adoption, 1974–1987 ... 72

4 An Adoptee for Every Lake: Multiculturalism, Minnesota, and the Korean Transracial Adoptee ... 92

5 Adoptees as White Koreans: Identity, Racial Visibility, and the Politics of Passing among Korean American Adoptees ... 121

6 *Uri Nara*, Our Country: Korean American Adoptees in the Global Age ... 150

Conclusion: The Ends of Korean Adoption ... 189

Notes 195
Bibliography 215
Index 225

ACKNOWLEDGMENTS

A project like this can never be completed without lots of help, and this one is certainly no exception. Many thanks to my mentor, Erika Lee, who took on me and my project many years ago. Thanks also to Jo Lee, Rich Lee, and Sara Dorow for their encouragement, feedback, advice, and support.

I never could have completed this project without the support of colleagues, some of whom have become good friends. Thanks to the many scholars who have discovered and rediscovered Adoption Studies with me and worked to critically think about adoption in the United States and around the world, including Tobias Hübinette, Lene Myong, Jae Ran Kim, Laura Briggs, Kim McKee, Sarah Park Dahlen, Hollee McGinnis, Lee Herrick, Liz Raleigh, and Kit Myers, whose insights on transnational adoption have much sharpened my own. I also so appreciate having been included in the community of adoption scholarship that is the Alliance for the Study of Adoption and Culture (ASAC). The biannual ASAC conferences began around the time I began studying adoption, and they always challenge and inspire me. Many thanks to Marianne Novy, Cynthia Callahan, Emily Hipchen, Mark Jerng, and Marina Fedosik.

The research in this project included field work in Minnesota, the American Pacific Northwest, and Seoul, South Korea. I was based in Minneapolis, but I could rely heavily on many friends who supported me while I was traveling. Thanks to Su-Yoon Ko for her generous hospitality in Seoul, to Tim Holm and Jane Mauk for introducing me throughout the Pacific Northwest, to Kate and Mike Donchi for hosting me in Portland, and to Mark Ruebel for hosting me in Seattle. Thanks also to Dae-Won Wenger and Nicole Sheppard at GOAL Korea for supporting my travel to Seoul in 2006.

Special recognition goes to everyone at the International Korean Adoptee Associations (IKAA) for supporting the first, second, and third Korean Adoption Studies Research Symposium, and to everyone from AK Connection, Asian Adult Adoptees of Washington (AAAW), and Also Known As for supporting me in my work in the States.

Work in an interdisciplinary field such as Korean Adoption Studies requires meeting with colleagues in faraway places, so I owe a debt of gratitude to those who invited me to speak at conferences, meetings, summits, and lectures that doubled as networking opportunities to develop this and other projects. In this regard, I offer my gratitude to Bill Meyer, Peter Selman, Indigo Willing, Sarah Kim Park, and Stephen Sohn.

This project would have looked much different without the assistance of some highly skilled and extremely helpful librarians. I am in particular debt to librarians in the newspaper departments in the libraries of University of Minnesota, Twin Cities, and the University of Washington, Seattle. A special thanks to David Klaassen, now retired from the University of Minnesota Social Welfare History Archives. Thanks also to Brian Drischell at the Academy of Motion Picture Arts and Sciences for help finding Korean War films. And a shout-out to the many librarians at Twin Cities–area public and university libraries who expressed their outrage that so many of the runs of our two local dailies are so poorly indexed.

In the time I was working on this project, I also had the opportunity to collaborate on other Korean adoption projects, and working with other artists and scholars certainly helped shape my thinking on this project. Thank you to Deann Borsay Liem, Kim Dalros Jackson, Kim Langrehr, Nate Kupel, and Katie Hae Leo.

I was also lucky enough to get some professional advice for this project from supportive friends, so thanks to Lisa Ellingson and Dainen Penta for their legal advice, and thanks to Paul Lai for feedback on the book proposal for this volume.

Thanks also to all who have taken time to read, review, and give feedback, including Catherine Ceniza Choy and other reviewers of this manuscript, and to Katie Keeran, Leslie Mitchner, and Lisa Boyajian at Rutgers University Press.

Many good friends who have been enormously helpful on this project have also become colleagues; all happen to also be Korean adoptees. Thanks to Lisa Ellingson, Heewon Lee, Jae Ran Kim, Lisa Medici, Sun Yung Shin, Jane Jeong Trenka, and Jennifer Weir for your support and feedback. You have helped me realize what it means to be part of a community of Korean adoptees. Your friendship, laughter, and tears have meant much to me.

Thanks also to the past and present members at Potluck for friendship and weekly sustenance. I've broken bread and been in conversation with this group on a weekly basis for over ten years, and its members have provided me both a sounding board for and a respite from the ideas I have worked out in this scholarship.

A special thanks to Eleana Kim, my longest colleague and collaborator. Her friendship has meant as much to me as her fine intellect.

I must also recognize Peter Bischoff, the first other adoptee with whom I discussed my thoughts on adoption, and with whom my critical assessment of the practice of transracial adoption began, many years ago. I am grateful to him for this experience.

A very special thank-you to each of the sixty-six adult Korean adoptees who officially participated in this research as oral history contributors, and to the many other adoptees who unofficially participated. This work would not have been possible without these adoptees and the generosity with which they shared their life experiences.

Finally, I wish to thank and acknowledge Peter Park Nelson, whose faith in me and this project began with its inception and has never wavered. He has read these pages more often than anyone save myself. He has been a precise editor as well as an ardent supporter of this work in every way. He is a cherished spouse who has been both remarkably tolerant of my many absences related to this work, and exceptionally loving, helpful, and supportive. I am so grateful to have found him.

NOTE ON TEXT

Transracial or *interracial* adoptions are the adoptions of children of one race by parents of another race; these adoptions take place *domestically* or *in-country* (used interchangeably here). *Transnational, international, or intercountry* (used interchangeably here) *adoptions* are the adoptions of children with citizenship in one country by parents with citizenship in another, and are often also transracial adoptions. In this book, as in much of the related literature, transracial adoption can refer to both domestic and transnational transracial adoptions; most (but not all) transnational adoptions are transracial.

I acknowledge that the terms *adoptee* and *birth parent* are considered politically inappropriate by some when used to refer to, respectively, adopted persons and biological parents of adoptees, and that sometimes *adopted Korean* or *adopted person,* and *first mother, first family*, or *biological parent*, respectively, is preferred terminology. I use these terms without intent to attach political or social significance to them. I prefer the term *adoptee,* in particular, partly because it is still in common parlance inside adoption communities and in the general public, and simply because it is a single word that simplifies the task of writing about this population. I use the terms *birth family/birth mother/birth father* because these are the terms interview subjects used most commonly when referring to biological family. I do not use these terms with the intention of opposing any group or groups of activists in adoption-related communities.

Except where noted, a reference to *Korea* is meant to indicate *South Korea.* This is not intended to suggest a primacy of South Korea over North Korea, but instead reflects the way Korean American adoptees, who have only ever been adopted from South Korea, refer to the nation of their birth.

Invisible Asians

Introduction

A History of Korean American Adoption in Print

On May 25, 1953, during the last weeks of fighting of the Korean War, a pictorial with the headline "100,000 Korean Children Are War Orphans" ran in the *Minneapolis Morning Tribune*. The brief article described the plight of children in Korea separated from their families ("orphaned," in the language of the article) during the war (see fig. 1). Buried on page 20 of the paper, the article was as much a call to action as war reportage. The focus on the children of war was nothing new, but articles like this, in newspapers across the country, ultimately led to a completely new method of family building: transnational adoption on demand and without end, supported by a new globalized adoption industry. Overseas adoption from South Korea would continue for the next sixty years—long after the country had recovered from the effects of war—and the South Korean adoption program with the United States would serve as a model for many other countries that sought to send children away for overseas adoption, as well as for richer and more powerful nations where desire for adoptable children would fuel the most privileged form of contemporary immigration to the global West and North. Beginning at a time when Asian immigration to the United States was virtually prohibited, this population of Asian child migrants to America would eventually number over 100,000; advocacy for them as the children of White Americans would give them easy access to immigration and citizenship in comparison to most other immigrants.

Newspaper coverage continued to document the arrival of Korean children to the United States as the adopted sons and daughters of American citizens.[1] As the practice of Korean-to-American adoption became more and more common, certain tropes used to explain and normalize the practice of Korean adoption became established: the miserable Asian orphan; the child rescued by a valiant American family; and the completely assimilated Americanized adoptee.[2]

FIGURE 1. Full article layout, "100,000 Korean Children Are War Orphans," *Minneapolis Morning Tribune*, May 25, 1953.

INTRODUCTION

[handwritten annotation: narrative of American moral & economic superiority]

The depiction of the pitiful orphan in Korean adoption discourse is part of a long-established practice of sentimental media depictions of children in order to develop political will around nationalist policies by eliciting sympathies for children caught in far-away conflicts.[3] In drawing attention to these victims of America's Cold War ambitions, who would be invisible otherwise, coverage of the suffering children in postwar South Korea reinforced a narrative of American moral and economic superiority.

Early media coverage of Korean adoption frequently focused on the actions of American military personnel as child rescuers. This accurately reflected the military's role in the very earliest Korean adoptions, those of so-called mascots, children unofficially adopted by military units in Korea and who went on to be among the first officially adopted into American families.[4] Emphasis on the humanitarian qualities of American military involvement in Korea also served to drum up popular support for participation in a conflict that divided opinion in an America still war-weary after the end of the Second World War.

In a typical example, from the *Seattle Times* in 1958, "Korean Child Welcomes Rescuer Here"[5] documents the arrival of Korean adoptee Joy Lynn, née Chun Cha, to the United States to join her American new family, but mostly focuses on Army Captain Boyd Clearwater, her supposed savior (see fig. 2). In the article, Clearwater is described as "adopting" an orphanage in Taegu, Korea, helping

FIGURE 2. Photograph from *Seattle Times* article "Korean Child Welcomes Rescuer Here," *Seattle Times*, October 26, 1958.

to support it by arranging for donations from the United States, then making arrangements for Chun Cha's legal adoption by the Bollinger family shortly before his own return to the United States. The article highlights a special relationship between Chun Cha and Clearwater, reporting that the child "thought that he had deserted her when he was making arrangements for her adoption,"[6] underlining the parental duty of the United States through its army. Appearing five years after the Korean armistice, this depiction of the relationship between the adoptee and the soldier symbolically represents the relationship between infantilized, war-torn Korea and the paternal figure of the American military, at a time when Americans were already beginning to forget the first U.S. failure to achieve military victory in Asia.[7] News accounts of Korean adoption with similar pro-military overtones continued to appear throughout the Vietnam War and well into the 1970s, reinforcing the narrative of America's Cold War military engagements as humanitarian acts and contributing to the image of American soldiers as the "good guys," despite increasing public opposition to U.S. military intervention in Asia.

"Adopted Koreans Fully 'Americanized,'" published in 1975 in the *Seattle Times*, made strong connections both to the military beginnings of Korean adoption and to the successful assimilation of Korean adoptees, positioning them as all-American (though the quotation marks in 'Americanized' in the article's title leaves some room for question), remarking on the kids' love of baseball and hot dogs (see fig. 3).[8] The article profiles several Korean adoptees who arrived in the United States in the late 1950s, one of whom is the adult Joy Lynn/Chun Cha from the 1958 article. Six joined the family of U.S. Army Sergeant Ogan, which is positioned as exceptional for taking on so many extra children. Journalist Chet Skreen even lists the amount the Ogans paid in adoption fees, but makes sure to note that the Ogan parents have no regrets. The article, written to compare the Vietnamese Operation Babylift, to Korean adoption twenty-plus years before, reassures readers that Vietnamese adoptees will grow up well-adjusted, well-assimilated, and happy. The article ends with a quote from Mrs. Bergstrom, the parent of another profiled Korean adoptee, who recommends adopting additional children from Asia as protection against any problems they might experience. She remarks, "They can at least share the hurts. Actually you forget they are adopted."[9] Calling attention to the Korean-ness of adoptees, in articles like this one, is necessary only to highlight the much more important greatness of the American military and nuclear family; it is the purposeful overlooking of the adoptees' Asianness that makes the adoptive family heroic. Forgetting the reality of adoption was a key part of normalizing adoptive families, and, to forget adoption, the most visible sign of difference between parents and children, race, had to be overlooked. This forgetting also rendered the stories of adoptees themselves less visible when compared to stories of adoptive parents. In this

FIGURE 3. Image emphasizing the Americanization of Korean adoptees in the United States, from Chet Skreen's August 10, 1975, *Seattle Times Magazine* article. The original caption reads: "Philip Ogen, and his brother, Peter, prepared for a Little League baseball game."

way, adoptee Asianness is elided, except to remind readers that adoptees were rescued from a bad (Asian) place. By 1975, the American story of transnational adoption was already framed, in articles such as this, as a win-win situation for Asian adoptees and their White American parents: adoptive parents are celebrated, assimilation is easy, and adoptees are happy.

The idea of adoption as win-win for both adoptive family and adoptee had taken shape: adoptive parents gaining much-wanted children and fulfilling the role of American heroes by saving children from backward and faraway places; adoptees, configured as onetime pitiful orphans, enjoying better lives and greater opportunities through adoption, the fortunate fall of their abandonment and displacement allowing them to become Americans. Not surprisingly, in this configuration, Korean adoption fit neatly into larger American ideologies privileging the primacy of the United States and the American family, the backwardness of the global East and South, and the power of an individual to make a difference.

As adoption from Korea to the United States increased throughout the 1970s and 1980s, newspaper coverage shifted from news sections to lifestyle sections. In articles of this period, international adoption in the United States, still dominated by adoption from Korea, was practically sold to the public both through the depiction of the heroism of internationally adoptive parents (as in the 1981 St. Paul Dispatch article "Adoptive Parents Find Love Has No Race or Color") and as a way for American families to be culturally enriched at a time of increasing interest in multiculturalism (as in the 1970 Minneapolis Star article "Interracial Adoption Could Enrich Lives, Suburb Women Told"). Although the focus of reporting remained on child salvation and the heroism of child-saviors, the role of savior shifted from the American military to the (almost always White) American family. Until recently, transnational adoption has been consistently portrayed in feel-good terms, in marked contrast to the treatment of other racial issues in American public discourse. Large multinational and multiracial families were celebrated both for taking in children not biologically related to the parents, and for these parents' ability to look past race in their choice of family formation. Adopted children are depicted as lucky, and also as normal, largely unracialized in their White families, living just as White children would. Implied is that not only are these adopted children lucky to have been adopted, they are lucky to have escaped race, which doesn't exist in their adoptive homes. In newspaper articles such as these, transnational adoptees are held up as a racial exception, a rare bright spot in the difficult history of American race relations.

Although much of the news coverage of transnational and transracial adoption from the 1970s to the 1990s emphasized the benefits of multiculturalism and progressive ideology in adoptive families, indications of White privilege, cultural appropriation, and the problematic implications of racial colorblindness can be discerned between the lines. In the 1970 Minneapolis Star article "Interracial Adoption Could Enrich Lives, Suburb Women Told," transracial adoption is explicitly configured as an antiracist act. The article details how problems of racism are brought into families by social institutions like schools and churches, and puts forward adopting a non-White child as one possible solution to racism. However, in the same article, an adoptive mother proudly states that "any child that doesn't have a home needs one, and it doesn't make any difference if they are blue-eyed Caucasians, or curly-haired Negroes, or slant-eyed Koreans."[10]

In the 1981 St. Paul Dispatch article "Adoptive Parents Find Love Has No Race or Color," reporter Kay Harvey maintains a focus on sentimental, colorblind love (see fig. 4).[11] The article opens with the poignant statement "Love has a long arm." Harvey continues, "And some Twin Cities couples have reached across oceans."[12] The Carter parents are depicted as raising their Korean children using the pro–birth culture attitude that adoption workers had, by that time, come to

the power of love over Racial difference

FIGURE 4. Full layout of first page of Kay Harvey's article "Adoptive Parents Find Love Has No Race or Color," *St. Paul Dispatch*, April 21, 1981.

embrace and encourage. Still, the emphasis remains on the power of love over racial difference. While the Carters themselves mostly speak about the logistical procedures of transnational adoption and the advances in adoption practice ("not secretive like it used to be"),[13] Harvey highlights the Carters' success in family building despite racial differences. The Carters themselves never mention race in the article, but the reportage keeps its focus on the racial dynamics, or the absence thereof, nonetheless.

Although news stories about the racial harmony of transnationally adoptive families continue to be published today, a more complex discussion of the racial and cultural identities of Korean adoptees began to appear in the 1990s, when a sizeable number of Korean adoptees had reached adulthood, and adoptees themselves began to figure as primary sources for reporters. Some articles continued to focus on adoption as a method of family building, such as the 1999 article "Native Instincts: More Foreign Adoptees Are Returning to Their Homelands When They Choose to Adopt, Themselves," about a Korean adoptee who chose to adopt from Korea.[14] Other articles began to examine questions of identity in the context of transracial adoption. A 1996 article, "Now I'm Found" (see fig. 5), authored by *Star Tribune* staff writer and Korean adoptee Crystal Lee Hyun Chappell, provides an early example of an adoptee perspective on Korean adoption. Chappell opens with her own adoption story, which features elements common to many Korean adoptee life stories: tragedy in the biological family, culture shock in the United States, deep feelings of loss, racial awakening, birth

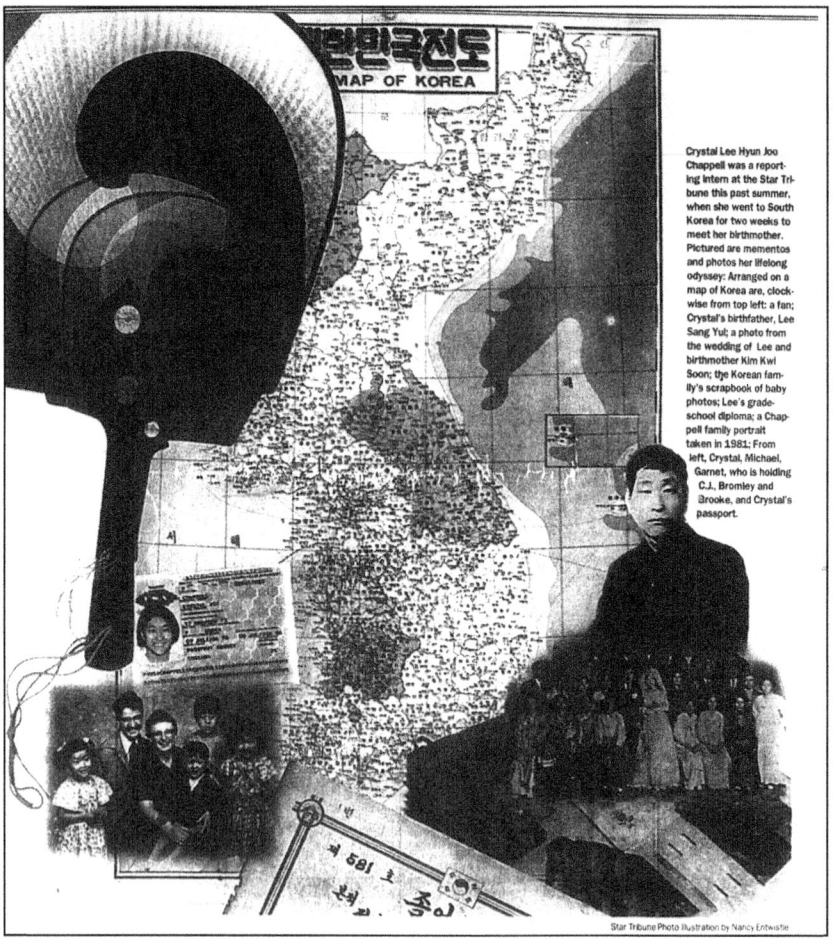

FIGURE 5. Graphic collage of materials provided by Korean adoptee journalist Crystal Lee Hyun Joo Chappell to accompany her autobiographical story, "Now I'm Found," *Minneapolis Star Tribune*, December 29, 1996.

search, and return to Korea. The title, evoking the lines "I once was lost, but now I'm found," from the well-known spiritual "Amazing Grace," represents a reversal of the way Korean adoption stories had been reported in the past, when readers were to understand Korean children to have been lost in Korea and found in America. Chappell's article is the story of her finding herself by reconnecting with Korea and Korean family, begging the question: was Chappell lost in the United States?

Accompanying graphics in "Now I'm Found" are notable in depicting the multiple facets of Korean adoptee identity, rather than a more typical happy family portrait (still included as one part of the collage). Although much past coverage of Korean adoption had focused on the positive impacts of adoption, later adoptee-focused stories turned the spotlight on losses inherent in the adoption process and experienced by both adoptees and biological family. Chappell's story is accompanied by a list of organizations that assist adoptees in the birth search process, as well as an additional article (also authored by Chappell) about local Korean adoptee-run organizations established to support the large Korean adoptee population in Minnesota (estimated by Chappell to be 12,000 at the time).[15] Although Chappell never makes an explicit critique of Korean adoption policy or practice, the appearance—after forty years of reportage on international adoption as a "win-win-win" solution for birth countries, birth parents, receiving countries, adoptive parents, and adoptees themselves—of an adoptee perspective that reflects loss of any kind represents a remarkable change in coverage of Korean adoption. Chappell's article and other early narratives by Korean adoptees presage the arrival of a wave of Korean adoptee voices that would reshape American adoption discourses and foreground adoptee experiences in our understanding of transnational adoption.

In reading news accounts, the dominant narrative of transnational and transracial adoption as a remedy for racism, or at least as evidence that racial divides in the United States are mending, comes into sharp focus. Literary scholar Mark Jerng describes this phenomenon as transracial and transnational adoption implicitly constructing a narrative of racial and national integration, measuring adoption in terms of ideals of racial equality and national integrity.[16] The belief that transnational or transracial adoption could be a "cure" racism has been strongly critiqued by scholars who trace the racist origins and heavily racialized practice of transnational adoption. Catherine Ceniza Choy points out the ironic fact that the adoptees in question would probably have never experienced themselves as negatively racialized had they stayed in their birth countries, and that a history of racialized American military action created the very situation the media claimed the American military could solve.[17] Recent ethnographic research on Korean adoption makes it clear that transracial adoptive families have not been "cured of racism" through transracial adoption; many adoptees report racist beliefs and attitudes in their White families. As summarized by Mia Tuan and Jiannbin Lee Shiao, "White parents and kin with questionable racial views were able to fully love the nonwhite children in their lives without having to examine their own prejudice or alter their attitudes toward other groups. In fact, they could point to their children as proof of their tolerance without ever owning up to the fact that they had all but recast them as white."[18] Kristi Brian identifies racism toward African Americans within Korean adoptive families.[19]

There is another way of thinking about Korean adoption in the context of American racial politics. Through experiences of Korean adoption, I critically examine race, both as it is understood by Korean adoptees within their (usually) White families, and as it is understood and produced in American society. Popular understanding of the importance of race has shifted since the 1950s, and I pay special attention to the mainstream embrace of popular concepts of multiculturalism in the 1980s and 1990s. As Americans have changed from being color-conscious to being colorblind, Korean adoptees—who often describe themselves as "raised White"—see themselves racially in every possible permutation of Asianness, Whiteness, and racelessness, even though most grow up in almost entirely White families and communities.

Most Korean adoptees, whether they are part of the small group of biracial adoptees, or are (to the best of their knowledge) so-called full-blooded Koreans, appear to others to be Korean, or at least Asian. Their outward appearance, which is usually markedly different from other members of their American adoptive families, is an important factor in their self-understanding, because it plays a large part in how they are perceived by those around them. When they are seen by people outside the family, they are often immediately understood to have been adopted, for there seems no other explanation for a White family to have Asian offspring. This is especially true in places like Minnesota, where many people either know Asian adoptees or have friends, neighbors, or family members who have adopted Asian children. Away from their adoptive families, Korean adoptees are understood as Asian or Asian American, and are subject to all the stereotypes that accompany that racial designation. Within the family and immediate community, Korean adoptees are often seen as White. Sometimes this can help reinforce the belonging of adoptees as part of White families and communities, instead of placing them in the awkward position of being the racial odd ones out.

There is little agreement on the meaning of racial identity within Korean adoptee communities. Although some adoptees welcome the opportunity to be identified with Asian or Asian American populations, others reject such identities, perhaps because of the heavy burden of racialization in America. Until recently, the discipline of Asian American Studies was largely silent on the existence of Korean and other Asian adoptees, despite the fact that Korean adoptees comprise a significant fraction of the Korean American population in the United States, and Asian adoptees have been made highly visible in the American media.

If we accept race as a social construct, identity formations of Korean adoptees force us to ponder whether Korean adoptees are Asian American, or if they are White if they claim they are White. Similar questions arise for Korean American adoptive families, who claim they are Asian American. In addition, we must question why and how the performance of race (Whiteness or Asianness), or the lack of such a performance, may be beneficial or detrimental to racialized individuals like Korean adoptees. Though an examination of Korean adoption, we can better understand the effects of race and colorblindness on the individuals who are asked to enact it, largely in the absence of a community of people of the same race.

Chapter Descriptions

The participants in my research were adult adoptees born between 1949 and 1983. Although I had not originally intended to look at Korean adoption from a historical perspective, I found that the practice had changed so much over its history that adoptees' experiences could not be understood without reference to the changes in American culture since the mid-twentieth century. This exploration has led me to understand Korean American adoption in multiple contexts: as a social phenomenon that reflects the evolution of American race relations; as a frequently overlooked yet historically significant aspect of the geopolitical relationship between South Korea and the United States during and after the Cold War; as a bellwether of increasing economic and cultural globalization; and as a foundation of a worldwide community of people deeply touched by personal experiences of adoption.

All these contexts have affected Korean American adoptees' life experiences as American people of color, as Korean Americans, and as adoptees. The Korean War produced the first Korean adoptees as war orphans and GI babies. The Cold War gave cultural impetus to humanitarian projects in Asia such as child-saving through adoption. The changing state of American race relations carried Korean adoptees and their families through mainstream ideologies of assimilation, color consciousness, and then colorblindness, changing how Korean adoptees experienced their racial identities through the years. Finally, as a sustained project of immigration and transmigration that began even before the liberalization of American immigration law in 1965, Korean adoption anticipated globalization movements that emerged at the close of the twentieth century. In the current practice of Korean adoption, wherein adoptees easily cross borders back and forth between the United States and Korea, many adoptees see the gaps between Korean birth families and American adoptive families as more significant than the division of countries by citizenship, borders, or oceans.

Several themes emerged from the rich and voluminous ethnographic material that the many Korean adoptee participants in this project volunteered. Since Korean adoption has been ongoing since 1953, adult adoptee populations today span at least two generations, and adoptees are generationally marked in their understandings of race, identity, and adoption itself. The oldest Korean adoptees, born of the Korean War and the early Cold War, are a small minority among Korean adoptees, yet this generation has greatly influenced public perceptions of those who came later. Many Americans still understand Korean and other transnational adoptees as the pitiable orphans of sad circumstance, even though South Korea is over sixty years removed from war and is now one of the richest nations in Asia. As American society increasingly embraced multiculturalism, a later, larger generation of adoptees grappled with issues around identity as Asian Americans, Koreans, and adoptees. Their experiences led them to create a number of Korean adoptee social organizations, and laid the foundations for a growing adoptee culture. A small subset of this generation has moved back to South Korea, permanently or semi-permanently, and their experiences place them at the leading edge of an emergent Korean adoptee transnationality as they live, work, and travel back and forth between the United States and South Korea.

Chapter 1, "A Korean American Adoption Ethnography: Method, Theory, and Experience," describes my position as a Korean American adoptee researching adoption, and explains how my position as a within-group researcher has influenced my approach to this research. As a multidisciplinary scholar, I have drawn on practices and methods that best serve the subject matter, whether they come from history, narrative studies, popular culture studies, economics, political theory, or ethnography, so as to understand the depth and breadth of a long and complex story. Although the core of this work is ethnographic material in the form of adult Korean adoptee oral histories, I have also explored cultural production by and about Korean adoptees, delved into the archives of organizations involved in adoption, and researched the geopolitics, history, and cultural theory of Korean American adoption. I rely on oral history narrative as an important tool to understand meaning in the everyday details, the social and political beliefs, and the behaviors of this vibrant community within the larger changing American society. Throughout my ethnographic research on Korean American adult adoptees, I have made adjustments as my position relative to my work and to the adoptee community of which I am a part has changed. A key concept in interpreting these shifting positions is my location as either (and sometimes neither) an insider (n)or an outsider in the community and world of Korean American adoption. This is especially true in regard to communities of Korean adoptees, within which my access to so-called native informants is complicated by the possibility of my own position as a native informant.

Chapter 2, "'Eligible Alien Orphan': The Cold War Korean Adoptee," focuses on the experiences of the first generation of Korean adoptees, those adopted in the 1950s and 1960s. Many of these adoptees were Korean War orphans in the immediate aftermath of that Cold War conflict. In many ways, the current cultural role of the Korean American adoptee was set during the 1950s and 1960s, largely as a result of popular media coverage. The broadly understood narrative of the child orphaned by war and rescued through adoption by benevolent

Americans has its roots in this generation. The victim-orphans, enmeshed in a web of Cold War political upheaval, needed advocates, and were imagined to have a place in American society under the protective care of White American families. These initial adoptees were powerful symbols of American superiority in the cultural Cold War, and their hypervisibility as Asian foreigners quickly transitioned as these children became a Cold War success story as all-American children in loving American families. Thus, the trope of the Korean adoptee as exceptional (in terms of cultural assimilation, psychological adjustment, and/or social success) among American peoples of color and/or among immigrant populations began with this small group of adoptees—who are now the elders of the Korean adoptee community in the United States and throughout the world.

Chapter 3, "Adoption Research Discourse and the Rise of Transnational Adoption, 1974–1987," reviews and analyzes applied research on transnational and transracial adoption from the 1970s and 1980s in order to confront biases and assumptions that would lead to outcomes recommending the continuation and expansion of transnational adoption. These ingrained biases have greatly influenced social policy decisions and public perceptions of transracial adoptees; here I analyze this body of work as an important influence on public discourse and beliefs about transnational adoption. In many cases, researchers in this period have chosen to base their definition of success in transracial adoption on the experiences of White adoptive parents rather than on the experiences of adoptees. Although issues of race, class, and gender have been discussed frequently, in-depth exploration of the meaning of race in the lives of transracial and transnational adoptees and in American society has been largely absent. A large volume of research on transracial and transnational adoption has been completed since this period, and this work, especially since 2000, has been much more nuanced and thoughtful around issues of race, gender, and class; as a result, research since 2000 is much less enthusiastic about the expansion of transnational adoption. However, the outdated social work and social policy research published in the 1970s and 1980s remains more influential than this newer work on public perceptions of transracial and transnational adoption.

Chapter 4, "An Adoptee for Every Lake: Minnesota, Multiculturalism, and the Korean Transracial Adoptee," describes Korean adoptee experiences in Minnesota, home to the largest per capita population of Korean adoptees in the United States, and highlights ways this population is failed by popular forms of multiculturalism that celebrate diversity. Using ethnographic materials, this chapter explores Korean adoptee experiences in Minnesota, and the many historical and sociocultural structures that have produced the high concentration of Korean adoptees in this state. Many Minnesotan adult adoptees in their thirties and forties worked through the complicated process of identity formation in an environment of weak liberal multiculturalism, and the identities that emerged incorporated critiques of multiculturalist ideologies, critiques that celebrated adoptees' difference but did not protect them from overt anti-Asian racism or the effects of racial isolation in a state that remains overwhelmingly White.

Chapter 5, "Adoptees as White Koreans: Identity, Racial Visibility, and the Politics of Passing among Korean American Adoptees," theorizes the racial position of Korean adoptees between the poles of Whiteness and Asianness. In this chapter, I discuss the politics of colorblindness in adoptive family formations and in greater society, and contextualize Korean adoptees (only some of whom consider themselves Asian American) within common stereotypes of Asian Americans. The intrafamilial structures that emphasize sameness to reinforce family unity—including White acculturation within family experiences, the minimization of adoptees' experiences of discrimination, the absence of positive Asian American racial identity, and relative racial isolation, in addition to poplar stereotypes of Asians as model minorities—all contribute to the choice made by many Korean adoptees to self-identity as White. Whether adoptees choose to enact a White or a non-White identity, they exist at the edge of a White/Asian American color line; I argue that they often cross and recross that line, enacting identities that are sometimes White, sometimes Asian. In this way, Korean American adoptee identity defies dominant racial or cultural categorizations, embodying truly multiracial and multicultural experiences,.

Chapter 6, "*Uri Nara*, Our Country: Korean American Adoptees in the Global Age," focuses on the experiences of Korean adoptees who were child migrants to the United States and returned as adults to South Korea, overlaying this ethnographic material with a critical examination of changing immigration regulations in both countries. The personal stories and immigration experiences of these return migrants connect transnational exchanges, American race relations, and Asian American experiences. Korean American adoptees who have returned to live and work in the nation of their birth are in a sense global citizens who possess both the American economic and cultural capital to live as expatriates and the Korean ethnic connections to gain a foothold in South Korea. But despite these apparent advantages, adoptees face exclusion as foreigners in both countries.

A (Final) Introductory Note

On Monday, October 14, 1974, an article titled "Multiracial Adoption Was Couple's Need" (see fig. 6) ran in the Family Life section of the *St. Paul Pioneer Press*. The article was similar to other stories written at the time about Korean and other transracial adoptions. These articles, in contrast to others focusing on

FIGURE 6. The Gregg family, from "Multiracial Adoption Was Couple's Need," by Cynthia Boyd, *St. Paul Pioneer Press*, October 14, 1974.

praising "successful" assimilation, were influenced by the progressive race politics of recent civil rights struggles. Instead of championing racelessness as a strategy to smooth out differences in adoptive families, the article highlighted the new (in 1974) race-and-culture-aware thinking in adoption agencies and in society. The family profiled, the Greggs, were portrayed as the model transracially and transnationally adoptive family, having adopted a Korean girl and mixed-race African American boy not because of infertility but out of humanitarian interests, and because their own lives were immersed in racial and cultural pluralisms. Families such as this were held up as embodiments of progressive thinking about race. The Greggs lived in a mixed-race and mixed-class neighborhood, attended an inner-city church with a mixed-race congregation, and both worked as educators in the racially diverse Twin Cities public school systems. The parents were proud of the racial awareness their young children already had and acknowledged the racism the kids were already facing. Through one family's story, this article seemed to promise a bright future for children raised in multicultural adoptive families in a new pluralistic and race-aware society.

I found this article while collecting newspaper reports about Korean adoption in the Twin Cities, but I was already familiar with its contents because it had been clipped from the newspaper in 1974 and tucked into a brown folder with all the other papers relevant to my own adoption. My scholarly interest in adoption began as a natural outgrowth of my own experiences as an adoptee, and I share the experience of being written about, surveyed, and studied as a Korean American adoptee. The Greggs, my parents, were profiled when I was three years old, and this article was the first piece of published writing about my adoption. This volume represents the most recent writing about my, and many other Korean adoptee experiences. As part of the first generation of Korean adoptee scholars writing about adoption, I am both professionally and personally aware of the shifting representations of transnational and transracial adoption in the popular press and in academic research. I am very pleased to have had the opportunity to speak to so many other Korean American adoptees and to expand on the meanings of Korean adoption in America both as a scholar and as an adoptee.

1

A Korean American Adoption Ethnography

Method, Theory, and Experience

[I] can see you can understand . . . why I feel the way I do and why I'm talking about what I'm talking [about]. . . . Thank you . . . I don't have to worry about explaining myself. . . . I think a lot . . . I think you know 99.9 percent of it all is . . . [Sighs.] I was a misplaced human being. I don't think that I should have come here.

Nadine, fifty-two years old,
on why she chose to participate in this oral history project[1]

When I embarked on the project of collecting oral histories from a population (Korean adoptees) of which I am a member, I had two major goals. The first was to understand, and help others to understand, the experience of Korean American adoptees as a powerful lens through which to understand the multiplicities of Asian American identity, American race relations, U.S.-Asian foreign relations, and historical changes in the American family. The second goal was to expand, correct, and augment stories about transnational and transracial adoptees. Much of the previous research in this area has been positioned to influence policy affecting transracial and transnational adoption, but, despite claims that these studies are undertaken for adoptees, the perspectives of transracial and transnational adoptees themselves are often deemphasized. In an industry (and, I would argue, a body of research) that privileges adoptive parents and rich nations over birth parents and poor nations, supporting adoptees in a research context is crucial. In the course of this project, I have come to realize that I also have a third goal: to develop a methodological niche as a within-group researcher, and to understand and describe the benefits and liabilities of such a position.

In the interest of transparency, it is necessary for me to disclose my position as a Korean adoptee active within the local transracial/transnational adoption community, and as a scholar at odds with many methods and findings within transracial/transnational adoption research. I am a former board member of my local adult adopted Korean organization, am an organizer for research conferences for adoptees, and have a broad network of connections to many others in the Korean adoptee community nationally and internationally. My central criticism of past transracial adoption research is that it tends to focus on parents as the primary agents of adoption processes, even when the researchers claim to be focusing on adoptees. In addition, I have critical concerns about the tendency within the American adoption industry (including adoption agencies, social workers, parent groups, and national governments) to interpret high cultural assimilation and normalization of adoptees as a measure of adoption success. I am ambivalent toward the practice of transnational adoptions (which are often also transracial adoptions); the more I have learned, the more objections I have to how the vast majority of adoptions are carried out. However, I also understand that transnational adoptions continue to take place, and the overall rate of transnational adoptions may continue to increase; as the number of children adopted from one sending country falls, other countries take its place. I continue to advocate for changes in the profoundly flawed structures of transnational adoption, changes that acknowledge the difficulty of the transracial adoption experience for many adoptees, and the sense of nonbelonging and alienation many experience within their families and communities. Nevertheless, a blanket rejection of the practice of transnational and transracial adoption does not, in my view, help adoptees or those who will become adoptees, whose interests I most deeply share.

This research has deep personal implications for me. My initial motivation was born of my impassioned response to the lack of information about my own experience. I felt that my experience had been overlooked and that the experience of thousands of transracial adoptees was being disregarded and subsumed into a middle-American (which I broadly defined as White, heterosexual, and middle-class) experience even though, I strongly believed, the life experience of transracial adoptees was generally distinct from that of most White Americans. (Of course, for many transracial adoptees, the envelopment into Whiteness was the prescribed goal.) As I became more intellectually engaged in these topics, I saw transracial adoption as a lens through which to understand intersections of race, culture, class, gender, and sexuality. Particularly in regard to race and culture, transracial adoptees are in the unusual position of developing our racial identities separately from our cultural identities. Further, transracial adoption, which today is often transnational adoption, complicates projects of imperialism and nationalism as transnational adoptees become visible markers of differences between the global West and East, North and South, rich and poor, imperial and colonized, and White and non-White.

The Decision to Collect Oral Histories

In his introduction to *Cultural Compass: Ethnographic Explorations of Asian America*, Martin Manalansan notes that much of Asian American Studies research and theory has focused on literary and popular media rather than on ethnographic work. As an Asian Americanist anthropologist, Manalansan articulates the need for ethnographic work in Asian American Studies as a meaningful way of knowing. Although his discussion of the influence of postmodern theory on ethnographic work acknowledges the importance of literary and cultural criticism to the field, he calls for multi-sited ethnographic work and "community-based research" in Asian American Studies.[2] Likewise, Jeffrey W. Burroughs and Paul Spickard stress the importance of community narrative in the understanding of ethnicity, particularly in groups with multiple ethnic or racial identities.[3] France Winddance Twine, in her introduction to *Racing Research, Researching Race: Methodological Dilemmas in Critical Race Studies*, advocates a transformation of ethnic studies fieldwork by considering complexities around the significance of insider and outsider positions occupied by researchers working in community contexts.[4] Both Manalansan and Twine consider the critical importance of native researchers; Manalansan writes that both researchers and their subjects "are now apprehended as producers as well as products of history, and shapers and builders of culture."[5] Their suggestion that researchers from within communities may empower those communities is critically tempered with the reality that this situation also necessarily complicates research.

The focus of my research is on adult adoptee oral histories, and in choosing these as the most important source, I am consciously privileging adoptee voices. In addition, the oral history methodology I have chosen gives me access to subjects who have not previously been heard from; several of the adoptees I worked with told me that they would not consider participating in research with any other format than the oral history, or with anyone not adopted themselves. This might be partially explained by the fact that the oral history process is not totally outside cultural norms within the Korean adoptee community: exchanging adoption stories is an informal ritual of socialization among Korean adoptees. Making connections based on personal adoption histories forges relationships that become the foundation of adoptee community. The process of giving an oral life history (especially to another adoptee) mirrors this practice, to a degree. My overall research design and methodology here answers Manalansan's call for critical native multi-sited research, in that it is a response to my own knowledge of, and connections with, a local and global Korean adoptee community.

I chose to learn the stories of transnational adoptees by collecting oral histories (rather than completing traditional interviews) because I wanted my adoptee informants to have as much autonomy and as little imposed structure as possible in telling their stories. After obtaining human-subject consent from each narrator, I told them that the choice of what to include or exclude from their oral histories belonged to them. They were each told that they could stop whenever they wanted to and that they could structure their stories however they wished. I did tell them I would ask clarifying questions if something was not apparent, or if I felt the topic of identity development was not coming forth. I also invited them to ask questions about my research or my experience as an adoptee. When compared to less messy methods such as surveys, this method can appear imprecise, but I subscribe to the position taken by historian Gary Okihiro, who advocates for oral history's significance in contributing to the history and knowledge of an ethnic group whose histories may not have been valued enough to be preserved in mainstream history and society.[6] If history's winners are also its authors and owners, members of ethnic minorities and other marginalized groups must take ownership of their own histories, and oral histories are uniquely suited to this task. Through the telling of our own stories, we take control of the making of our histories. In the case of Korean adoptees, the question is not only who owns history, but, more precisely, who owns Korean adoptees' histories in terms of birth records and birth country culture and experiences. The question is also one of understanding the adoption experience within Asian American experience and within the histories of American family and society. In addition, I have been influenced by a long tradition of feminist ethnographers who acknowledge their positions as women so as to access other women's experiences, and who use so-called feminized interviewing skills in order to gather information. Feminist approaches to ethnographic work include research design that acknowledges research participants as empowered and knowledgeable actors, rather than treating them as positioned beneath the so-called expert researcher; such feminist approaches include the encouragement of open-ended responses.[7]

Ensuring that my subjects retained their autonomy was important for several reasons. First, the stories of Korean and other transracial adoptees have not often been told (especially in the academic arena) from the perspectives of adoptees. Instead, the perspectives of parents, social workers, and adoption advocates have taken center stage, even in research that supposedly focuses on the experiences of adoptees. Work carried out under the banner of improving adoption practice comes to mind most immediately, although in my experience even work purporting to focus on "the best interest of the child" usually does not take actual adoptee perspectives into account. I am motivated to fill this significant gap in transracial/transnational adoptee research with adoptee voices and perspectives, my own included. If this body of research describes and analyzes us, and will play a role in determining what happens to future generations of adoptees, our voices should be a major part of the discussion—and though they are increasingly included in the scholarly literature, they are still marginalized within broader discourses around adoption practice.

I also wanted to guard against shaping the replies of my subjects though the interview process. This is an important consideration for any qualitative researcher using interviews; recognizing subjective biases and attempting to remove them from research questions is delicate business and always warrants close attention. For me, this is a concern of special importance because I am conducting research within my own group. Because I cannot expunge my own experiences as a Korean adoptee, I may be susceptible to fusing my own story with the stories of other adoptees. I have hoped to avoid this by asking participants to tell their own stories outside the context of my experience. Although I did ask some clarifying questions in which I included some of my own experiences, I tried to make clear to my sources that the oral histories were about them, not about me or my questions. In addition, I knew that presenting myself as someone who, because of my own experience as an adoptee, understands the Korean adoptee experience in its entirety (or at least more than I do) could be leading or censuring for other adoptees. Avoiding interview conversations (as opposed to oral history conversations) where I might be in any position to control content seemed a good way to protect against these types of transgressions.

Finally, the oral history process seemed to put most subjects at ease. Because the adoptee subjects were in control (and had been told they were in control) of the process of telling their stories, they seemed to be relatively unconcerned about how they would be represented or how what they were telling me would be used. The narrators' feeling of power and autonomy seemed to allow them greater expressive freedom in describing their lives. This autonomy, in combination with a trusted listener with similar experiences, elicited extremely detailed and very personal histories. I expected to hear a lot of personal information but was still surprised at how much these informants opened up. In addition, several adoptees remarked that they had never been given the opportunity to tell their stories at such length or in such detail: they considered my interest in their lives a great compliment. The experience of telling their stories seemed to be both cathartic and difficult for them at times, and I have no doubt the narrators' personal investments in the oral history process added to the experience both for me as a researcher and for them as narrators.

In making these choices to frame my research, I focus on oral history narrative as a way to understand meaning in the everyday details, the social and political beliefs, and the self-reported behaviors of this vibrant community. The oral histories central to this research are meaningful in political, social, and intimate spheres, as lived experiences of adoptees in the many overlapping Korean adoptee communities in the United States and around the world. Because these stories examine the ambiguous and in-between positions of

Asian American transracial adoptees, they reveal much about the complicated nature of Asian American identity, American race relations, and transnational crossings between the United States and South Korea. Through their stories, adoptees explain how they have coped with and taken control of their identity formation, despite the absence of ready-made roles for them in the strictly enforced and categorized world of racial and national identity. This methodology is particularly useful in illuminating the balances and imbalances of power that exist between adoptees, as real and symbolic racial and national entities, and the respective racial (White, Asian American) and national (American, Korean) groups to which Korean American adoptees ostensibly belong—despite the fact that they are frequently excluded from these groups because of their perceived status as racial, cultural, or national minorities.

Accessing Korean American Adoptees

When I decided to take on this project, I was fairly certain that I would be able to access adult Korean adoptees locally who would be willing to give their oral histories. I grew up and resided during my research in the Minneapolis-St. Paul, Minnesota, area, which is the largest metropolitan area in the American state with the largest concentration of Korean adoptees. The large population of Korean adoptees in this area makes it a particularly rich location for this work. Two large adoption agencies, Children's Home Society (CHS) and Lutheran Social Services (LSS), both located in St. Paul, facilitated transnational adoption in the area for over thirty years. Many people making the decision to adopt in Minnesota or in the adjacent states of the Upper Midwest had likely considered using one of these agencies, and anyone in the area wanting to adopt transnationally more than twenty years ago would almost certainly have had to adopt through one of them. Local adoption agencies that facilitate Korean transnational adoptions estimate that more than ten thousand Korean adoptees currently live in Minnesota (more than in any other state), and the possibility of transnational adoption through LSS or CHS is certainly at least a contributing factor. For these reasons, any survey of Korean adoption in the United States would have to include Minnesota. I myself was adopted though LSS and attribute my Minnesota upbringing partly to this fact. I considered myself lucky to be among so many other Korean adoptees, and to have preeminent access to the local Korean adoptee community.

Partly because of my own interest as a Korean adoptee, and partly in anticipation of my research interests, I had become more active in the Korean adoptee community in the years before I formally began my research; I attended and eventually helped to plan national and international Korean adoptee conferences, frequented Korean adoptee social and educational events, and served on the board of the local adult Korean adoptee nonprofit organization, AK Connection (AK is an abbreviation for "Adopted Korean"). My personal and professional relationships with a recognizable community of Korean adoptees (and, for this research, especially Korean American adoptees) has been instrumental in securing access to adoptee interview subjects, information about organizational history and conflict, and knowledge of community events, all of which I have utilized heavily in my research process.

Perhaps contrary to conventional wisdom, this relationship has been neither lifelong nor innate for me; though I am a Korean American adoptee, I did not seek to develop personal or professional relationships with other adoptees until well into my adult life. Although I well understood the experiences of growing up transracially and transnationally adopted in America, I learned, like many other adoptees of my age group, what it meant to be part of a community and a generation of Korean adoptees not from my adoptive parents and the White community in which I was raised, but from other adoptees, whom I only found through my own initiative, as an adult. That said, it was not difficult for me to get involved once I decided to do so. Adult Korean adoptee organizations are constantly welcoming new members, including some who are very young adults taking their first steps toward exploring adult identities as transracial adoptees, and others who are older and seeking community around their adoptee identities for the first time.

In many ways, the four years I served on the board of AK Connection paved the way for my research. When I joined the board in 2001, social events organized by AK Connection were well attended by adoptees from the Twin Cities and the surrounding region, thanks in part to the organization's strong web presence. I initially saw my volunteer work with the group's board as a way to contribute to the community of adoptees with whom I had begun to identify, but my tenure also enabled me to develop relationships that established my credibility within this community, one to which I had been an outsider for most of my life, even though technically been a member since infancy. By the time I began my formal research, a few years later, I had met most of those Korean adoptees in and around the Twin Cities active in Korean adoptee networking efforts, as well as many adoptees around the country who were doing similar work in their own regions. This organizational volunteer work, and the friendships and networking relationships that grew out of it, helped me gain access to many adoptees interested in contributing to my research, through their oral histories. Most of these relationships, at least initially, depended to some degree on my identity as a Korean adoptee. However, the organizational efforts and the support I lent to fellow Korean adoptees, as individuals and as a community, made accessing others in the Korean adoptee community easier when I began to collect oral histories.

In addition to the information I collected directly from oral histories, my work has been informed by my interest in, connections with, and interactions within and outside Korean adoptee communities. Some (but not all) of this information was available through my own status as an adoptee. As a (sometimes) insider in Korean adoptee communities, I have had steady access to groups and networks probably not readily available to most non-adoptee researchers. My participation in the AK Connection board provided a window onto the issues and problems affecting Korean adoptee organizations in the United States and, to some extent, throughout the world.

Choosing to study adoptees in the Twin Cities area was easy, but deciding whether and how to use my personal contacts within the Korean adoptee community was more difficult. Many adult adoptees I met during my volunteer work became my friends as well as my professional acquaintances. I was acutely aware that involving them in my work could affect both the research and the relationships. In the end, I chose to collect oral histories from adoptees I already knew, and over a period of two to three years asked virtually all the adult Korean American adoptees with whom I had become acquainted to participate in the project (unless logistical factors made collecting someone's oral history difficult or impossible).

When I began this project, I was overwhelmed by many things. Most of all, I was concerned with the responsibility of doing it right. I keenly felt a huge responsibility in representing my community, which I believe has been so frequently misrepresented in research. However, at the beginning of any large project, when new ideas serve to broaden rather than narrow, the huge scope of the work can obscure the best next steps to get the project rolling. I needed to figure out how to handle both the logistics of a large ethnographic project and the emotional issues the work would raise. I also needed to stake out my position within the work, personally and professionally, as a within-group researcher, and use this position to define my work to my subjects, my audience, and myself, even as I conducted it. With all these research concerns, I thought, at least I shouldn't saddle myself with finding new subjects. This is how I decided to work with people I already knew.

Of course, this decision also created problems, though I think they were more manageable than the problems I would have encountered had I chosen to seek adoptee subjects that I did not previously know. Because I sat on the board of AK Connection and the majority of my personal relationships with adoptees at that time had developed through that organization, I had the responsibility of discussing my research plans with the other board members to make sure they did not feel my membership on the board created a conflict of interest. All of them had always known that I had research interests within the field of transnational adoption, and they had always expressed support. However, collecting my first oral histories was the first real work I had done, and I wanted to explicitly acknowledge the difference between saying I would do research and actually doing it. If any board members had felt that my position on the board could be exploitive or inappropriate, I was prepared to step down and reexamine my research design. But after I spoke to each board member individually and presented my project to the board as a group, all approved as long as adoptees were protected by confidentiality. I assured them that this was part of my research protocol. So I stayed on the board, and in the end several board members gave me their oral histories. It was in these initial oral histories that I began to understand the work that I was undertaking, and the enormous privilege I was being granted by those who agreed to share the details of their lives with me.

As I continued to collect oral histories over the next four years, my relationship with different adoptee groups and individuals deepened and broadened. Eventually, I made the decision to collect oral histories in the Pacific Northwest of the United States, in order to include populations of adoptees demographically or experientially distinct from those in Minnesota. I also collected oral histories in Seoul, South Korea, from adoptees living there. The methods I used to find informants did not change in the two other locations I eventually worked in: I used my own social and organizational networks to spread the word about my project and collected oral histories from adoptees who responded. I also asked most adoptees with whom I became acquainted, and most agreed to participate, as well. About half of the sixty-five oral histories I have collected to date for this research have been given by adoptees who I knew socially or organizationally beforehand. The other half volunteered without having known me first.

The Oral History Encounter

After identifying informants, the next step was to start collecting the oral histories from those who volunteered, which I started as soon as I could schedule the subjects. In the first several weeks, I took one or two oral histories each week and prepared transcripts afterward, but eventually, especially when I traveled to distant locations, I found myself taking one, sometimes even two, oral histories a day and waiting to transcribe until later. I would not recommend taking so many oral histories in a short time, but it was necessary because I could only be in the Pacific Northwest and in Seoul for limited amounts of time (about a month at each location).

Even though I had at the outset staked out a position as a within-group researcher wishing to excavate and advocate for my group, my position shifted as my informants' stories changed my view of the adoptee experience. Much in the tradition of feminist social researcher Marjorie DeVault, I capitalized on my position within my group of study, and, borrowing from historian Peter Friedlander, I maintained flexibility and adaptation to my subjects by listening and responding to what I was hearing.[8] Through this process, I came to better understand the additive nature of self-reflexive and community-based research; even though I necessarily came to the research with some knowledge and assumptions based on my own and other adoptees' experiences, each oral history added to my idea of what constitutes the transnational adoptee experience and informed my beliefs about the significance of events in my life and other adoptees' lives. That my foundational ideas about the adoptee experience were moving targets complicated the research, but I believe that to bind myself to a rigid ideology throughout an ethnographic project in which I was both a researcher and a member of the study group would have been an act of dishonesty.

My greatest concern in working with adoptee subjects who were also my friends was that they might censor themselves to maintain a comfortable friendship with me after giving their oral histories. Even though I thought my narrators were more open to me than strangers might have been, I knew strangers can sometimes be more honest than friends. Each adoptee friend had to gauge how my judgment of their story might affect my view of them. On my end, I was and am invested in my relationships with my subjects and have considered them my friends both before and after the oral history process. It occurred to me that I might be in for a rude awakening when I began working with people I didn't previously know.

Although I considered many of my initial subjects friends, our friendships were relatively young when I began my research. I believe that being unfamiliar with the details of their lives before beginning the oral history process improved the research and also deepened my friendships with many of them. While I knew some details of their lives, I knew much more after they had told their life stories. I now know things about them that, as a friend, I probably would not have known until we had known each other longer. In most oral history encounters, I felt the adoptee subject wanted to tell me their story at least partly to get to know me better as a fellow adoptee.

The most awkward difference between the exchange of adoption stories that is common between adoptee friends and an oral history is that the oral history process is mostly a one-way flow of information. I found out about the subjects, but they did not find out much about me. Not wanting to fall back on the rules of formalized research (which makes life easier for the researcher, but does not adequately acknowledge the emotional content or exchange in the oral history process), I tried to compensate for this imbalance by acknowledging it and asking each adoptee, at the end of their oral history, if they had any questions about me or my experiences. Some had questions, most did not, and I suspect that most were too exhausted from giving their own oral histories to want to talk more.

Although I have no doubt that all of these adoptees have exchanged stories with other adoptees, most remarked that they had never before been asked or had the opportunity to talk about their lives at such length in one sitting.

Though the process of giving and receiving oral histories was often difficult, I hoped that my oral history project would strengthen the idea that adoptees' stories were indeed important. In this way, one of my personal goals would help build community by including its members in my work.

On the other hand, I also felt the responsibility of evoking honest responses in these oral histories. Many of my subjects, I believe, thought they were signing up for a conversation with me, in the course of which they would tell their stories. I suspect that some found the process difficult in unexpected ways. Often, the narrators' candor stirred up emotional reactions in them as they talked about difficult events in their lives. Certainly the process was exhausting for all of my narrators. Many oral histories I heard were intensely sad; this was true even for adoptees who didn't seem sad at the time of their narration. I was surprised at first, but soon learned to expect this. After I had completed several oral histories, I wondered if I should change the terms of my subjects' consent form, which states that participants "will be subjected to no harm," to include the possibility of emotional trauma. In the end, I chose not to make this change, because I thought it presumed too much. Since not all of my informants had sad stories, I did not want to hint that this was a necessary or expected part of the process.

This research is similar in methodological considerations to other community-based studies, such as Elizabeth Lapovsky Kennedy and Madeline Davis's work in the Buffalo lesbian community.[9] Numerous researchers note the intellectual and social importance of processing emotional issues around fieldwork (see Reinharz's chapter "The Stress of Detached Fieldwork," in *On Becoming a Social Scientist,* as well as work by Marjorie DeVault, Norman Denzin, and Susan Krieger).[10] Because of the high emotional content of many of the life stories I heard, this work was exhausting for me as well. This phenomenon has been identified among psychological workers as "compassion fatigue," caused by (usually therapeutic) listening to a subject whose experiences the listener connects with closely. Even though this project was not designed to have a therapeutic benefit for adoptee participants, several participants remarked that telling their life stories to an interested listener did have just this kind of effect. In any case, to safeguard my own psychological well-being, and to protect my ability to continue the project in the future, I had to find ways to release the emotional pressures the oral histories brought out in me; failure to do so would have risked sabotaging the project and damaging my relationships with my subject-friends. The work of processing the experiential and emotional content was present after each interview, and I soon learned to take time to comprehend what I had heard, intellectually and emotionally.

For me, one of the most difficult tasks of working with adoptee subjects, especially with friends and acquaintances, has been judging without judgment. As a researcher, I must judge the material I collect; I need to assess what my subjects say, how they say it, what it means—both by listening to exactly what is said during the oral histories and by reading between the lines afterward for other meanings. As suggested by Kim V. L. England,[11] this work is dialogical—based on dialogues between me and the project participants as I digest their life stories. Because I also have an adoptee experience, I had to avoid projecting my own experience and opinions onto my subjects—but I couldn't allow myself to become paralyzed by this concern, because without judging and assessing the material, I would have no research project, just a set of interesting conversations.

At the same time, I wanted not to exercise too much judgment, either during the process of collecting oral histories or while analyzing them. I heard a number of things I personally disagreed with or objected to as a Korean adoptee, as a scholar with left-to-radical political leanings, and as a woman of color. I believe that honesty and transparency as a researcher are essential to the success of this project, but my values and politics areareas where I believed it was crucial that I attempt to keep my personal opinions from my subjects, because any offer of unsolicited advice or proselytizing could prevent subjects from being completely truthful or break the trust between myself and the subject. And, though I am interested in the positive development of the adoptee community, this was not a project of ideological recruitment; I remained pointedly aware of that fact.

I did find it easier to proclaim my ethics in this project than to follow them absolutely. Certainly one of the grave problems in transracial adoption is racism or racist misunderstanding within the family, and I know this is a painful difficulty for many adoptees. Many adoptees described painful experiences with family members they saw as racist or bigoted (against one racial group or another) and who did not acknowledge that such beliefs were hurtful to adoptees, themselves people of color. In one case, in an effort to support a subject as a friend and a fellow adoptee, I verbally passed judgment on her father. The following is an abridged version of part of the oral history in question:

Q: So did you feel like you experienced racism in your family, and obviously I'm thinking of a different kind of racism than name-calling?
A: Right. I didn't feel racism. Because my parents, like a lot of other parents I've heard talk, said, "Well we just love you for who you are." I don't think there was that kind of racism, but there was racism in our family. My dad is racist.
Q: He would express racist ideas about other people . . . but not about you?
A: Right. About other people but not about me. And I've always struggled with that, and I struggle with that today. We don't talk about it too much anymore.
Q: What kind of stuff does he say?
A: A big thing for my dad is that he was in the Vietnam War and I think that he, because of the time, being in the '60s and early '70s, there was [the] civil

rights movement and there was a lot of tension between Whites and Blacks and he developed a very negative feeling toward African Americans. I think he's done a lot to curb that, but it's always bothered me. He knows it's bad behavior, so he doesn't act on it, but he still thinks . . . he harbors it. He harbors it. And I never got that, just as long as I ever remember knowing it: "You don't get it. If you're racist toward them, then you have to understand how that affects me. Because somebody else could be racist toward me because of the way I look." We just go around and around and around.

Q: But you don't think he harbors racism toward you.

A: Oh no . . . [Here she talked several minutes about the other acts of racism she has seen her father has perpetuated, and what she has done to educate both her parents.] I'd rather take the time to teach my parents, but there are clearly things that we just don't talk about because they're not going to . . .

Q: Like the fact that your dad is a racist.

A: Right, I know who he is and I know that he means well, I don't agree but he's going to harbor it inside, but he wouldn't do anything.

Q: He's never going to hurt anybody.

A: Right. He's never going to hurt anybody.

Q: Right, but I do think it's an important thing. I mean, it hurts you.

A: It does. And I think that what he's been able to realize is how and why it hurts me. Because I can articulate that now in a way that I couldn't when I was fifteen and sixteen. They are starting to get that association that maybe, because I'm Korean, I may experience things this way or that way. I think we have a really positive relationship now, and I think that they've been really supportive, which is I know more than a lot of people have.[12]

In this example, because I knew that this is an area where adoptees (including the friend-informant cited) have difficulty, I found myself positioning the subject's father against her in an effort to support her. Even though she herself had referred to her father's statements as racist earlier in the conversation, my reappropriation to "a racist" from "racist," not of my subject but of her father, was certainly a moment of judgment on my part. The phrase "a racist" is more damning, suggesting a person essentialized in their racism, while "racist" is more expressive of racist tendencies or beliefs as part of a whole. Even though I did not perceive this transgression as causing any problems between myself and this subject, the example shows one reason why the ethic of nonjudgment is so crucial. In the messy world of interpersonal relations, it is a hard ethic to maintain consistently, and I have to make a constant effort to acknowledge any lapse in order to keep this ethic from slipping away. Nevertheless, I realize that, in the interview just cited, my transgression of this important rule was also telling about my position at that moment; the impulse to support fellow adoptees, even if by judging parents as racist, outweighed, for me, the rule of nonjudgment.

Another potential problem with working with this group of adoptees, my friends and acquaintances, concerns how I came to know them. I met many of them through an adopted-Korean social and informational organization. Thus, even though I make no claims of representing all adopted Koreans in my research, I must assume there is some selection bias at work here; these subjects, because of their involvement with an adopted Korean group, are likely to possess a high degree of so-called adoptee identity, meaning they view the adoption experience as an important part of their identities; this may be less true of the adopted Korean population as a whole. The majority of my subjects have been back to visit Korea, an experience that seems to further cement the adoptive experience as formative for adoptees. It is unknown how many Korean adoptees have returned to Korea; less than 8 percent of the worldwide Korean adoptee population returned in the five-year period between 2000 and 2005,[13] though it is unclear if multiple visits by any given individual were counted as separate visits or one. Even using a liberal estimate, I would surmise perhaps one in four (or fewer) will return to visit Korea in their lifetimes.

Finally, one benefit of working with friends and acquaintances early in the oral history collection process was that I knew these subjects would be more forgiving of the mistakes I was bound to make as I learned how to carry out this research. My initial subjects were most kind in entrusting me with their stories, even though I was new to the work, and what I learned from them proved invaluable in collecting the later oral histories.

Variable Positionalities

Throughout the ethnographic process that built this research (and in this, I include everything from the conception of the project to writing it up), I have made adjustments as my position relative to my own work and to the adoptee community of which I am a part has changed. A key concept in interpreting these shifting sands of positionality is my location as either an insider or an outsider (and sometimes neither) in the community and world of Korean American adoption. This is especially true in communities of Korean adoptees, within which I have access to so-called native informants, yet have also the possibility of my own position as a native informant.

I see myself as part of a generation of ethnographers, as acknowledged by Andrea Fontana and James H. Frey, who "have realized . . . that researchers are not invisible, neutral entities; rather, they are a part of the interactions they seek to study."[14] Much of my work with and within groups of Korean adoptees depends on my own understanding of the complexities of individual and group identity within Korean adoptee discourses. This understanding is likely as much a product of my own life experiences as it is a result of my academic training, but I suspect it represents the fusion of the many elements that constitute my own layered identity. When I ponder the scholarly and sociocultural significance of the research I write about here, the question of the importance of my position as an adoptee is ever present: to what degree do my experiences as a Korean adoptee and an Asian American shape this work as both an intellectual and a community project? To answer this question, I have tracked the many ways in which my position as a member of the community that I am researching is both an asset and a liability.

Insider/Outsider

In *Decolonizing Methodologies*, Linda Tuhiwai Smith provides a thorough discussion of the complexities of being an insider researcher and the benefits and detriments of being either insider or outsider. She writes that "insider research has to be as ethical and respectful, as reflexive and critical, as outsider research. It also needs to be humble. It needs to be humble because the researcher belongs to the community as a member with a different set of roles and relationships, status and position."[15] Like Smith, Norma Williams acknowledges that being an insider on some aspects of her research did not make her an insider all the time, or free her from the responsibilities incurred by outsiders doing research.[16] Treading the razor's edge of insider/outsider has been a major consideration of my work in my community. Certainly, the most obvious benefit of my position is the access I have to other Korean American adoptees, but this does not mean nonadopted researchers could not or have not produced insightful and important work about this community, especially if they have worked to gain the trust of the adoptee individuals they study.

In the more than sixty-year history of Korean adoption to the United States, there have been several survey and interview studies of Korean adoptees; most have aimed at ascertaining whether adoptees were adjusting well in their adoptive placements, and assessing the "success" of the practice of transnational and transracial placement. The agencies facilitating these adoptions are almost always private, and the fact that most (very appropriately) do not allow access to adoption records, even for the purpose of research, presents an additional barrier for identifying transnational adoptees. Therefore, much of the research on Korean adoptees has instead relied on calls for volunteers, disseminated through public channels. As a result, Korean adoptees who participate in research on Korean adoption tend to be publicly identifiable, meaning they are part of Korean adoptee networking groups, attend adoption-related conferences, or use adoption-related Internet discussion groups, blogs, or e-mail lists. Not surprisingly, this means that there are some Korean adoptees who have been approached and/or surveyed multiple times for research purposes;

some of these adoptees are sharply critical of how this research has been conducted, or of the fact that it is conducted at all, mostly because of a perception that adoptees are objectified in the research or used as "lab rats." I had to work to gain and maintain the trust of adoptees who held this opinion in order to obtain their participation in my study. This was probably easier for me than it would have been for a nonadoptee researcher, but only because I was able to access adoptee-only spaces. Once in these spaces, I think I did no more than any other conscientious ethnographer allowed into the space of any subculture. Other adoptees recognize me as a fellow adoptee almost without exception, but I also know a few other Korean American academics who study Korean adoption in the United States who are erroneously assumed to be adoptees. These researchers make a point to reveal themselves as nonadopted, but have enjoyed similar access to Korean adoptee communities when they have been supportive, respectful, and responsive to the wishes of these individuals and groups.

For this project, I cannot exclude some explanation of my emotional state and its effect on the intellectual and theoretical processes that intimately inform my work.[17] As a Korean adoptee, each story I heard from another adoptee evoked an emotional, psychological, and intellectual reaction. Whether the elements of other adoptees' lives echoed my own or were very different, I compared what I heard repeatedly to my own story, and eventually to the stories of other subjects. Some moments in other adoptees' oral histories were especially meaningful or poignant for me, and it has been a challenge to figure out why. Unraveling whether a particular experience resonated with me emotionally or intellectually often proved impossible because so much of what was emotionally charged for me was also of intellectual significance.

The most striking example of this was the sorrow that descended over me as I began to collect and transcribe the oral histories. Although the stories I was hearing did have sad elements, I did not recognize these as particularly sad when I first heard them, so I did not understand why the collection process was affecting me this way. Only after other researchers read some of my transcripts and reacted with sadness did I realize that much of my subject matter was indeed sad. In retrospect, I think I had so normalized the painful events of adoptees' lives in light of my own experience that I did not immediately recognize these stories as painful. This realization further defined my position as a researcher; since then, I have listened more attentively to the painful experiences I have heard in oral histories. Understanding this initial reaction of extreme sadness led me to realize that tracking my emotional states throughout the life of this project would be an essential task. Even as the work of collecting oral histories from other Korean adoptees eventually became less emotionally trying for me, I learned to acknowledge the depth of emotional labor required, and began to allow for my own needs in preparing and recovering from each oral history collection session; doing this helped me progress more effectively. Because my emotional and intellectual processes were constantly informing one another, failure to understand and manage either process caused the other to suffer.

At first glance, it might seem obvious that a researcher who is a Korean American adoptee would be an "insider" within the population of Korean American adoptees, but this is not always the case. The role of the sociocultural researcher is inherently an outsider role; regarding a social group with academic scrutiny and analysis is not usually part of standard social relations, and the value of such activities to the subject group is often called into question. Although my intention has always been to conduct, create, and share my work within my Korean adoptee community, the process of doing intensive research within the community was sometimes met with suspicion, despite my adoptee status.

In addition, when I began the oral history collection process in 2003, few other Korean adoptees were engaged in Korean adoption research, so I was very much outside the imagined normal experience and interest of other adoptees. In fact, because most academic research on Korean adoptees has been conducted by researchers who are themselves either adoptive parents or adoption professionals (both groups made up primarily of White people), Korean adoption research was in many ways a White act until the early 2000s and not part of the "insider" activities of Korean adoptee society—though this has started to change in the past five years as more Korean adoptees have pursued their own research projects.

The Native Informant

The importance of the native informant, described by ethnographer and scholar Shahnaz Khan as "the person who translates her culture for the researcher, the outsider,"[18] has long been established in the ethnographic methodologies of social science disciplines such as anthropology and sociology. The native informant is the person who allows the (Western, usually White, often male, always positioned as objective) researcher to "discover" her culture, or at least to describe it for an academic audience. Therefore, the native informant is a valuable asset for a researcher in search of the cultural truth of a community, society, or other subculture. Although the researcher might be indebted to the native informant, during much of the positivistic history of ethnographic inquiry (what Norman Denzin calls the "Traditional Period" and "Modern Phase" of qualitative research, which together spanned a period from the late nineteenth century until about 1970),[19] the intellectual and cultural superposition of the researcher over the native informant was implicit in the tendency for ethnographers to "study down" in cultures considered less advanced than their own, and in the assumption that the researcher was objective and therefore able to discern the true nature of the native informant's culture. The native informant was seen as too immersed in her culture to be objective, and therefore could serve only as the window through which the objective researcher could explain that culture to others.

With the formalization of the new disciplines of ethnic studies and women's/gender/sexuality studies, and entrance of scholars from these disciplines into mainstream academic discourses, the separation between researcher and researched began to close. This marked the "fourth moment," in Denzin's history of qualitative research, the Crisis of Representation, in which qualitative research becomes more reflexive and the objectivity of the ethnographer can no longer be assumed, as the researcher often becomes part of the story he or she tells. This "moment" was to open the possibility of the researcher *as* native informant and/or the possibility that the figure of the native informant could disappear altogether.

Khan writes about her position working with Pakistani women in Pakistan as a Pakistani Canadian woman, and her position as both an outsider and an insider, a native informant. Khan discusses the condition of mutable positionality and its effects on research and the researcher, explaining how she is considered a native and an expert (as both a scholar of and a native to the experiences of Pakistani women) by her Canadian colleagues, but as an outsider who lives in the West by the Pakistani women whom she studies; she understands her position as one of high access relative to other researchers, but also knows she is often misread, and her work misused, in popular political discourses about the Muslim East. She states, "Situated as the other of the other, I am reminded that the position of the native informant is precarious."[20] Here Khan acknowledges that her positions as researcher, co-ethnic, academic, Westerner, and woman are always changing—not because she herself is in a constant state of flux, but because of different understandings of her position from the various perspectives of individuals and groups around her. In Khan's example, as in my own, it has become increasingly clear that it is often the context in which research is rendered, much more than the content of the research, that speaks most meaningfully to the reader. The situation of the reader, whether another academic, a person in or related to the community being researched, or a member of the general public, influences how she will understand and identify with the work being produced.

The Adoptee/Adoption Expert

I have attempted to create a research project that incorporates communitarian, feminist, ethnic studies, and postmodern methodologies—partly because the values in these ideologies fit with my own intellectual and ethical sensibilities, but more importantly in an effort to do justice to the complex and multilayered reality of Korean adoptee communities and individuals in the United States and around the world. In my approach, communitarian (or community-based) research must also be ethnically sensitive and feminist—not only because the population of informants with whom I am working is majority female and ethnically Korean. The reflexivity of feminist qualitative methodologies has guided my work as a member of the group I am researching. A commitment to making available the voices of Korean adoptees, long silenced in White-dominated popular discourses as well as, until recently, within the discipline of Asian American Studies, binds me to ideologies and methodologies in ethnic studies and to the overarching goals within that discipline of documenting and correcting lost or silenced histories of American people of color. Finally, postmodernist ideology and methodology is reflected in my work through my understanding of the oral history as a constructed narrative, and one that has complicated, intersectional, and multilayered meanings. The meanings in the autobiographical life stories of adult Korean American adoptees may be understood differently by the adoptee as storyteller, by myself as a fellow adult Korean American adoptee and as a researcher, by the reader of my finished work (who will add their own contextualization) and by the communities and individuals I discuss.

It was (and is) important to me as a researcher and an adoptee to give back to the individuals and groups that have so generously facilitated my research; even though the role of the researcher has long been the role of an outsider (both from a social standpoint and, historically, in practice), it is of great importance to me to behave as an insider in my work with the adoptee community. On the individual scale, this means treating each study participant with respect and warmth, making sure the process is as comfortable as possible, and honoring the participants' needs and wants with respect to the use of their life stories; from an ethical and methodological standpoint, this should be no different than the relationship between any qualitative researcher and her or his subject(s). At larger scales, the role of the insider becomes more important and complicated, as well as—I would argue—more complex. Although ethical researchers always treat their human subjects with respect, academics rarely take the initiative to share their research with the communities they study, and thus in order to create collaborative work and to improve the base of knowledge about that community. This situation is commonly said to result from barriers around academic knowledge and expression, but I fear it is also often due to the tendency of researchers to become isolated "experts" positioned to analyze and comment on the communities they study from a supposedly objective perspective outside the group.

Because there is a small (but growing) body of scholarly research available about transracial and transnational adoption, academics who study adoption are frequently called upon as experts by adoption agencies, groups of prospective and current adoptive parents, and, to a lesser degree, adoptee organizations. Such is the dearth of current information available to these very interested publics that the designation "adoption expert" could be (and is) applied to almost anyone in an adoption triad (meaning birth parents, adoptees, and adoptive parents) who is willing to talk about adoption, as well as to adoption professionals. Adoptees or adoptive parents who have produced creative work in the form of books, films, or Web content are especially likely to be identified as experts. Even though academics who study adoption are also called upon to talk about adoption at adoption agencies, at culture camps, in classrooms, and in the media, it is noteworthy that the role of academics usually differs from the roles of these other experts. The voices of academics can carry more weight, due to the perceived depth of their investment in the topic as researchers, scholars, and intellectuals. However, in the world of so-called adoption experts the respect afforded academics is often tied to a presumption, generally unwarranted, that their views are objective. This view is bolstered by the fact that many academics who research adoption are not adoptees and therefore can be assumed not negatively affected by the adoption experience. So, while the adoptee is commonly read as being one kind of expert, the transition for an adoptees to also be understood as a scholarly authority is challenging.

In my case, this discontinuity is particularly salient when dealing with journalists; as I have become more widely known as both a Korean adoption researcher and a Korean adoptee myself, I have been contacted more and more by journalists looking for a new angle on Korean or transnational adoption. In many ways I am well equipped to operate as an adoption expert (for instance, I developed and taught the first semester-long undergraduate course on Korean adoption, and in preparation for this project have compiled a reasonably comprehensive corpus of information about the history of Korean and other transracial adoption in America), but most journalists who contact me are not interested in my knowledge bank, but in hearing of my personal experiences growing up as a Korean adoptee. I always marvel that reporters seek me out, usually because they have been directed to me as an adoption expert, only to ask what they could ask any adopted person. In dealing with journalists, the "inside" position of adoptee always trumps the "outside" position of researcher, and I get asked the same stock questions: "How old were you when you were adopted?" "Did you have any problems being adopted?" "Have you found your Korean family?" "Do you speak any Korean?" I have come to believe that this is not because the position of researcher or expert is unimportant, but rather because my work as a researcher makes me a "super-insider," extra qualified to tell the (hopefully) melodramatic tale of my adoption and subsequent assimilation into America. If I tell reporters I am happy to talk about my work or to be a source for information about Korean adoption history, policy, or community and identity formation, but am not willing to speak about my personal life, I seldom hear from them again. The decision not to discuss my personal adoption story thus restricts my access to popular media outlets.

To blur the lines between my insider and outsider status even further, I have also participated as an adult adoptee subject in other people's research. Because I have depended on the participation of adoptees to complete my research, and because I believe that research on adoption and adoptees could and should be informative and important to the community under study, I feel obliged to volunteer for such research. To date, I have been interviewed three times and filled out many survey questionnaires. The most prominent of these research projects is that of anthropologist Eleana Kim, whose dissertation "Remembering Loss: The Cultural Politics of Overseas Adoption from Korea" and book *Adopted Territory: Transnational Korean Adoptees and the Politics of Belonging*, have been valuable resources and touchstones for me.[21] We met through a mutual Korean adoptee acquaintance who recognized similarities in our work, and quickly developed a friendship and a valuable collegial relationship. Although Kim is not an adoptee, she is probably my closest colleague, both because of our shared area of expertise and because we take similar methodological approaches. In Kim's research, I am positioned firmly as an insider within the adoptee community, both through my introduction as a member of the AK Connection board and through quotes from an interview at the very beginning of our acquaintance.

In the end, whether or not researchers are themselves adoptees, I can probably claim insider status with them as a researcher myself. However, although they maintain collegial relations with me (which I appreciate greatly), none (to my knowledge) has ever accounted for my position as an insider in the community of academics to which we belong. Although none of the research in which I have participated has been focused on the small community of adoptee researchers, and I never expected it to, I do wonder what their research might have looked like if this question of "inside" and "outside" in the changeable and overlapping positions of researcher, community member, Asian American, and adoptee was more prominently in play.

Adult Korean adoptee organizing can also be understood through the international gatherings of adult Korean adoptees. The first of these gatherings (all referred to in Korean adoptee parlance simply as "The Gatherings") took place in 1999 in Washington, DC, the second two years later in Oslo, Norway, and the third, fourth, fifth, and sixth in Seoul, South Korea, in 2004, 2007, 2010, and 2013. These Gatherings, which brought together unprecedented numbers of adult Korean adoptees, were the result of extraordinary community-building efforts by a few Korean adoptee volunteer leaders. Each Gathering has grown in scope, and hundreds of adoptees from many countries attend.

I only heard about the first Gathering in 1999 after the event occurred, despite the fact that I was living within driving distance of Washington, DC, at that time; and for the second, I was unable to attend because of work obligations.

So the first time I attended a Gathering was in 2004 in Seoul. Although I had, by that time, begun my research efforts in earnest, and had already collected several oral histories in the Twin Cities, I was determined to refrain from collecting any at the Gathering. I think adoptee conferences are one of the worst locations for taking an oral history or conducting most other types of research. Although the logistical opportunities to meet adoptees are tremendous at such events, attendees are likely to have an extremely overdetermined sense of their identity as adoptees; such a conference, with its adoptee-centered programming and huge numbers of adoptees in close quarters, is not in any way a typical experience for most Korean adoptees. I prefer that adoptees tell their life stories in settings that are as normal and comfortable as possible (for instance, in their own homes). For my first Gathering, too, I very much wanted to experience the event as an adoptee—which at the time meant not working too much while there.

By the 2007 Gathering, my situation and outlook had changed. In 2004, I was still on the AK Connection board, had only marginal organizational connections to the Gathering, and attended the organizational leadership meeting but did not participate in the planning or execution of programming. In 2007, despite no longer being formally part of any Korean adoptee organization, I had been asked to chair the organizing committee for the First International Korean Adoption Studies Research Symposium, a one-day academic conference devoted to Korean adoption research from several disciplines, which was specifically planned to coincide with the fourth Gathering so that the research being presented would be available to the hundreds of Korean adoptees from around the world who would be in attendance. In many ways, the work of presenting academic research back to a population of adoptees was the ultimate culmination of my shared but rarely overlapping roles as adoptee and researcher.

The organizers of the Gathering made clear to me during the planning process that they preferred to highlight and support the work of adoptee academics. After all, the Gatherings are and have always been a venue by, for, and about adult Korean adoptees. Certainly, my status as a Korean adoptee was a key factor in the organizers' decision to ask me to lead the symposium. Although I was and am excited about the entry of other adoptee-scholars into the arena of adoption studies (or at least studies that include a discussion of adoption) I recognize that many academics leading the way in Korean adoption studies are not adoptees. I concluded that a symposium of Korean adoption studies could never be intellectually complete without including nonadopted scholars, and had to argue (though not very hard) for their equal inclusion. So in this example, the values of being an academic guided my decision to position myself not too far inside the adoptee-only perspective of the Gathering planners, though my own status as an adoptee probably helped legitimize my claim that nonadopted scholars were as important to include in our symposium as the adopted ones.

The Illusion of Objectivity

When humans study each other, they always bring their own cultural attitudes and beliefs into the process. This makes objectivity difficult, if not impossible, to maintain. In that light, I believe that as an active participant in my current community of study (as one who may share the community's cultural attitudes and beliefs based on life experience), I will almost always know more about my community than an outsider. What I already know and what I want to learn will almost always be substantively different from what an outsider researcher knows and wants to learn, because my knowledge and my curiosity are informed by my experience within the community. If, as an active participant, I am trained in human research methodologies and in cultural theory, my potential to learn more about my community is even greater. Scholars from outside my community can still know and learn about my community, but will probably lack the inside information necessary to develop the same body of knowledge as I.

I don't expect all cultural communities to be researched only by insiders, but I am an ardent advocate of the practice for several reasons. If insider and outsider scholars were given, and had always been given, equal access to cultural research, I imagine each would fill gaps left by the other. In fact, however, outsider research and objective methodologies are far more common in social and cultural research. This is not to say I do not believe in the validity of outsider research, but that I have always formulated (even in my previous life as a natural scientist) critiques of objective or outsider research. For my research on Korean adoptees, I am advantaged for the reasons discussed above and disadvantaged only by the doubts of those who question the validity of my work as lacking the outsider's presumed objectivity. I believe that all scholars of culture should have access to the topics of their choice, but that the researcher's status as outsider or insider should be considered at the inception of any cultural research project and throughout its execution. There is an element of self-interest in this belief; I may one day want to end my own research on Korean adoptees and turn to other topics outside my cultural group. Ideally, cultural topics should be researched and analyzed by persons of varying levels of subjectivity, to yield the most complete set of observations and investigations. At the very least, cultural researchers should take fundamental considerations of positionality and subjectivity into account.

The remedy I envision to help mitigate problems resulting from researcher subjectivity is virtually total methodological transparency. Research methodology, including an assessment of researcher subjectivity, should be made available as a part of the research project. Ideally, this should include the position of the researcher within the community, the motivations for the research, the personal beliefs of the researcher concerning the research, the issues and problems of the research potentially present in a community context, and the impact of research on the community studied. Transparency in methodology does nothing to lessen researcher subjectivity, but does provide context within which scholars, students and other readers may place the research and researcher.

Within my community, I often also know more about my community than other adoptees, but this knowledge, rather than the cultural knowledge or understandings that Korean adoptees share, is usually historical knowledge, knowledge that anyone could amass if only they had access to information. The only reason I have this knowledge, when my fellow adoptees might not, is because most adoptees have little or no access to the history of Korean adoption or aggregated demographic, social, or cultural information about the Korean adoptee experience. Korean adoptees, as social minorities within a racial minority, tend not to see themselves in textbooks, in popular culture, or in the rest of mainstream society.

Conclusion

About two weeks into the oral history process, after I had taken three oral histories and finished transcribing one, I had a telling dream. At the time, I was concerned about how the process was going and was just starting to have very emotional reactions to the work. I also had the flu and was feverish.

In the dream, I was taking an oral history from myself and realized as a researcher that I the narrator was telling three different stories. As the researcher, I was having trouble keeping these three stories straight. I was not just talking to myself, but was actually two different people—a listener and a narrator. There was no visual element to the dream; rather, I was listening to the recording of an oral history that I had given to myself the researcher. I responded to my voice as a narrator with the sound of my thoughts as a researcher. As the researcher/listener, I was not conscious of myself as the narrator, and, as the narrator, I was not conscious of myself as the researcher. I was a subject and I was a researcher, and, as the researcher, I was confused. This situation was so frustrating for me that I eventually woke up. I never figured out what my three stories were or what they represented, but I know ths dream was a meaningful message from myself to myself.

I am still not sure exactly what this dream meant, but I think that through the research process I have reclaimed myself as both an adoptee and a researcher. The confusion and frustration I felt in the dream are mirrored by the anxieties and challenges evoked by this project in my waking life, but I feel certain that any reclamation I have made will generate enormous returns in my work. This work of self-reclamation will undoubtedly facilitate my role in the reclamation of the transnational adoptee experience, through my ability to understand myself as researcher and subject and to understand the lives of my subjects as significant, complicated, and profound.

2

"Eligible Alien Orphan"

The Cold War Korean Adoptee

I was definitely United States material. I didn't fit in so well . . . in Korea. I spoke English and I adapted and assimilated . . . readily. And I wasn't accepted. . . . I was really taunted by the Korean children and spit at 'cause I was told I was White and things. And this was my chance. This was my ticket to come.

Mabel, fifty-three, adopted in 1956[1]

A Post-Korean-War Adoptee

The first generation of Korean adoptees was made up of Korean War orphans in the immediate aftermath of that conflict. Tracing the history of intercountry adoption, Alexandra Young characterizes the years between 1945 and 1975 as the Humanitarian Response period, a time in which governments around the world responded to wartime devastation in Europe and Asia, and when the practice of transnational adoption was developed as one of those responses.[2] Although they constitute a tiny fraction of the current overall population of Korean adoptees (less than 4 percent of the current Korean American adoptee population was adopted before 1962),[3] these adoptees have become iconic in Americans' understandings of Korean adoption and adoptees. The broadly understood narrative of the child orphaned by war and rescued through adoption by benevolent Americans has its roots in this generation. In many ways, the current cultural role of the Korean American adoptee was set during the 1950s and 1960s, largely as a result of popular media coverage of this small group of Korean immigrants who came to the United States when almost all other Asian nationals were barred from legal American immigration by a strict policy of Asian exclusion (in effect in some form since 1882). In a time when Asians were understood to be so unfit for inclusion into American society that they were excluded from entry and permanent residence, these child migrants would redefine what it meant to be Asian in America, first through their racial isolation in predominantly White communities and then through their assimilation into White society. It follows that the trope of the Korean adoptee as exceptional (in terms of cultural assimilation, psychological adjustment, and social success) among American peoples of color and among immigrants began with this small group—who are now the elders of the Korean adoptee community in the United States and throughout the world.

Although they have not been as heavily studied as the larger population of Korean adoptees who came to the United States starting in the late 1960s, it is this generation that social work and adoption researchers, as they began their examination of adoption in the 1970s (described in chapter 3), had in mind when they argued that adoption should continue. The victim-orphans, enmeshed in a web of Cold War political upheaval, needed advocates, and were imagined to have a place in American society under the protective care of White Americans whose love could overcome the violence of war.[4]

Wartime Origins of Korean Adoption

In examining this first generation of Korean American adoptees, it is essential to consider the political, historical, and cultural realities of the Korean War. Among these was a growing interest in Asia by the government of the United States as Cold War geopolitical battle lines were drawn following the end of the Second World War. In order to secure the strategically located Korean peninsula against communism, the United States deployed American troops, and the limited occupation of South Korea by American troops has continued to the present day. The transnational adoption program that began between the United States and South Korea in 1953 was a direct response to American involvement in the Korean War.

Ramsay Liem characterizes the Korean War as the "first 'hot' war of the Cold War . . . [the United States'] first encounter on the Asian mainland; it was also the first failure to achieve victory [for the United States],"[5] and this is a common popular perception of the war. However, other scholars, such as William Stueck, argue that, in ideological terms, the West won the Korean War because it "averted the global bloodbath of the previous decade and positioned the West advantageously in the ongoing Cold War,"[6] when compared to its Soviet adversary. Certainly the Korean War served to heighten Cold War anxieties stateside, as the first conflict in the Cold War in which the United States was to support a foreign government to exercise anticommunist foreign policy. In so doing, the United States had to maintain a delicate balance between domestic and foreign policy while working with the relatively young political power of the United Nations.[7] Stueck notes that the level of anticommunist sentiment in the United States during the 1950s was disproportionate to the actual military threat of North Korean and Soviet aggression.[8] This sentiment fueled American anticommunist political action in Korea as well as anticommunist social, cultural, and ideological action in the States.⁹ Although America only engaged in a limited war in Korea, it was more fully committed to anticommunist ideologies at home, including salvation of Korean children through adoption. Eleana Kim highlights the history of Korean adoption as an anticommunist effort when she notes that "Bob Pierce, the founder of World Vision International, an evangelical Christian aid organization . . . explicitly used the adoption of [racially] mixed Korean children as part of an anti-Communist, Christian propaganda program"¹⁰ by using ads in American newspapers headlined "A Korean Orphan for You. Yours for the Asking!"¹¹

The portrayal of Korean adoption as child salvation belongs to a long history of using images of suffering children to support political ends.¹² The poverty of Korea in the first years of Korean adoption was very real, and war orphans were commonplace. Korean historian Bruce Cumings notes that "South Korea in the 1950s was a terribly depressing place, where extreme privation and degradation touched everyone. . . . Cadres of orphans ran through the streets, forming little protective and predatory bands . . . [and there were] beggars . . . often traveling in bunches of maimed or starved adults holding children or babies."¹³ By the end of the Korean War, American sympathies toward South Korea, America's ragged ally in the fight against communism in Asia, ran high.¹⁴ The image of the orphaned Korean War waif became a key image in the American emotional and ideological struggle against communism.¹⁵ The symbolic value of humanitarian action in Korea, through which America reinforced its self-perception of superiority over its communist adversaries, is especially significant in light of the muddy resolution to the Korean War. From an American perspective, North and South Korean forces seemed to move back and forth over the Korean peninsula with neither side securing a clear victory. Indeed, the war never officially ended; instead entering an armistice that continues to this day. Is it surprising, then, that Korean adoptions began immediately after the war ended, perhaps as a remedy to the ambiguity of the resolution of the war and the shame of failing to achieve American victory? Adoptions of Korean children could be the bright spot, a visible reminder of the goodness of American involvement in what would soon become the Forgotten War.

American understandings of Korea through the aftermath of the Korean War were shaped by many different sources, including several kinds of news media, and certainly through film. Although the Korean War has not been as widely celebrated in film as other American conflicts, the fact that ten of the ninety-one English-language feature films made about the Korean War have plots or subplots concerning war orphans reveals that the war orphan was a significant element in the American popular understanding of the Korean War.¹⁶ Between 1951 and 1966, as Korean transnational adoptions were being negotiated and codified in Korean and American law as international economic, immigration, and social exchanges, six English-language features (*The Steel Helmet, Mission over Korea, Battle Hymn, War Hunt, The Young and the Brave,* and *Marine Battleground*)[17] were released that included Korean orphans as an important part of the plot. The very first feature film about the Korean War, *The Steel Helmet* (1951), included a Korean orphan subplot, and in *Battle Hymn* (1957), one of the best-known feature films about the war, the plight of Korean orphans was a primary focus. In each of these films, the Korean orphan character or characters, who are often metaphorically adopted by American military units as mascots, symbolically represent Americans' responsibility toward children, and by extension toward war-torn Korea. The films valorize sympathy toward Korean child-victims as a sign of the American soldiers' humanity; conversely, American characters who lack this sympathy are depicted as having already lost themselves, and the war. By the early 1960s, the United States began to position itself in a helper role in South Korean politics, and promoted itself in a parental role in which South Korea would become an economic dependent.[18] By the 1970s, when the number of Korean adoptions began to increase dramatically, the symbolic relationship between America the parent and Korea the child was firmly established; "Korean orphans," writes Arissa Oh, "could be thought of as a metaphor for Korea itself."[19]

The Korean War separated as many as ten million Koreans from family members.[20] Through oral histories of Korean Americans in the United States, Liem finds that the trauma of civil war for Korean Americans is very much a part of the memories of first- and second-generation Korean American immigrants.[21] However, the Korean War also served as the germinal event that has led to the permanent separation of over tens of thousands of Korean children from their biological parents through adoption abroad. War orphans were configured as (and sometimes emigrated as) refugees from war, and many were stigmatized for being born of mixed Korean and American parentage, a socially unacceptable situation in Korean society. Although early evangelical efforts promoted Korean transnational adoption as both humanitarian and anticommunist, the Korean people were also depicted as intolerant of mixed-race children, striking a chord among Americans who saw themselves as tolerant and progressive.[22] It was (and in many cases, still is) believed that it would be far better for these children to be placed in the United States than to remain in Korea, a nation imagined as not only war-torn and impoverished, but also culturally backward, in the American consciousness.[23] Whether the political motivation for adoption was right-wing anticommunism or left-wing antiracism, Korean transnational adoption was a way for Americans to reinstate their pride in being American in the face of the humiliation of the lost Korean War.

Even though some of the first adoptions from Korea can be seen as a direct result of American military action, in that the adoptees were biracial children fathered by American soldiers, transnational adoption from Korea was expanded and sustained by demand from the American public—whether motivated by sympathy, a sense of obligation, national pride, or convenience. In Korea, postwar social changes, including rapid industrialization and political upheaval, produced a ready supply of children for international adoption, the infrastructure for which was established immediately after armistice.[24] And although the policies and the outcomes of the relationship between the United States and South Korea have been hotly debated in both nations (though probably more so in Korea), both the occupation of South Korea by American military personnel and the emigration of Korean children for transnational adoption have continued without interruption since the Korean War, reflecting the political and sociocultural influences of American expansionist hegemony in Korea.

From its origins as a solution for children in crisis, transnational adoption has become something of a national custom in Korea; it is estimated that over two hundred thousand Korean children have now been transnationally adopted worldwide. Although this is reflective of demand from American parents willing to pay for adoptable children, the South Korean government has been, for the most part, extremely compliant in meeting this demand. Many accounts link South Korea's lack of a comprehensive social welfare system to the export of babies and children by the thousands despite the nation's falling birth rate and a rising GNP that is now among the highest of any adoption-sending country in the transnational adoption network.[25]

Korean transnational adoption was the first sustained transnational adoption program in history (all previous transnational adoption programs were temporary, in response to national disasters or emergencies); the current permanent practice of transnational adoption, whereby prospective adoptive parents in the United States or another receiving country can expect to have a choice of countries from which to adopt children, can be traced to Korean adoption. Indeed, most countries that have sought to develop transnational adoption programs have used the South Korean model, on some level, since South Korea has the longest-running, most reliable, and most stable overseas adoption program in the world.

The trickle of Korean adoptees to the United States, which was to become a constant stream, initially defied American policy and social norms in the 1950s and 1960s. Immigration policy which barred Asians from entry into the United States was excepted, then overturned, as the symbolic value of the rescued Korean war waif outstripped the value of racist exclusion policies designed to "keep America American," and buoyed America's morale after its first lost war in the new Cold War. The fact that transnational adoption has sustained itself for more than sixty years is also attributable to changing racial preferences and beliefs among Americans, and to social changes in the public perception of what constitutes an acceptable American family, changes that began in this time period. Today, transnational adoption is encouraged by immigration policy that privileges transnational adoptees over other types of immigrant. However, the current migration of thousands of children per year for the purposes of transnational adoption can all be traced to the first wave of Korean adoptees who arrived, shortly after the Korean War, into a U.S. cultural environment of racial assimilation, social conformity, and Cold War sentimentalism about Asia and its children.

Life Stories of Korean Adoptee Elders

I decided to collect oral histories from Korean adoptees outside Minnesota because I wanted to hear the experiences of older adoptees—that is, older than most of the adoptees I had found in Minnesota. Only one adoptee who participated in my Minnesota-based research was over forty at the time of the interview. While I knew the first generation of Korean adoptees would be significantly smaller (about ten times smaller) than the twenty- and thirty-something generation prevalent in Minnesota, since approximately 6,500, or 6 percent of Korean adoptees, were over the age of forty at the time of my research, and the population of Korean adoptees in their twenties and thirties was over 68,000, or about 63 percent of the Korean adoptee population,[26] I also suspected that these older adoptees, having grown up in an America with different attitudes toward race and racial difference than later generations, would report different life experiences than later generations. This proved to be the case, and I soon came to understand the experiences of this first generation as formative both for the Korean American adoptee community and as a population in whose image the identity of all later Korean adoptees would be cast in the American popular imagination.

During the summer of 2005, I spent approximately one month collecting oral histories from Korean adoptees over age forty in the U.S. Pacific Northwest states. As I did with the other participants in my research, I found these adoptees through word of mouth with the help of a few adoptee friends and colleagues. Only one of the adoptees I contacted declined to meet with me. In all, I interviewed twelve Korean adoptees over age forty on this trip. Before that summer, I had met one of the Pacific Northwest participants, and I reinterviewed that person while in the region. After collecting oral histories in the Pacific Northwest, I met two additional adoptees over age forty who volunteered oral histories.

Choosing the age of forty to separate this group of Korean adoptees from the others who participated in the project was somewhat arbitrary, but there was a natural break in age between this older generation in the Pacific Northwest, and the younger group in Minnesota. I did interview a single subject in Minnesota who was thirty-nine at the time of the interview, but all the members of the over-forty group were forty-four or older. So, aside from the one person aged thirty-nine, the next oldest subject was thirty-seven, seven years younger than the youngest member of the over-forty group; there were no significant gaps in the ages of the adoptee informants in their twenties and thirties. I also found some social and cultural differences between the older and younger generations, as members of the older generation often had been adopted under different circumstances than those who came later. Of course, the social climate in the United States also changed between the time Korean adoption started in the mid-1950s and when it became more popular in the 1970s; these changes are also reflected in the stories of this oldest generation of Korean American adoptees.

Altogether, the collection of oral histories upon which this chapter is based consists of fifteen life stories: twelve collected in the Pacific Northwest, two collected in the Midwest, and one collected in South Korea. The oldest participant was fifty-six years old at the time of interview, the youngest forty-four; the median age of the group was forty-eight. Thus, although these Korean adoptees are, demographically, the "elders" in the Korean adoptee population, they can be described as middle-aged. There were eleven women and four men in this group, which is consistent with the overall group of study subjects, containing forty-four women and nineteen men. The gender composition of the older generation in this study is also similar to the overall gender breakdown of Korean adoption during the period when this generation was adopted: until 1971, 69 to 71 percent of Korean adoptees were girls.[27] Ten interviewees in this group were married or in long-term partnerships, seven had been divorced, and ten were parents.

Memories of Korea

Because the practice of Korean transnational adoption has changed to accommodate demands of adoptive parents, who increasingly have wanted to adopt infants rather than children, most Korean adoptees who participated in my oral history research were adopted as infants. However, in the over-forty population, many had been adopted as children and retained clear memories of Korea or of Korean family; members of this age group were the only study participants who had such memories. Vivian, age fifty-six, recalls her Korean mother:

> I do remember my Korean mother and I know it was hard for her to keep me because I'm obviously not full Korean and it was very evident in Korea; it's not so evident here, I don't think, but in Korea I would be

just walking down the street and other people would be passing by, and I would always expect, or at least be on my guard, thinking that, well, they are either going to yell at me or hit me or, if I'm really fortunate, they'll just not see me at all, so I would always try to hang my head and hope that they wouldn't see me because—I think and most people have heard and that it—and it's true—that when you're not full Korean, and if you're a by-product of a Korean woman getting together with Caucasian men, they just won't accept . . . either you're just an outcast everywhere and . . . if I was with her, yes, they would yell at her because they would assume that she was a prostitute and, you know, I'm thankful that she kept me for so long as she did.[28]

David, aged fifty-two, also remembers his Korean mother and the circumstances of her death, which led directly to his being adopted:

My mother that had me, she started getting sick and she knew she was going to probably die, and I think it was TB or something . . . it was some kind of lung disease. . . . There was an army base right there, so . . . she, ah, she just got sick and, um, they wanted, um, she wanted someone to take care of me because she did not want me to go to America. . . . She wanted, she wanted me to be with her forever. And I think that perhaps that she, you know, loved my father or whatever and that I was, you know, a part of that so she didn't want me to go. So she tried everything she could to keep me, you know, keep me there, and it just didn't work out, then, when she died . . . when I was three-and-a-half, so she was eighteen, nineteen years old.[29]

Even though he was young when his mother died, David stayed in Korea for some time after her death. When he returned to Korea in 2004, the return to his childhood home town stirred additional memories for him:

But I went back into my village. Then I remembered. I remembered many things. They showed me places where, "Well, you lived here, and you lived here, and you lived here" . . . It came together, everything that had been in there all these years and I had never, ever told anybody about it 'cause my memory pretty much stopped then, after . . . but, after I got over there, I remember the plane. I remember. I can remember GIs giving us candy bars. I remember a little girl who sat next to me. They dropped eight of us off at SeaTac on that day on Thanksgiving Day, and I can remember crying because I can remember wanting to hang on to her. . . . I told people about that, and "Oh no no you're crazy you don't remember that." And I was reading, I was reading on one of the sites, this Korean niece was looking for this woman. . . . She was born in '52, taken to the orphanage in '57, adopted to the U.S. in '57. You know, of course, I was born in '53, and taken into the orphanage in '57, adopted in '57, so to me that's proof that that's her. And I remember her sitting next to me.³⁰

Such clear and detailed memories are uncommon among the adult Korean adoptees who volunteered life stories for this research. Much more common are stories about Korea and the circumstances of adoptees' relinquishment that the adoptees do not actually recall, but which have been passed to adoptees, presumably by adoptive parents. However, these constructed memories of Korea are very important in many adoptees' understandings of their adoption and origin stories. The effect of the poverty and destruction of the Korean War is apparent in the stories of this generation of Korean adoptees, whose adoption stories were filled with reports of scarcity, illness, and stigmatization for being mixed-race. Edward, fifty-two, told his pre-adoption story, which consisted mostly of memories of his orphanage placement:

> I was only there [at the orphanage] for a couple of months. Few months and I was shipped right back out again. And a lot of the stuff that I have knowledge [of], no one knows the accuracy. . . . I was told I was abandoned at birth and my grandma raised me as long as she could. And then she couldn't take care of me anymore. And that's how I ended up at the Holt, uh, the Seoul Sanitarium. . . . When I first came from Korea, I of course remembered it real well. Things faded, but they weren't real happy memories either, so, because there was never enough food and people weren't happy to see us . . . because I looked light. I didn't look very Korean, at least not then I didn't. . . . If you look at the mortality rate, the babies that were born in '52, '53, that whole era. The mortality rate was pretty high. So, no, I am extremely thankful that I am adopted. . . . At that point it was such a stigma to have mixed-race children . . . and I wanted to really fit in, but I didn't fit into that orphanage. And I, um, was kind of spit at, as being White. You know, I was, and that was like a bad word. . . . The Korean children in the orphanage gave me a bad time, because I was lighter.³¹

Pam, forty-nine, shared her adoption story:

> I have no way to verify this but my understanding is this is the story: that I was found in a ditch or something like that in Korea, half frozen, half—well . . . very cold, very hungry . . . basically half frozen, half starved, and who knows, and I was in . . . two different orphanages before I was sent . . . World Vision, sent from World Vision to an orphanage in Seoul, Korea, . . . for Holt, so as soon as I was adopted through Holt International Services Children Services and the date that I was given for my date of

birth was one that was given to me, since there was no way to determine exactly when I was born.³²

Both adoptees talk about the lack of resources: there being very little food and being, "half frozen." Many adoptees born in the 1950s talked about these kinds of conditions. Some remember it this way, and others were told of these hardships.

Mabel, fifty-three, recalled what she was told about her adoption: "The story was, is, that my mother was in an affluent family.... She had—she was married to a Korean soldier, kind of a high-ranking official. And ... I don't know if my mother was raped or if she fell in love with an American soldier. But she was reduced to kitchen help. And, so, uh, ... I think she kept me as long as she could, and it might [have] been a few years. [This is] what I had been told [b]y my [adoptive] mother."³³

In all of the examples above, another remarkable characteristic is the lack of certainty with which any of these adoptees claim they can know what happened before their adoptions. In the first example, even though the narrator has memories of the Korean orphanage/hospital from which he was adopted, he is still unsure of details of his story and has to rely on his adoptive mother, whom he seems to doubt when he says, "I think sometimes my [adoptive] mother just assumed that some of this stuff." The women in the second and third examples don't claim to have any memories before they were adopted, so their pre-adoption stories were almost certainly relayed to them by adoptive parents, who may or may not have received accurate information about their children. The adoptee in the second example was told of the physical jeopardy she was in while living in Korea, and of the several institutions through which she passed, but was not given any information about her Korean family or even her own birthday. In the last example, the adoptee's pre-adoption story is quite detailed in its account of the married Korean mother who either committed adultery with, or was raped by, an American soldier, but lacks much more easily knowable details such as the amount of time the adoptee spent with her birth mother. In this particular story, the victimization of the Korean mother provides a simple reason for the relinquishment of the child. In such examples, it is easy to wonder if adoptive parents don't create part of their children's stories, replete with drama and intrigue, or if these stories were created by adoption agencies for the purpose of helping adoptive parents understand the perilous nature of their children's lives in Korea.

Barry, age forty-four, who was adopted with a twin brother, told me of his first few days in the United States:

> Our parents came and met us. Um, we were eight months old but we were only ten pounds each ... we were very, very ill, and we were actually rushed to the hospital.... And we were in the hospital for at least six

weeks.... They [the adoption agency] had made our parents sign papers saying that no one was liable if we [died in transit] or if we died as soon as we [arrived].... My parents wanted to have us as soon as possible.... Thinking about the situation from afar, the thing was, they were paying people in an orphanage to care for us when of course they wanted to be our parents and care for us ... they really wanted us and, you know, desperately wanted children.... What we were told was that our mother died in childbirth. We weren't told anything about our father. Now, I have since found out, uh, through a friend, who, you know, who lives in Korea and helps facilitate uh, birth searches that, um, ... while it's plausible that our birth mother died in childbirth, it's equally plausible that we were given up for adoption. Uh, in fact she told me a couple of years ago that twins are considered a bad omen.[34]

It might seem questionable that twin infants with such low body weights and who were obviously in poor health would be deemed fit for overseas travel (which, at the time, was much more arduous than the eleven-hour journey from Seoul to the West Coast today), but this account is consistent with Holt International practices of the time; the chance of survival for ailing children was estimated to be greater in the United States than in South Korea, so, despite the health risks of travel, many children were sent to the United States though sick in transit.[35] From the details of this adoptee's story, it is clear that the agency facilitating the adoption was aware of the risks of transporting these very ill infants, because the adoptive parents were asked to sign liability waivers to limit the agency's responsibility in the event that one or both boys died en route or shortly after arrival.

These memories of survivors dovetail with public understandings of adoption from Korea as an act of child salvation and patriotic duty in aiding victims of the war, as well as the symbolic paternal duty of American servicemen who may very well have had biological fathers of some of these war waifs in their ranks. In her examination of 1950s images of Korean adoptees in the American media, Rebecca Burditt notes depictions of Korean adoptees progressing from "war waifs, the homeless, the parent-less, often filthy and malnourished children who wandered the streets [to images which] ... stressed the emotional connection between orphans and their American father figures,"[36] who operated as symbolic fathers but could possibly literally be the orphans' fathers as well.

For these adoptee war survivors, painful memories of Korea helped to cement the American experience as positive, in comparison. Although they may not have specifically desired it, their own memories and understandings of Korea, overlaid with popular perceptions of poor living conditions in postwar

South Korea, helped create the longstanding image of Korean American adoptees as saved children, lucky to have been embraced by a stable, civilized, and prosperous America. This is despite the fact that later and larger generations of Korean adoptees were adopted from far less desperate conditions: by the end of the twentieth century, South Korea became the most prosperous country that still sent large numbers of children abroad for adoption. But by the time Korean adoption had become more common (and, therefore, less newsworthy), public perceptions about Korean adoptees and their role in American culture had been set.

Immigration Policy for Korean Adoptees

Against the background of Asian exclusion practiced by the United States before 1965, significant legal changes had to be enacted to allow Korean children into the United States for adoption and naturalization. Because of the family-oriented nature of the transnational adoption-related immigration measures, transnational adoption immigration policies of the 1950s and 1960s represented a departure from older, more established anti-Asian immigration policy.

Provisions specifically barring immigration from Asian nations, a policy known as Asian exclusion, had been part of United States law since 1882 for China, 1907–1908 for Japan, and since 1924 for most other Asian nations. As Korean nationals, the first Korean adoptees were effectively barred from obtaining permanent residence visas. Beginning in 1953, Korean children were admitted to the United States under the 1953 Refugee Relief Act. When the act expired in 1957, adoptees slated for travel to the United States had, for most of that year, no legal way to immigrate, and some first-generation adoptees had to be individually admitted into the United States by special acts of Congress during this period. The Refugee-Escapee Act of 1957 was the first legislation to specifically address the admission of foreign adopted children to the United States as refugees.[37] Grassroots lobbying efforts by American adoptive parents and adoption agencies led to the 1957 law being extended three times between 1957 and 1961. This legislation was enacted specifically to allow Korean adoption to the United States, as Korea was the only country sending significant numbers of children to the United States through adoption during this period. After the expiration of the Fair Share Refugee Act in June 1961, several more Korean children were adopted through individual special acts of U.S. Congress; then, in September of that year, the Orphan Eligibility Clause of the Immigration and Nationality Act of 1961 permanently guaranteed visas for transnational adoptees to enter the United States in anticipation of their adoption by American parents. It is notable that this legislation was passed four years before the Immigration and Nationality Act of 1965, which liberalized American immigration law and effectively lifted the policy of exclusion that had barred most Asians from legally entering the United States.

These changes in immigration policy served the mission of engaging the American public in the Cold War through sentimental acts. At the same time that adoption of Korean War orphans was being sold to American women as a patriotic and humanitarian duty, such policy changes were designed to serve adoptive parents and prospective adoptive parents involved in child-rescue-through-adoption efforts.[38] Making exception for a group of immigrants long barred from entry to the United States made sense in enabling their deployment as humanitarian reminders of American superiority, while posing "neither the economic nor political threat of the adult refugee."[39] White Americans' desire to adopt from Korea operated largely outside Asian-exclusion discourses; accordingly, the race and national origin of the adoptee immigrant could be all but erased, both in the eyes of the law and in the eyes of society, as White American families assimilated their adopted Korean children. The social naturalization that the first generation of Korean adoptees experienced in the highly assimilative 1950s and 1960s helped ensure their social and legal separation from other groups of Asian Americans and immigrants, especially in light of the fact that other Asian immigrants were not allowed entry into the United States in significant numbers until the reform of national immigration policy in 1965.

In addition to changes in laws governing immigration from Asian nations, another innovation in Korean adoption was the regular use of adoption by proxy, a technique first used in the immediate aftermath of the Second World War to facilitate the adoption of children from Greece and Japan.[40] Adoption by proxy allowed Harry Holt to bypass many of the economic and logistical barriers to adoption, for adoptive parents deemed suitable by his organization, often on the basis of the families' evangelical Christian beliefs. In proxy adoption, an agent of the adoption agency becomes a child's legal guardian in Korea; following transport to the United States, the child is then readopted from the proxy agent by the adoptive parents. The introduction of proxy adoption made it possible for American families to adopt without traveling to Korea, and often without even leaving their home states. The costs and inconvenience of travel outside the country no longer had to be barriers to adoption of Korean children by Americans. Proxy adoption became controversial because child welfare social workers took issue with the lack of child welfare protocols in some proxy adoption schemes, including Holt's.[41] Holt was compelled to remove as many Korean children to American families as possible, and worked closely with legislators in his home state of Oregon to encourage the passage of federal legislation that would permit entry into the United States by Korean adoptees, including those adopted by proxy.[42] Among the opponents of the measure was International

Social Service, an international social and family welfare and aid organization. International Social Service first formally opposed the practice of proxy adoption in 1954, having documented several cases of adoption by proxy in which the adoption failed because adoptive parents rejected their Korean children after adoptive placement.⁴³

Changes in immigration policy that created exceptions for Asian immigration in the case of adoption made it possible for Korean transnational adoptive families to exist, and the Korean adoptees from this generation with whom I spoke experienced these policy changes as important parts of their adoption stories. Mabel, adopted with her sister in 1956, explained the legislative maneuvering that facilitated their adoption, and believes that she and her sister were the first to come by proxy. She explained, "My sister and I were the first that came from Seoul Korea Orphanage. . . . And we were the first children that came adopted by proxy. Senator Wayne Morris was the . . . senator, then, of Oregon. And he helped pass legislation to, um, for us to be adopted by proxy. We came—we were quite newsworthy because we came after the Holts. . . . So we . . . got a lot [of] news attention."⁴⁴

For many, the special legislation necessary to facilitate their adoptions made them feel special and privileged because of the high contact they (through their adoptive parents) had with their U.S. legislators, as if laws were being enacted just for them—which, in many ways, was true.⁴⁵

Forty-seven-year-old Frances talked about the legal acrobatics that her parents, with their U.S. senators, went through in order to adopt her from Korea. Her family had kept all the paperwork that they had from the time of her adoption and passed these documents to her. Unlike the adoption files of transnational adoptees today, hers also contained numerous legislative documents concerning her travel and admission to the United States. Like many other prospective adoptive parents of Korean children at the time, Frances's parents had asked their senators to sponsor legislation that would allow the infant they wanted to adopt from Korea into the United States. As she recalls, "We had two Democratic . . . senators and [they] put together a bill that specifically would allow me only to come to the United States because I was dying. . . . So here's the bill . . . see, this was all because at that time everything was all through proxy . . . all the bills were written so it was enabling the parents to adopt the child via proxy."⁴⁶

While the bill that would allow Frances—and only Frances—into the country was being ratified, new legislation according non-quota immigrant visa status to foreign orphans was also being drafted. This temporary measure allowed Korean adoptees to bypass prohibitions against Asian immigration by permitting Korean orphans under age fourteen to be admitted as refugees. In the end, Frances was among the first to be adopted under the new legislation, passed in 1957, making the bill for her singular entry obsolete. Referring to additional legislative documentation, she continues:

> [On] September 11th, [1957], that is the day Eisenhower signed it, during the closing days of this session of Congress. [Reading from a letter from her U.S. senator] "Among other things, this bill provides for the issuance of special non-quota immigrant visas to certain eligible alien orphans under 14 years of age who are adopted by United States citizens or who are coming to the United States to be adopted. The President approves this bill to date, consequently the private legislation that I introduced for [name of adoptive parents]'s daughter will no longer be necessary. They will be able to bring her into the United States under the provisions of the new law as outlined in the above paragraph. I am happy that I was able to co-sponsor and co-support this legislation and make it possible to bring [the adoptee, referred to by her American first and middle name] into this country. With all good wishes, sincerely, Henry M. Jackson, U.S.S." I was on the first plane under the new legislation. . . . At the time that they were waiting to get Eisenhower to sign that legislation they had over 250 orphans waiting to go and the majority of those were already assigned. They were just waiting . . . for . . . when Eisenhower signed it. It was only good for two years so they had to redo all of the letter writing for '59 and do it again for '61; every two years, they had to constantly send all of these newsletters out to parents to write letters to . . . congressmen and get those bills passed again. So it was a huge undertaking; it was like a grassroots process . . . every two years to get the legislation to build to the top of the heap to get it signed so more babies could come through.[47]

I found it striking that none of the adoptees with whom I spoke indicated that these legal and immigration difficulties had given their adoptive parents pause, considering that the existence of such policies could have indicated just how isolated their Korean children might be in a country where Asians had been deemed inadmissible for so long. Instead, they often talked about the help their parents had requested and received from their U.S. legislators, to whom they appealed in entirely sentimental terms in order to obtain custody of children they had never met. Barry, age forty-four, talked about legal difficulties in his adoption in 1961 that must have concerned his immigration status. He remarks, "I should also mention my . . . mother . . . told me that it had become so difficult that they needed . . . our, their congressman to help them facilitate the adoption. And even though my mother was a Republican, . . . she always worked for the reelection of our congressman who helped the adoption."[48]

For others, issues of immigration were more easily understandable than issues of naturalization. Although Korean adoptees since 1961 have had fairly easy access to visas, all foreign-born adoptees admitted prior to the year 2001 had to be naturalized in order to become U.S. citizens. The naturalization process, if completed before age eighteen, was fairly simple—but not all were naturalized, or even knew that this was required. Candice, age forty-four, explains, "They [her adoptive parents] thought that, um, I would become [an] American citizen because of my dad being American. . . . My mom [was] Korean, yeah. But my dad was a U.S. serviceman. My [adoptive] parents thought, because my dad was an American, that I would be considered an American. But I wasn't. And so when I was ten, they found this out."[49]

This confusion is especially understandable because Candice herself is of mixed race, and her family had been told that her biological father was a member of the American military. Because under many circumstances American citizenship can be conferred through either parent, it makes sense that this adoptee's adoptive parents would think that their half-White (and therefore half-American) daughter should not have to apply for naturalization. However, the total legal break with her biological family, and the secrecy or uncertainty surrounding the identity of her biological parents, may have delegitimized this adoptive family's claim to automatic citizenship for their Korean daughter, and she had to be naturalized.

Eligible Alien Orphan

I have only heard the term "eligible alien orphan," used by Korean adoptees in reference to how American government entities referred to them. Although the term is not in current use, it comes from language used by U.S. immigration agencies—their official name for Korean American adoptees in the immigration process. Today, prospective adoptive parents can apply for immigration visas for foreign-born adoptees as aliens, through U.S. State Department Form I-600, "Petition to Classify Orphan as an Immediate Relative," or through Form I-130, "Petition for an Alien Relative." This term also resonates with many adoptees in their common feeling of alienation from both American and Korean societies.[50] The word "eligible" appears throughout U.S. immigration forms where it functions as a gatekeeper, describing who may or may not be admitted to the United States. So, though the term "eligible alien orphan" may have been deemed too clinical or insensitive to American adoptive parents to remain in common use by the U.S. State Department, I use it to describe the way early Korean adoptees understand how they were viewed by the American government. This term describes child immigrants selected to come to the United States for permanent residence as part of American adoptive families. In immigration terms, the adjective "eligible" modifies (linguistically and legally) the noun *alien*, a foreign person who might not otherwise be appropriate for inclusion in the nation, followed by the noun *orphan*, which marks the reason this particular alien is eligible for entrance into the United States. The *orphan* status applied to adoptees before their immigration makes them eligible for both adoption and American citizenship.

The popular understanding of the orphan as a child with no living parents has prevailed, even though most Korean adoptees who have entered the United States as "eligible alien orphans" have at least one living biological parent (the paradoxical "orphan with two mothers").[51] The word *orphan* also connotes an object of pity, and a subject for charity and salvation, and so meshes well with popular and political understandings of Korean adoptees as international Cold War charity projects and usefully obscures the coercion and exploitation of vulnerable populations in sending countries and the forced migration of children eligible for adoption.[52]

Within Korean adoptee communities, there is considerable discussion of the term *orphan* as adoptees reflect about their own legal, social, or psychological status: children whose one-time orphan status has been the reason for the largest life change that most adoptees can expect to experience. For Caleb, age forty-eight, the popular understanding of an orphan as a person with no living parents is accurate for some adoptees, especially older adoptees who were adopted because they lost parents as a result of the devastation of the Korean War and the hardships that followed:

> The orphan phrase was there because the adoptees from the Korea War were for the most part orphans. And *orphan* typically means without parents. Nowadays, that's not true, and, even from back then, a lot of the adoptees were thought to have been orphans because they were displaced from their families and, if they couldn't find a family member relatively quickly, then the child was considered to be an orphan without parents.... I think really calling us *orphans* anymore isn't really accurate. Because so many have [living Korean] parents.... Whether they've met them or not doesn't necessarily matter.... [As far as being called *war orphan*,] that's what everyone said at the beginning and that's what I've felt because they've never been able to find a birth relative. They say that most likely that's what happened. She [his Korean mother] hadn't died when she gave me up, but she may have been dying or died shortly afterward. But since I've got a birth certificate and her name, I've never considered myself an orphan because I was placed by a parent. My sister was abandoned, somebody had to have abandoned her, but she may have been abandoned by someone else. Maybe the chance of her being an

orphan is greater than me being an orphan. But some adoptees I've met who were ten, twelve, fourteen years old, who knew their parents and were placed because of economic reasons, and they know that they're not orphans because they have since found their birth families. [In the Korean language], I've heard that translated; it means *nonperson* or something? Way back when, Molly or Bertha Holt had mentioned something, Koreans didn't have a very good word for orphan, but if you had no parents you were considered a nonperson; that's how they explained it to me.[53]

Caleb identifies several different definitions of an *orphan*: a person with no living parents; a person who was separated from parents and was unable to find them again; a person who was adopted and never found any Korean family; and someone who is considered a nonperson in Korean society. He also specifies who he considers not to be an orphan, including those who do have living Korean family or who, like himself, were placed for adoption by known Korean parents. Although the legal definition of the Korean adoptee *orphan* (a person legally relinquished by parents or other legal guardian and therefore available for adoption) is more clear-cut, for adoptees, the predominant popular understanding of the *orphan* as a child with no living parents has much more tragic and sympathetic connotations. So the descriptions of adoptees as *orphans* sometimes elicit more complicated responses from adoptees like Caleb, for whom historical location within or outside the context of the Korean War and its aftermath, as well as connections maintained or lost to Korean birth family, both contribute to the meaning of the term *orphan* when applied to Korean adoptees. In addition, Caleb notes the social location of the orphan in Korean society. His understanding is that the Korean word for *orphan* is synonymous with *non-person*, underlining the importance of family lineage in Korea. Caleb's statements reflect an explanation commonly offered to adoptees as evidence that it is better for Korean orphans to be adopted abroad than domestically in Korea. He recalls that his understanding of the Korean term for *orphan* was received from Molly or Bertha Holt—biological daughter and wife, respectively, of Harry Holt, who initiated the institutionalization of Korean adoption after the Korean War and founded Holt International, the adoption agency that has placed more Korean adoptees in the United States than any other.

Celebrity Adoptees: Salvation and Isolation in the 1950s

The arrival of the first Korean adoptees in the United States was a newsworthy event. Many children who were adopted in the 1950s and 1960s were written about in local newspapers, and some were even featured in national publications; much of the news coverage had an unmistakably promotional quality. These were usually congratulatory human interest stories marveling over this new and unusual method of family formation.

Between 1951 and 1956, *Life* magazine published coverage of Kang Koo Ri, a Korean War orphan dubbed "The Little Boy Who Wouldn't Smile," who lived in a U.S.-sponsored orphanage before being adopted in the United States in 1956. Rebecca Burditt traces *Life*'s treatment of Kang through follow-up articles over five years as he is reported to be "completely transformed from the solemn, weak and unhappy child he once was," into "the 'new' Kang . . . a lively and healthy subject."[54] This transformation was attributed by *Life* to the fortunate trajectory of American humanitarian intervention followed by American family involvement, the ultimate form of humanitarian aid to less fortunate children.

Eleana Kim also notes the proliferation of stories about Korean adoption in newspapers, magazines, books, and film during the 1950s. She cites the story of Lieutenant Colonel Dean Hess, who orchestrated the evacuation of one thousand children from Seoul in 1950; Hess's story was popularized through his 1956 memoir, which was adapted into the feature film *Battle Hymn* (1956).[55] Kim also notes the many stories of American GIs serving in South Korea symbolically adopting Korean waifs as platoon mascots, beloved and protected by the soldiers.[56] She also describes the adoptive family drama depicted in the pages of *McCall's* women's magazine, in which a reader attempted to adopt a child she saw in a 1953 *McCall's* article featuring Korean orphans, circling the child she wanted and making her request directly to South Korean president Syngman Rhee in a letter with the magazine clipping enclosed.[57]

Many of those adopted in the first generation talked about news coverage of Korean adoption as a factor in their parents' decision to adopt from Korea. Frances, age forty-seven, had kept clippings of the newspaper articles about her and the other adoptees who flew to the United States on the same plane in 1957. During her oral history, she read to me from these clippings:

> We were written up in the *Bellingham Herald* and the *Linden Tribune,* which were local papers. . . . Now, . . . this is the *Seattle Times,* . . . this is the Seattle one and this is in October 31st . . . and what happened was . . . there were eighty children on the plane from Korea and they stopped first in Portland and they dropped people off here, and then they went to Seattle and dropped off the rest. So, even though it says October 31st, it's still the first shipment of eighty in 1957, but it dropped off in both places. . . . So . . . that's from the *Seattle Times*. So the beginning of being able to have

the babies transported was a big story, so this is a picture of us. That's my dad . . . and my mom . . . and that's me and my sister.[58]

Olga experienced the news coverage as evidence of her own celebrity and popularity in her small Pacific Northwest hometown:

I was a celebrity in my own home town . . . it was a little town. You know, a thousand people, and I was a Holt adoptee. And I was a celebrity! I was in the—my dad was a plywood worker and I was in the—plywood newsletter, I was in the hometown paper, I was everywhere . . . And I won a contest down at the . . . drugstore and I won an E-Z Bake Oven! Because they gave points and every time you bought something . . . for every point you bought, you could put somebody's name down, to have those points go to. And because I was [a local citizen's] Korean adopted daughter, they all knew me, and I got to get the points. So I won! And everybody knew me. So when I was little before I started school, I was everybody's favorite pet, because I was different and I was popular and I was just the best thing that ever happened since sliced bread, because I was an adopted Holt kid.[59]

Olga and Frances, both first-generation Korean adoptees, play dual roles in news coverage of their arrival; celebratory and congratulatory news stories used adoptee arrivals to serve as instruction to general readers on how to respond to this triumph of American humanitarian achievement through adoption over Cold War adversaries; in addition, the news coverage clearly instructed adoptive families and adoptees themselves on how to understand their adoption stories.

However, public knowledge about what it meant to be a Korean child who had come to be adopted in the United States was also sometimes interspersed with more troubling signifiers. The perceived spiritual and earthly salvation of Korean orphans from postwar Korea put pressure on some adoptees during this period. Rachel, for instance, recalled her mother's classification of her adoption as a "missionary project," a characterization supported in much of the news coverage of Korean adoption.

I had always grown up with my mom saying, "Y'know, you were our little missionary project." . . . I'd always known I was adopted. That was never a big deal and when you're brought up, raised with your parents . . . your mother always saying, "You're a missionary project; that's what we did for the Lord" and that kind of stuff, . . . it never occurred to me that there was anything different about that. But when I told that to my second husband, he said, "I can't believe that she would say something like that." . . . I don't get what the big deal is, either, because I've always heard it.[60]

The Price of Assimilative Salvation

Among adoptees who immigrated to the United States in the 1950s, much more than among younger generations of Korean American adoptees, the understanding that they were saved is almost ubiquitous. This salvation was multiply configured as having been saved: from the horrors of postwar Korea; from the disadvantage of having been born poor, biracial, or disabled; or from just having been born Korean, in a country imagined far less technically and socially advanced than the United States. However, salvation has a price, and in 1950s and 1960s America, that price included leaving behind Korea and things Korean in order to assimilate into American society and culture. Olga put her understanding of her salvation from Korea into the context of her American life and upbringing by downplaying the possible but unknown circumstances of her adoption. Instead, she talked about her efforts to refocus those White and Korean American acquaintances who badger her with questions and assumptions about her adoption, shifting the focus onto the essential sameness of all human beings:

> Why was I one of the ones that was saved? But you also wonder too, you know people say, "Well are you full-blooded Korean, or what?" And I said "I don't know" you know, I, I have friends who are, who came over and they were older, or I've had, um, war brides and they look at me and she says, "You look really full Korean" and, um, I said "Hmm, well whatever, that's kind of nice." Or I'll tell people, "You know I'm probably the daughter of a hooker." [Laughs] They go "Oh really?" and I thought you know or I'm the daughter of a rape or I'm the daughter of two very poor Korean people. [People ask] "Doesn't it bother you?" and I said "Why? You know we're all sinners, what difference does it make, you know? And I'm just here, they [her Korean family] couldn't take care of me."[61]

Implicit in Olga's explanation of her common identity with others, as she wonders aloud what difference all the speculations about her personal history makes, is an acknowledgment of her lack of knowledge about her past, her parentage, even her racial heritage. For Olga, as for many adoptees, these details about her past do not matter. Although she admits that she does not know the circumstances that led to her adoption, her speculations that her mother was a prostitute, a rape victim, or very poor closely parallel common American explanations of the circumstances of Korean adoption. While a casual listener might respond with shock, Olga has already developed a response: "We're all sinners. What difference does it make?" If these doubts about her parentage have been internalized, she has also learned how to deflect others' assumptions about her unknown history.

By minimizing the importance of the past, some of the adoptees in the project isolated themselves, even from other adoptees. David, age fifty-two, tells of his response to having met a fellow Korean adoptee in high school. He said, "And I had no idea. Probably the last contact I had with her was when I was a junior in high school and I still had no idea she was a Korean adoptee. No, I thought she was just some kind of Asian. [Laughs] It was like, you know, oh you didn't tell people about it. So it was my secret and it was, back in those days, you don't tell anybody about it. And I kind of lost contact with her."[62] Even though on some level David might have suspected (enough to figure it out later in life) that the woman he met as a high school student was also a Korean adoptee, at the time, he was so secretive about his identity as an adoptee that he even denied the possibility that other Asian Americans he encountered could also be Korean adoptees.

Mabel, fifty-three, talks about a different kind of not fitting in, recalling being ostracized by schoolmates, and notes that, by contrast, she feels accepted by Korean adoptees. She explains, "In our immediate social settings, in school and in our neighborhoods and things, kids were just like mean. . . . It was so confusing; I didn't fit in, I wasn't picked or chosen for groups or sports or anything, I was really athletic, but I was picked last and everything. I was so cute and lovable! It was very confusing. . . . The one thing, though, without a doubt: when I am around other Korean adoptees, whether they are all Korean or mixed [race], I don't have to tell my story, I feel like I so fit in."[63] The harsh treatment by (presumably White) peers seemed connected to the kind and understanding treatment she subsequently experienced with fellow Korean adoptees.

Sally, age forty-five, describes a transition from wanting very badly to fit into mainstream (presumably White) America as a younger person growing up in the 1960s and 1970s, to becoming more interested in her Korean and Asian heritage when she gave birth to a son as an adult:

> I think of . . . my identity in being Korean American, being an adoptee and I think about my childhood at the time growing up in a very small town and being Korean, being Asian, being different. But, at the time, all . . . I wanted to do was fit in. I just wanted to be like everyone else, and, you know, even to this day, when people ask, well, what are you, and I say, well, I'm American, and then I say, well, I'm Korean American. But I never just say I'm Korean. Or I don't say I'm a Korean adoptee. I just generally say I'm an American or Korean American. But growing up, [I was] never really . . . thinking of myself as Korean or Asian or as an adoptee, but thinking of myself as being American. . . . And it wasn't until I had my first son when I was twenty-nine that I started to think about my, um, heritage.[64]

Like Sally, several other Korean adoptees used changes in self-description, contrasts in how they once described themselves to others and how they describe themselves now, to talk about their changing identities as Korean adoptees. Linda, age forty-four, remarked:

> I've always considered myself—believe it or not—Korean. When people ask me on the street, you know, "Oh, what are you?" Because I've gotten that a lot. You know, I say, "I'm Korean." Um, I never say, "Well, I'm Korean American." I never say, "I'm American," . . . I just, I just always say, "I'm Korean." . . . I still, I still say that, because that's as much as I know. When I came, I was born in Korea . . . I believe that my mother was Korean, and that my father was, you know, uh, Caucasian. I'm, I'm not sure, maybe he was an American Caucasian. But because I don't have any other, . . . you know, identifying information, I just say, "I'm Korean." And, you know, it's kind of, it's kind of . . . like, it's, it's too much to explain the whole story to people. . . . So . . . I think people who know what their ethnicity is, are extremely fortunate, you know? It's not a question for them, and, as difficult as it is to not know who your parents are, at least you know . . . who your ancestors were.[65]

Although younger adoptees have often expressed how offensive they found it to be asked by strangers, "What are you?" Linda simply always answers the questions, and always the same way. She uses her self-description, "Korean" as a way to claim the place of her birth, even though she believes she is biracial and thinks her birth father was White and probably American. Saying she is Korean is the only factual information she feels she can claim about her identity, since so much information about her past has been lost to her, and she remarks that an identifying characteristic that most people can take for granted—ethnicity—is something she has had to guess at. It is as if the act of self-identifying as Korean is a way for her to mark the one thing that she does know about her past: she was born in Korea. When she says that she considers people who know their ethnicity to be fortunate, she is also touching on another important fact of life for adoptees: even the most basic and important information about adoptees' identities is often lost in the adoption transaction.

Sally talks about the significance of a change in her self-description:

> I view myself as being an American, Korean American, whereas when I was younger, [I looked] at myself as White. Now dubbing myself as Asian and having a real sense of pride now about being Asian, whereas I didn't when I was younger. And, and just visually, like my office, is all this kind of Asian theme and Asian . . . kind of flavor to it. My home . . . is decorated, or accessorized or whatever, furnished with a lot of an Asian theme

... I wear a lot of ... I have a lot of Asian apparel that would be probably traditional Asian wear.⁶⁶

...y, a change from self-description as White to Asian or Korean American signifies her pride in a Korean heritage that has become important to her as she has grown older. Visual cues of her personal identity, like her choice of clothing and home decoration, have become another way for her to embrace her Asian identity. But this process took time, as she had to unlearn the assimilative norms of her youth, when she was expected to consider herself White.

Barry, age forty-four, talked about feeling "culturally American":

Certainly the United States has been where I've lived all my life; I am culturally American. The country has many faults but it also is a wonderful place.... From the standpoint of multiculturalism, ... growing up as we have, as adoptees in this country, [one has] to somehow find [one's] identity here, I think, and be at peace with it, and I'm very much at peace with it. So yes, I'm very much an American. For many years I was comfortable saying I was Asian American but not Korean American. I've talked to other adoptees who have said this, too, but growing up we used to call ourselves "fake Koreans," ... and I felt, somehow, I was inauthentic. So now I realize, ... getting to know many Korean Americans who are not adoptees but grew up second generation, or even third generation now, and didn't have a very deep experience with Korean culture or interaction with it, [that] they feel ... not completely authentic either.⁶⁷

Although Barry does not discuss his changing identity in terms of assimilation, he does indicate that his understanding of what a Korean American identity is deepened after he became an adult. He discusses his understanding of his identity as an American, and how he does not feel that he fits into the category Korean American, because as an adoptee growing up in a White American family, he did not feel he could claim a Korean identity. It was through his contact with nonadopted Korean Americans as an adult that he came to understand that the experience he had imagined as "authentic Korean American" with "deep experience with Korean culture or interaction with it" might not exist, as he had once believed, for many Korean Americans. So, instead of feeling fraudulent in claiming a Korean identity for himself, he now sees flaws in the taxonomy of "fake" and "real" Koreans. For all of the adoptees I have discussed in this chapter, the understanding of what it means to have a visibly Korean body was important, especially in light of the assimilative pressures they must have faced, growing up in the 1950s and 1960s.

Edward told a story of how he discouraged his son from identifying as Korean, even though he has passed his own Korean heritage on to his son. He recalled, "When [my oldest son] was filling out his college app, I was just kinda looking over his shoulder, and he was going to be a freshman. And I see that, for nationality, he checked Korean. And I said, 'What's with that?' He said, 'Well I figured I'm more Korean, and so that's why I checked.' I said, 'Do you really identify with being Korean?' 'Oh, absolutely.' And I said, 'Well, I know, I hate to burst your bubble, but you actually have more Irish in you than you do Korean in you.'"[68] Although, at first glance, it might appear that this adoptee denies the importance of his own Korean heritage and therefore was troubled by his son's interest in having a Korean identity, this story can instead be understood as a father's attempt to give the benefit of his own experience to his son. Assimilation into the general American populace was an important survival skill for this generation of Korean adoptees. Some were able to assimilate physically because they were biracial, but most were successful in assimilating culturally. Assimilation was expected by many adoptive families and by the communities in which adoptees lived, and it reassured a Cold War–weary American public that humanitarian and Christian American principles could help win the Cold War, and save children, to boot.

The Cost of Exceptionalism: Navigating Racist Midcentury America, Alone

Historian Sarah Potter cites increases in transracial and transnational adoption as one of the factors contributing to the end of matching (based on phenotype, class background, and even IQ) in adoption by American social workers; the presence of completely racially mismatched children in White families was an utter rejection of this practice.[69] Changes in American society began to allow the existence of multiracial families, and the secrecy around adoption that racial matching allowed was replaced by the valorization of transnational adoptive parents, one sign that the stigmatization around adoption was decreasing. At the beginning of this chapter, I discussed how the value of early Korean adoptees to the American Cold War humanitarian image exempted them from policies of Asian exclusion. Although these individuals may have been symbolically important to an American identity built on humanitarian and egalitarian ideals, Korean adoptees of this era described a less welcoming American social landscape. Almost all participants described experiences of racism, either as overt discrimination or abuse or in more subtle forms. In addition to having grown up as racially isolated individuals (with the exception of some with siblings who were also Korean adoptees), those who were adopted in the 1950s and 1960s were also social curiosities. In these early Korean adoptions, the combination of racial mismatch with other family members and total linguistic and cultural Americanization often led to questioning by people outside the family. In

...n, social mores about racial difference allowed for more direct requests ...ial explanations around adoptees' circumstances, as well as for much more overtly racist remarks and teasing, than have been experienced by those adopted more recently.

Nadine, age fifty-two, was initially put into Chinese American preschool because her parents thought it would help her socially and emotionally to be around other Asian children. However, when she went to regular grade school, White children teased her viciously.

> When I started school I'd fit in at the Chinese American nursery school; it was in downtown Portland, I fit in there, and I was happy there. I used to have a good time with the kids there. But when I got into grade school—it was when I was got into second and third grade—this one kid used to follow me home with two, three kids, three boys. They'd call me "ching chong chinamo," um, "chink, slant eyes," um, they'd call me "jap . . . Tokyo Rose," uh, that was a compliment. She had a lot to do with the Japanese war. . . . You know, that to me was a compliment, because she was Asian.[70]

Despite having been in a mostly Asian American preschool, Nadine was so harassed that she began to construe some of the name-calling she endured as positive; even though "Tokyo Rose" was certainly intended as a slur (referring to the Asian, English-speaking female host of a Japanese propaganda program during World War II), Nadine considered this name a compliment, because at least her attackers were correctly associating her with Asian women, collectively known as "Tokyo Rose" during the war. Although this subversion of the cruel intent behind this name-calling might have been a good coping tactic, it also underlines the racial isolation that Nadine experienced, since it makes clear she did not understand the full meaning behind the name other children called her.

David related similar experiences growing up in a predominantly White school:

> They'd corner me and say, "We're going to send you back to where you came from!" which kind of terrified me. . . . Couple of them were saying, "Your mother was nothing but a whore," or whatever, and I was defending that because I still had really good memories of my mother and it just really, really bothered me, but I learned to keep my mouth shut. You know, going to school, it was the same for so many of us, . . . 'cause I looked more Korean when I was younger. . . . I can remember being chased home, you know. And called any kind of Asian ethnic name that there is. . . . And I told my parents about it once. And they said, "Don't worry about it, whatever, they didn't mean it," . . . so I never told them

again and I just never told anyone about it ever again. And I just . . . , you know, just kind of accept[ed] that's the way it's going to be. And I just kind of wanted to fit in; I wanted to have friends; I wanted people to like me. So it was, just growing up—I guess it was late fifties and then into the sixties. . . . It's kinda hard to think back on that.[71]

Even though David experienced some racial teasing that became quite violent, his White parents' responses, when he reported it to them, further reinforced the racism that he'd told them about, because they minimized his experience and went so far as to take the side of his assailants, making the excuse, "They didn't mean it" in their defense. After hearing this response, David quickly learned to never tell his parents or anyone else about racial incidents or attacks. Instead, he learned to accept that he would have to endure this kind of harassment alone. Today, he describes these conditions as a part of growing up in the 1950s and 1960s. This parental denial of racial issues and problems is also shared in the example below, recounted by Candice, age forty-four:

So it's—my family, too, whenever I would try to bring up racial issues that I was having problems [with]—in the family or outside the family, [it] was stopped. And if I talked about [this], [for instance], in an e-mail that I wrote my sister . . . she wrote me an e-mail back, saying, "It must be really hard, but we saved you and, you know, you should be, in a way, grateful that we did this," and all this stuff. So, I can't really talk to my family about it. They really don't understand, they think that I should just be able to get over it.[72]

In this example, the adoptive family does not support Candice when she tells them of her experiences of racialization. Specifically, while not denying the truth of the adoptee's claims of racial harassment, the sister shuts Candice down instead by claiming that, as an adoptee, Candice does not have the right to complain about these experiences because to do so would signify the adoptee's ingratitude for having been adopted into the family in the first place. Paradoxically, even though the idea that adoption constitutes salvation for Korean adoptees is specifically configured on racial difference between family and adoptee (insofar as the adoption of a racially and socially subordinate Korean adoptee into the superior world of the White adoptive family is an act of generosity for the family and a boon for the adoptee), any claim of racial mistreatment by the adoptee is carefully dismissed. The racial difference between Korean adoptee and White family can only be used to benefit the family, not as a grievance for the adoptee.

David's athletic prowess enabled him to fit in at school, but it also created other problems for him. In this example, he describes internalizing the social pressure to avoid acknowledging the racial difference between himself and his parents by eventually making sure no one ever saw him with his parents, which also left him emotionally isolated with unspoken issues around his race and identity; he had many stories about how emotionally raw he was around racial incidents, such as the ones below:

> Thinking back . . . my parents never, never watched me wrestle or play football; they might have watched me play baseball. And then it got to be, as I got older I didn't want them to come to any games because [people] would see White parents with me and then they would know that there was something wrong. You know, and it was like "Well, what are you?" . . . And I would get so tired of that. "What are you?" I [never answered that]. Naw. I turned around and cried. You know, I'd run. Even back in high school I can remember this time this cheerleader . . . I was getting into my locker, and she came up behind me and I thought, I thought she was going to be nice, and she, you know, she mocking me, kind of saying some kind of Asian language, you know, like they do, and I was so frozen that I couldn't believe that, you know, I was seventeen years old and this was still happening to me. So I think I set the lock and I just took off and ran away. [Laughs.] So I never really dealt with it very well at all.[73]

When I asked him, "So you never told anybody that you were adopted?" he replied, "No . . . they couldn't figure it out. . . . You know, then, of course, I was rebelling. . . . I played so many sports and I was so good at it, but it got to be . . . tough, and I found out it was a lot easier to take drugs than play sports because . . . I was hurt and it was all just trying to kill my pain."[74]

In the examples above, community and/or parental denials about the difficulty of racial difference were painful for adoptees, to varying degrees. This response to racial difference by White family and community was reported by many Korean adoptees of this first generation, as well as by members of younger generations.

Dating was another experience that brought race and racial identity to the fore for many first-generation Korean adoptees. Sally had very different experiences when she was in high school than when she was in college:

> So when I grew up, and all the way through high school, first I wasn't allowed to date until I was sixteen, I think it was. And then I was all excited that I was sixteen, I was gonna have all these, these dates; well, it never materialized. . . . I did feel it was race related. Yeah, especially in a town that was predominantly White . . . and not that I felt discriminated against, but just, again, the . . . visual, or the interest of other White guys, their interest just of wanting to date, you know, people that look

like them I guess ... that type of thing. So what was interesting was that, when I went to college, ... that was also kind of a, *whoaaaa*, there was ... all this kind of attention from men. [It was] 1977. Fall of 1977. So that was like, *whoaaa*, ... and that was new, and just managing all of that and trying to figure out what that meant.⁷⁵

Sally expected to have dating options once her parents allowed her to date, but no one ended up showing any interest, which she eventually understood as reluctance among White boys in her high school to date a Korean girl. However, when she went off to college in 1977, she was surprised to find, once she arrived, a total reversal of her high school experiences: many White men were interested in dating her. David described similar experiences of being shunned by White girls and harassed by White boys in high school during his teen years:

> I just felt like nobody wanted to date me. Because I wasn't normal. ... I think [some had interest], but I was stupid, I couldn't see it. I was just afraid. Just so, just so afraid. [Once] there was a group of White boys going down the hall. I think I was looking at some girls, and they came up to me and said ... "Don't be looking at White girls ever again." So I just kind of put my head down and kind of like, kind of walked away. And you know, yeah, I was really afraid. But the equalizer was to get on the sports field and the football field and whatever and, you know, then I could kick their ass 'cause I was a lot thicker and stronger and I was in good shape. It was the only way. I was not a violent person at all. I did not start a fight, ever. They'd always want to start fights with me. Which happened quite a bit. [Laughs.] Because I was different.⁷⁶

With all the social pressure to minimize and deny their own experiences of racial difference, it is not surprising that many adoptees in this generation ended up internalizing their responses to the active, but out of bounds, racialized social world around them. Sally spoke about her thoughts on "nature versus nurture," perhaps a coded way to talk about race; she saw some characteristics as inborn and perhaps racially determined, while believing that others were learned from adoptive parents and adoptive culture. However, most of the characteristics she associated with "nature" are social behaviors that are stereotypically Asian.

> It's also interesting, this whole nature versus nurture, because [sometimes] I think I have a lot of characteristics of my adoptive mother: being outgoing, gregarious, assertive, aggressive, you know, whatever. But then, as I've gotten older, especially in my job, where I interact a lot with different Asian cultures, I've realized that there's a lot of me that's also just nature. But I have found an affinity, with dealing with, in my

job, . . . Asian cultures. . . . So there's a lot of this whole nature part of me. And it's interesting, even though I was raised [in America and] I consider myself American . . . , I am viewed here, particularly at work where I get feedback, as having a lot of . . .—not stereotyping, but generalizing—kind of Asian traits. In a group setting, I'm very reserved, and more quiet. I do tend to be more aware of a formal hierarchy and seniority and age, and I wasn't raised that way, but I seem to have this kind of orientation toward that. So it's always interesting—was that, yeah, the nature or the nature part of me.[77]

Nadine told me a similar theory about her similarity to the nonadopted Asian and Asian American women she knows. She said, "I've worked with a lot of Korean women. I've worked in electronics for almost twenty years—and the way they act and react to certain situations and things is not that much different than the way I act and react. And how defensive I get, and how loud I get, and how abrasive or vulgar. You know, Korean women are the same way. So are Vietnamese women; so are Lao and Thai women."[78]

Although in both examples, these women are interpreting stereotypically Asian social behaviors as being naturally inborn in them as Koreans, I do not want to suggest that either woman has some kind of racial false consciousness. Perhaps they have internalized messages about their Asianness that they have picked up from cultural cues received over a lifetime. These messages, sometimes pushing a denial of race-based identity, sometimes heightening race-based identity, would have been particularly confusing for this generation of adoptees, who grew up in a cultural period that did not support a complicated rendering of social, cultural, and racial identity.[79]

Conclusion

The experience of first generation of Korean American adoptees, those who were brought to the United States in the 1950s as an extension of America's investment and interests in South Korea following the Korean War, is both similar to, and different from, that of younger generations of Korean adoptees. While many of the oldest generation's stories of growing up racially isolated and culturally assimilated are similar to the stories that younger Korean adoptees have told me (and to experiences reported in other research, and in written and filmed accounts of Korean adoptee experiences), this generation also had more specific memories of Korea that complemented their imaginations of their birth country. Most significantly, adoption immigration policy, and popular understandings about Korean adoptees that still prevail today, are based on the experiences—whether real, reported, or imagined—of this generation. The first generation adoptees, more than later generations, were socially pressured to assimilate, and had little or no opportunity to connect with other Asians or Asian Americans. As some of the only Asians allowed to immigrate to the United States at the time, they were almost totally racially isolated, within their predominantly White families, in racially segregated 1950s' and 1960s America. Copious press coverage of Korean adoptee arrivals throughout the 1950s and 1960s emphasized the salvation of Korean children by generous and kindhearted adoptive parents who offered the shelter of American family placement. Although this well-meaning media attention valorizing adoptive parents served to explain the circumstances of family formation for Korean adoptive families, it also restricted the options available to adoptees as they grappled with their identity formations as Asian Americans, as Koreans, or even as adoptees. Despite huge changes in American society over the past sixty years, popular understandings of transracial adoption that developed around the first generation of Korean adoptees have proved remarkably durable and continue to be applied to later generations of transnational adoptees from Korea and other countries. The fates of the first generation of Korean adoptees would also be broadly accepted as a litmus test for whether the adoption of children so different from their White American families could be "successful," a question that would evolve into a subject of intense social work and behavioral science research over the next several decades.

3

Adoption Research Discourse and the Rise of Transnational Adoption, 1974–1987

> At each phase of the study, we reported the problems, setbacks, and disappointments, as well as the successes, joys, and optimism about the future . . . there are no differences between the birth children and adopted children in the likelihood of problems occurring . . . they feel that their lives were enriched by the transracial adoption experience.[1]
>
> Rita J. Simon and Howard Altstein, *Adoption, Race, and Identity*

Several bodies of literature about transnational and/or transracial adoption have been produced since both practices began in the middle of the twentieth century. There are narratives by adoptive parents detailing their experience of adoption. There are also narratives, including memoirs, documentary films, and creative writing, by adoptees presenting their own perspectives. There are self-help books that tell prospective parents the best ways to adopt transnationally or transracially, with answers to common questions and advice on resolving common problems when they arise. There are also a considerable number of scholarly publications based on studies of transracial and transnational adoptees. These include: writings about adoptees' physical and mental health and development; the history of transnational adoption and its possible future; sociological and legal perspectives on adoption practice; studies of adoptee identity; and social work and policy research.

Of the wide variety of published scholarly work on transracial adoption, I have chosen to highlight social work and social policy research in this chapter, for several reasons. Social workers (including adoption workers) were the first group of professionals to work with transracial adoptees and their families. Social work professionals and researchers made decisions that established adoption rules, guidelines, and recommendations. As a group, these researchers were the first to investigate the unique cultural implications of transracial adoption. They were among the first scholars to engage in public debates about transracial adoption, and it was in these debates that ideas of transracial adoption as a problem or a solution first took shape. Research on transracial adoption has a longer history in social work than in other disciplines—almost as long as the practice of transracial adoption, covering most of the lifetimes of early adoptees and the entire lifetimes of those born more recently. In addition, social work and social policy studies have produced more works in adoption studies than has any other discipline.

Although I sought to focus on research published between the first Korean transnational adoptions in the 1950s and the peak years in the mid-1980s, little was written about transracial or transnational adoption in this field until the 1970s. Administrative files of the international social work organization International Social Services reveal that the way Korean adoption was practiced initially drew sharp critiques from social workers within the organization and in state governments, but these assessments were not expressed in published research at the time.[2] By the time the research was published, the practice was over twenty years old. With a few notable exceptions, research outcomes supported the practice of transracial and/or transnational adoption. It was not until the 1990s that critiques of transnational and transracial adoption grounded in postcolonial theory and critical race studies would emerge. Although the number of transnational adoptions from Korea had begun to decline in the latter half of the 1980s, China developed a sizable overseas adoption program that peaked in the late 1990s, and overall transnational adoption rates ballooned into the 2000s. By this time, truly adoptee-centered research had appeared in the published record, and, during the time that critiques of the practice multiplied, transnational adoption rates worldwide fell. I am not suggesting here that changing research findings are solely responsible for what Peter Selman calls the "rise and fall of transnational adoption," but scholarly activity is certainly one element of the broader public discourse about transnational adoption.

I do assert that the almost universal support provided by early research for the novel practices of both transracial adoption (which began in the United States in 1948) and institutionalized transnational adoption (which began between the United States and South Korea in 1953) was a major factor in the expansion of transnational adoption in the United States, and is likely to have contributed to the later expansion of the practice to the rest of the Western world. Today, it seems as if adoption, including transnational adoption, has always been commonplace, but in fact only a few decades ago adoption without racial and phenotypic matching was an unusual practice, with outcomes unknown to behavioral science and child welfare researchers. Although transnational and transracial adoptions began in the United States at about the same time, it was not until transnational adoptions became more common, in the 1980s and 1990s, that this population of adoptees began to be studied apart from other transracial adoptees, who were adopted domestically. Against the backdrop of the civil rights struggles of the 1960s and 1970s, social work researchers may have chosen to focus on Black and Native American transracial adoptions as a more immediate concern. Ironically, it was criticism from African American and Native American communities that pushed the adoption industry to pursue sources of children outside the United States at a time when Asians were broadly understood in the American mindset to be largely exempt from the racial subjugation that affected other people of color. Although popular media like film, television, magazines, and newspapers educated the public about the growing population of Asian adoptees, encouraged families to adopt, and even instructed them to think of transnational and transracial adoption as a moral project, it was the adoption research on transracial and transnational adoptees in the 1970s and 1980s that gave American society permission to adopt across race and national borders, and assured them that they could expect few, if any, negative outcomes. Despite suspicions among social workers and others about the way Korean adoptions were being completed in the 1950s, the complete reversal within social work from an anti-to -a pro-adoption perspective in subsequent decades was believed completely scientific, validated the continued expansion of transnational adoption and the industry supporting it.

The Research

The articles and books I reviewed in this discourse analysis are those that reported research on transracial and/or transnational adoption in the United States. They include sixteen articles or books, seven from the 1970s, nine from the 1980s.[3] There was some research relevant to Korean American adoption prior to this time, but it consisted of dissertations, conference papers reported as summaries in proceedings, journalistic accounts, or reports performed by nonprofit organizations. Publication of research about transracial and transnational adoption as scholarly books or journal articles began in the 1970s, when the first Korean adoptees were already adults, but before the practice of transnational adoption had become commonplace. They are, in chronological order:

- 1974, *Black Children White Parents: A Study of Transracial Adoption*, by Lucielle J. Grow and Deborah Shapiro
- 1977, *Transracial Adoption*, by Rita Simon and Howard Altstein
- 1977, *Outcome of Black Children–White Parents Transracial Adoptions*, by Charles Zastrow
- 1978, "Issues in Transracial and Transcultural Adoption," by Dong Soo Kim, in *Social Casework*

1979, "Adoption of Korean Children by New York Area Couples: A Preliminary Study," by S. P. Kim, S. Hong, and B. S. Kim, in *Child Welfare United States*

1979, "The Identity, Adjustment, and Achievement of Transracially Adopted Children: A Review and Empirical Report," by Christopher Bagley and Loretta Young, in *Race, Education, and Identity*, edited by Gajendra K. Verma and Christopher Bagley

1979, "Identity in Transracial Adoption: A Study of Parental Dilemmas and Family Experiences," by Lela B. Costin and Shirley H. Wattenberg, in *Race, Education, and Identity*, edited by Gajendra K. Verma and Christopher Bagley

1979, "Racial and Cultural Issues in Adoption," by Charles E. Jones and John F. Else, in *Child Welfare United States*

1981, *Transracial Adoption: A Follow-Up*, by Rita Simon and Howard Altstein

1983, *Chosen Children: New Patterns of Adoptive Relationships*, by William Feigelman and Arnold R. Silverman

1983, *Adoption and Race: Black, Asian, and Mixed Race Children in White Families*, by Owen Gill and Barbara Jackson

1983 *Transracial and Inracial Adoptees: The Adolescent Years*, by Ruth McRoy and Louis A. Zurcher

1984, "The Long-Term Effects of Transracial Adoption," by William Feigelman and Arnold R. Silverman, in *Social Service Review*

1984, "Adoption of Black Children by White Parents in the USA," by Rita Simon, in *Adoption: Essays in Social Policy, Law, and Sociology*, edited by P. Bean

1986, "A Longitudinal Study of Black Adoptions: Single Parent Transracial, and Traditional," by J. F. Shireman and P. R. Johnson, in *Social Work*

1987, "Transracial Adoption and the Development of Black Identity at Age Eight," by P. R. Johnson, J. F. Shireman, and K. W. Watson, in *Child Welfare*

1987, *Transracial Adoptees and Their Families: A Study of Identity and Commitment*, by Rita Simon and Howard Altstein

With few exceptions, the reviewed research shares several characteristics: (1) adoptive parents are at the center of the research, and queries are made to them about the experience of adopted persons, even though adopted persons are the supposed subject of the research; (2) "adjustment," often coded language for racial, social, and cultural assimilation by the adoptee, is positively regarded as an indicator of success in the adoption context; and (3) possible problems associated with transracial adoption are assumed to be minor compared to the assured problems associated with the lack of a permanent family. In addition, there are also some similarities in factors that the reviewed research tends to disregard: (1) social and cultural theory that critiques dominant hegemonic and colonial practice with regard to race, class, and gender is not considered, and the whiteness of the adoption industry and of most adoptive parents is not acknowledged as a factor in findings or research design; (2) losses in the adoption process for adoptive parents, adoptees, or birth families are seldom considered; and (3) reported problems among study populations are discounted, and although some studies report that significant proportions of families studied experience problems, the question of what proportion would constitute grounds for concern is not discussed. Published research has a clear function within scholarly discourses; in this chapter, I analyze this material not only as research but also as it contributes to public discourses about adoption. In doing so, I follow the critiques of past and current transracial adoption research assumptions and methodologies put forward by Patricia Fronek and Denise Cuthbert and by Jonathan Dickens. Fronek and Cuthbert critique legal and welfare approaches to transnational adoption as necessarily focused on individuals rather than on community needs and social justice goals.[4] Dickens places different types of transnational adoption policy into distinct welfare regimes, attributing variances in policy and regulation of transnational adoption to the differing political and social attitudes about adoption in differing sending and receiving nations.[5] In my analysis, I frame understandings of transnational adoption in discursive rather than absolute terms.

In paying particular attention to adoption research as a contributor to public discourse that influences both public opinion and governmental policy, I argue that adoption research contributes to and may also be influenced by one-sided perspectives of adoption. Specifically, I refer to the broad beliefs that adoption, particularly transracial and transnational adoption, has only benefits and no costs; that adoptive parents are at the center of the adoption story as saviors; and that adoptees are lucky to have been rescued. In the work I analyze, the assumed overall social good of adoption and the unimportance of race in transracial adoptions are borne out as assumptions or outcomes in early transracial/transnational adoption research, some of which also contains significant unacknowledged racial and cultural bias. Using assumptions that bias toward adoptive parents' positive experiences, much of this research was, knowingly or unknowingly, designed to examine only to positive outcomes in transracial and transnational adoption practice, while ignoring actual or potential problems. Given these flaws in research design and methodology, it is not surprising that the majority of these works endorsed the novel practice of transracial and transnational adoption as unproblematic, thereby supporting its expansion.

Adoptive Parents at the Center

Several early transracial adoption research projects used parents' perceptions of their transracially adopted children to characterize the adoptees and to assess how the children were faring in the adoptive situations. Authors of the first studies deemed this necessary because the adoptee children were often too young to answer questions about their situations. But by the 1970s, when much of the academic research considered here was published, the population of adult transracial and transnational adoptees was certainly large enough to assess—though it may have been difficult for researchers to contact adoptees in the absence of the adoptee networking groups that have emerged relatively recently. In their review of historical adoption research, Jesús Palacios and David Brodzinsky identify the use of a "single respondent['s], typically one parent's, response" as a common methodological problem in research from this period.[6] In any case, methodologies in which parents assess and answer for their children inevitably introduce the parents' biases into the research. Even if the researcher's intent is to support the best interests of children within transracial adoptive settings, using data collected from parents about their children tends to privilege the best interests of White parents, rather than of their children of color. Most critically, the early research of Rita J. Simon and Howard Altstein (1974) and Charles Zastrow (1977)—now accepted as cornerstones of transracial adoption research—used these parent-assessment methods without adequately reporting the limitations of this methodology. This drew fire from later researchers, but Simon and Altstein made no real attempt over the course of their twenty-year study to explore the implications of parent-reported results that indicated overwhelmingly positive adoption experiences.

Simon and Altstein's interviews and assessments of 206 adoptive families in the 1970s revealed the families in their study to be uniformly middle-class and predominantly Christian, with 78 percent living in all-White neighborhoods and 90 percent or more considering themselves liberal.[7] All had adopted transracially. Some had also adopted White children, who were also assessed. The majority of participants in the study had adopted domestically, mostly African American or Native American children. Interviews using specific questions developed by the researchers began in 1971, and were repeated in 1979, 1984, and 1991. Initially, 206 families participated, but by the end of the study only 83 families could be located and were willing to participate. In addition to carrying out interviews, the researchers tested adoptees' self-esteem and family integration, using various testing instruments. The researchers assessed both self-esteem and family integration as generally good, and did not find significant differences between adoptees and nonadoptees for either characteristic. Most adoptees grew up in predominantly White settings, and most adoptees' closest friends were White.

The adoptees also answered questions about relationships to parents and siblings, and their responses were interpreted by Simon and Altstein as similar to those of nonadopted children. In the end, 90 percent of adoptive parents said they would urge others (White or not, despite the dubious possibility that parents of color would even be allowed to adopt a White child) to transracially adopt.[8]

Simon and Altstein revisited transracial adoption and the families who participated in their 1977 and 1981 study, in 1987. Reported in the book *Transracial Adoptees and Their Families*, the results were based on interviews with parents and with the children (who now had a median age of fifteen years). When comparing parent and child responses (even though the parents and children were not asked the same questions), the researchers reported finding "considerable consensus."[9] In this round of interviews, parents were asked about how their children were doing academically, socially, and within the family. Parents generally reported their children were doing well in school, considered them socially healthy, and called their relationships with their children and their children's relationships with siblings healthy. Parents were also asked what they remembered to have been their expectations about their children's racial identities when they first adopted. Simon and Altstein reported that 12 percent of parents expected the children to have the adoptive parents' racial identity, that 23 percent the children to have the children's own racial identity, and that 50 percent had no expectations about racial identity. Most said these expectations had not changed over the lives of the adoptees. When asked, 65 percent of parents said the children had talked to them about being the subject of racial incidents, but the parents generally did not think the incidents would leave a lasting impression on their children. When asked what they would advise others about transracial adoption, 40 percent warned against adopting out of a sense of social or political duty, and 25 percent mentioned that "handling 'the race issue'" should be a major consideration. Still, most (86 percent) said they would urge others to transracially adopt.[10]

In the article "Adoption of Black Children by White Parents in the USA" (1984), Simon summed up her own research and made the point that "almost all the mothers and fathers emphasized that that the transracial adoptions had enriched their lives."[11] She also acknowledged that, because very few transracial adoptees had even reached adolescence, it was still difficult to say how the adoption experience would influence adoptees as adults. She concluded by advocating for colorblindness in transracial adoption.[12]

Zastrow (1977) published a study on African American transracial adoptive families with preschool-age children, focusing on the satisfaction of these parents compared to that of in-race White adoptive parents, and on the overall success of the adoptions, based on parents' perceptions. He found that parents saw few special problems with transracial adoption,[13] but that they foresaw more complicated issues for their children as they entered later stages of adolescence and adulthood, and he noted that almost all the parents (99 percent) considered their adoption experience either extremely satisfying or more satisfying than dissatisfying. Zastrow used these results to support transracial placements as a good solution for African American children in need of adoptive placements.[14]

Lela B. Costin and Shirley H. Wattenberg (1979) studied parental and family experiences with transracially adopted children. They interviewed parents in families of twenty-one transracially adopted children in 1972 and 1973. In an acknowledgment that their research was about adoptive parents instead of adoptees, Costin and Wattenberg took an approach which considered parental dilemmas in transracial adoption: whether to integrate or differentiate transracially adopted children, and whether to instill knowledge of the transracial adoptee's cultural background. They concluded that, while parents do think about these dilemmas, there probably was not a typical transracial adoption parent profile.[15]

Nearing the end of their twenty-year longitudinal study, Simon and Altstein conceded that "much of what we have portrayed thus far has been gleaned from the perceptions and opinions of the parents."[16] The age of the children at the outset of the study necessitated this method, but the researchers' emphasis throughout their study, even when adoptees were reaching adulthood, was on parents. When adoptees moved away from home, little effort appears to have been made to reconnect with them for the later phases of the study. Zastrow, for his part, based the majority of his findings on parental perceptions of the success of their adoptions.

Unfortunately, several subsequent researchers replicated this methodology, further reinforcing the assumption that adoptive parent experiences are basically identical to those of their children, and that adoptive parents belong at the center of any inquiry on adoption. The use of adoptive parent experiences as proxies for those of their children complicates this research because it aligns researchers with the perspectives and concerns of these parents, whose goal is a successful transracial adoption, whose belief in the morality of transracial adoption is wholehearted, and whose White privilege is generally unrecognized, both by themselves and by the researchers. Although this methodology elides the actual experiences of adopted people, the research does unequivocally show that, in every study where the issue was assessed, adoptive parents have seen the adoption experience as beneficial to both themselves and their children.

Adjustment and the Slippage toward Racial and Cultural Assimilation

Since early in the history of transracial adoption, researchers have sought to evaluate the so-called success of transracial placements and to verify that adoptees benefit from their adoption experiences. Most of the evaluation has been empirical, using assessment instruments such as personality tests, racial identity tests, and questionnaires. The issue of adjustment has been paramount in many of these studies; many of the research questions have centered around how well the adoptee seems to be adjusting to the adoptive family and experience, or how generally well-adjusted the adoptee is. In addition, many studies have attempted to ascertain how adoptees racially self-identify. This is probably at least partly in response to the 1972 National Association of Black Social Workers' charge that only African American parents can instill a sense of self in African American children, and to the understanding that transracial adoption may be harmful to native communities and children, as implied in the Indian Child Welfare Act of 1978. But as early as the 1960s, adoption research had focused on the normalcy of adoptees in comparison to nonadopted persons, and on the possibility that adoption carried psychological risks for the child.[17] In the overall body of empirical adoption research, the question of possible harms to adoptees as a result of adoptive placement is yet unresolved, but studies of transracial placements in the 1970s and 1980s consistently found few or no adjustment problems among adoptees.

In 1974, Lucille Grow and Deborah Shapiro first reported the results of their comprehensive research on transracial adoption. They studied 125 families who had adopted African American children, all over the age of six, by twice interviewing parents and assessing child adjustment and parental management of race within the adoptions. Their major finding was that 77 percent of the children "had adjusted successfully."[18] William Feigelman and Arnold R. Silverman, in an effort to "investigate the long-term impact of transracial placement"[19] gathered information using questionnaires (presumably answered by parents, because most of the children in the study were too young to fill out questionnaires) from 372 adoptive families. They found that transracial adoptees adjusted as well or better than in-race adoptees, with Korean and Colombian adoptees scoring higher than in-race adoptees on the researchers' measure of adjustment.

The work of Grow and Shapiro and that of Feigelman and Silverman are examples of research that presents evidence of high child adjustment in the transracial adoption setting as a major finding, though it appears as a parameter in most of the transracial adoption research considered here, including that of Simon and Altstein and that of Zastrow. As noted by Hollingsworth, adjustment of children in their adoptive families was often gauged by asking parents how well *they* thought their children had adjusted. When this method was used, results indicating high adjustment of adoptees were unequivocal. Although high adjustment may indeed have been the norm for the populations studied, it is also possible that parents reported high adjustment because they *wanted* it to be true. Most (if not all) parents are highly motivated to say their children are happy and doing well; to report otherwise could be seen, consciously or subconsciously, as a parenting failure. Adoptive parents—and, arguably, *especially* transracial adoptive parents, in the face of criticism that transracial adoption might be harmful to their children—have high investment in the success of their adoptions. Even if all the parents in these studies are exceptionally reflective and honest, adopted children are also highly invested in demonstrating high adjustment into their adoptive families. Many researchers have reported that parents have emphasized sameness and downplayed difference to their transracially adopted children. Because parents recognize that their transracially adopted children's appearance is often strikingly different from that of other family members, parents often strive to continually demonstrate inclusion in an effort to minimize potential feelings of otherness and alienation. For adopted children, any claim that runs counter to this familial narrative of sameness and inclusion may seem a betrayal. For these reasons, I see the poorly defined criteria of adjustment as a poor indicator of successful adoption.

Cultural assimilation in the United States always refers to the assimilation of people of color or difference into the dominant White culture. The act of assimilation is often represented as a move toward greater personal or financial success. The loss of culture during assimilation is often considered worth the rewards. Adoptees are assumed to enter the adoption relationship as a population whose assimilation can be considered a fait accompli, thus sidestepping the moral complications of the loss of culture within the White family. The perceived success of transracial adoptees (in terms of adjustment and self-esteem) supports the notion that assimilation is the best path for people of difference. Even though the practice of transracial adoption on its surface may appear to be a rejection of the practice of matching (where adoptable children were matched to prospective adoptive parents by appearance, class, and even IQ), the broad practice of assimilation of adoptees into White families, and praise for assimilation by researchers in the early decades of transracial adoption, reveal assimilation as another kind of matching, one where adoptees are culturally indistinguishable from adoptive families despite their unmatched race. Mark Jerng remarks, "The tacit . . . rule of the 'sameness' of adoption . . . gives way to a vision of adoption accommodating racial difference out of necessity."[20]

When adoptees themselves, either as children or as adults, have been tested or asked to assess racial or cultural identity, most studies have produced results indicating a high degree of assimilation into White culture. This is to be expected, as most adoptees are raised in White families. Transracial adoptive parents often deemphasize the adoptee's race by practicing colorblindness in the family and by stressing the child's Americanness. As parents, they want their children to be like them. There is tremendous desire within families that become racially mixed through adoption for everyone in the family to be the same. Imagined homogeneity helps these families cope with their outward differences and be more like a normal, or racially homogeneous, family.

Simon and Altstein stated that one purpose of their study was "to find out how racial attitudes, awareness, and identity were or were not likely to be affected by the merging of different races within a nuclear family."[21] The majority of parents in the study reported that they wanted their children to racially identify as raceless or as White. This being the case, it is hardly surprising that many parents and children then reported either having no racial identity or having a White identity. Simon and Altstein's study paints a picture of adult adoptees living, dating, and socializing in a predominantly White world, and coming to a more racialized self-concept later in life. In the 1977 report, 62 percent of parents reported having no problems with adopted children and 63 percent reported a change in themselves. Some said they had become more racially and socially sensitive as a result of adopting, though most said it had made them "colorblind."[22] When asked about the racial identity of their children (who averaged five years old at the time of questioning), 32 percent of the parents of Black children thought their children identified as Black, and 30 to 38 percent of parents thought children of color were too young to consider their own race. A majority (65 to 69 percent) of parents said they wanted their children to identify as having no race, or as having race of both their birth parents and their adoptive parents. Most of the parents (75 percent) were doing things to involve children with their birth race cultures, but 12 percent were doing nothing differently and continued to live as they would have if they had not adopted a child of a different race. Of their own racial identity, 70 percent of parents said their racial identity did not change when they adopted, and 30 percent said they themselves changed to become raceless.[23]

The idea of racelessness, which features so strongly in the responses of adoptive parents in Simon and Altstein's study, merits closer examination. In a society where the dominant culture is White and non-Whites are "of color," to have no race is effectively to be White. Parents who described themselves or their children as "raceless" were likely attempting to protect their families from the difficulties of difference, but in creating an imagined racelessness, they were unwittingly Whitewashing their children.[24] In their 1987 follow-up report, Simon and Altstein also asked the children about their social and family relationships. The children reported having, mostly, White friends, and 60 percent said they exclusively dated Whites. When asked about transracial adoption policy, 70 percent of the adoptees questioned specifically disagreed with the position of the National Association of Black Social Workers. They also reported high integration into their adoptive families. Surveys of the transracial adoptees as adults continued to show a high level of family integration when compared to White adopted children adopted within-race.[25]

Dong Soo Kim's 1978 article "Issues in Transracial and Transcultural Adoption" is an early work that stands in contrast to the positive reports of adoptee adjustment in other studies. Kim outlined a critique of transracial adoption policy and of previous studies, suggesting that in studies that found Korean adoptee children to be as well-adjusted as other children, the children were "still in the adolescent stage with an anticipatory socialization." Kim also noted that some of the children in his study were unhappy with their Asian appearance, while "many adoptive parents [saw] 'no color or race or nationality' in their adopted foreign children" and that "frequent reports of foreign children are that 'they felt "totally American" except when people called them Asian,' which happens all the time."[26] Kim questioned the validity of adoptee adjustment studies, arguing that "the so-called good adjustment of these children is being accomplished at the cost of their unique ethnic cultural heritage and identity, partially reinforced by parents' innocent, yet inapt, expectations. However, the American cultural assimilation . . . is not fully accepted because of prevailing racism of the society."[27]

Researchers such as Simon and Altstein advocated for colorblindness as a "cure for racism," a position echoed by many parents, with the subsequent blending of difference into a melting-pot landscape of dominant White culture; Kristi Brian reports Korean adoptive parents see themselves as less discriminatory than in-race adoptive parents.[28] However, treating assimilation as a measure of success within transracial adoptions indicates a failure to acknowledge the loss of cultural heritage and racial identity in the transracial adoption process. Cultural anthropologist Barbara Yngvesson points to this kind of thinking in published adoption research leading to the problematic conclusion that "transracial adoptive homes would provide a model for a color-blind society."[29] In the minds of these researchers, the problems of childlessness on the part of parents and parentlessness on the part of children have been solved, so the loss of cultural and racial identity is not even mentionable—except by Dong Soo Kim, an ethnically Korean scholar. It was not until the 2000s that researchers, notably Rich M. Lee, also an ethnically Korean scholar, began to publish findings based on adoptee reports (rather than those of their parents) indicating that the racism that transracial adoptees experienced should be perceived as a harm specifically linked to the transracial placement itself.

Disregarding Reported Problems

Many researchers in this period appear to have ignored portions of their study populations who reported problems with or in their adoptive children. Although no researchers found problems in a majority of their study population, several reported problems among sizable minorities, which they explained as insignificant. Most of the researchers attributed these problems to factors other than the transracial nature of the adoption itself, or minimized the problems within the overall results. S. P. Kim, S. Hong, and B. S. Kim completed a study of fifteen White New York couples in 1979 through interviews and questionnaires. The couples had adopted twenty-one Korean children. Nine couples reported behavior problems in sixteen children. Among the twenty-one children, twelve were adopted over age three, and the researchers surmised that this fact contributed to the problems reported.[30] Simon and Altstein (1981) wrote a follow-up on the families they had researched five years earlier based on phone and mail correspondence with parents.[31] They found that one in six of the families now reported difficulties with their children that they attributed to the child's transracial adoption, with stealing being the most commonly reported problem behavior. Other problems included diagnoses, for some children, of disabilities that parents perceived to be genetic in origin. Some parents also expressed feelings of guilt that their decision to adopt had caused pain to their children. Overall, Simon and Altstein maintained their position in support of the practice of transracial adoption, stating that the great majority of families had few problems, as assessed by parents. Families with problems (also called "unhappy families") were assessed separately, and the researchers stressed that these families were a minority in the group, comprising eighteen of the eighty-eight families interviewed.[32] In Owen Gill and Barbara Jackson's study, six of thirty-six children were identified as having problems, yet the authors stressed that this was "only 17 percent."[33] None of this research specified what incidence of the types of problems reported by the adoptive parents would be cause for concern.

Deemphasizing Loss

Adoptive parent–focused studies of the 1970s and 1980s largely failed to capture adoptees' feelings of loneliness and alienation from both adoptive and birth cultures, and of loss of birth culture and security. Most adoptees do seem to cope with these feelings successfully, but these details are essential elements of the transracial adoptee experience. Most adoptees interviewed in my research and in other recent studies reported a profound sense of isolation, as if they were the only ones in their situations. Many transracial adoptees also discussed alienation from others of their birth race, as well. In their relationships with others of the same race, adoptees described not fitting in or not meeting expectations. Many said others of the same race could tell they were different, which led to their rejection. Some said they themselves could pick transracial adoptees out of a room by appearance and mannerisms. Other adoptees described feelings of loss and grief about their birth culture. This evidence suggests that the formation of racial identity in transracial adoptees is more complicated than just choosing a preferred affiliation. Navigating race as a person of color in a predominantly White society is always a challenge, but is unusually demanding for transracial adoptees because an exploration of birth race is sometimes seen as rejection of adoptive race and family. Because of this, adoptees have much to lose in racial exploration, and family support is often lacking in adoptees' efforts to this end.

The fact that fewer adult transracial or transnational subjects were available to researchers in the 1970s and 1980s than today may have limited researchers' ability to incorporate adoptee perspectives into their work during this period. However, although a body of scholarly literature dealing with loss in adoptive placements had definitely emerged by the 1980s, none of the findings of this literature found their way into research on transracial adoption at the time. Based on the body of research I have reviewed, it is impossible for me to draw a firm conclusion about why exploration of such an important facet of adoptee experience was ignored in the research design and findings from this period. I can't help wondering, however, if ethnocentric assumptions that transracial and transnational adoptees were lucky to have been adopted may have prevented both researchers and parents from imagining that adoptees would have experienced loss as a direct result of having been adopted.

Race Queries

Attention to race in adoption research of this period was based on attitude and identity testing of individuals, using a variety of methods. None of the works considered here explicitly acknowledged the existence of racialized power imbalances within transracial adoption structures. Perhaps to maintain the appearance of objectivity, the research was focused on the study populations out of social and cultural contexts. Most studies found that transracially adopted persons had acceptable levels of positive racial identity development, though none clearly defined an *un*acceptable level of racial identity development.

Simon and Altstein's 1977 identity assessment of children included 366 children aged between three and eight years, over half of whom were transracially adopted.[34] Children were asked to respond to a list of questions about white, black, and brown (meant to symbolize Asian or Native American) dolls and to associate qualities with Blacks and Whites in pictures. Results were inconclusive among the children with respect to preferences and attitudes toward the different dolls, where previous studies showed a strong preference for White dolls. Adopted Black children had a slightly more positive attitude toward photographs of African Americans than in previous studies (which had assessed Black children who had not been adopted), though all children still responded more negatively to photographs of Blacks.[35] Simon and Altstein attributed the difference in attitude between transracially adopted children and other African American children to the adoption experience, implying that being transracially adopted improved the children's perceptions of African Americans. This finding supports the rhetorical position that transracial adoption can help solve problems of racism.[36] A large minority of Asian and Native American transracial adoptees identified more readily with White than with medium- or dark-complexioned people and dolls. Simon and Altstein concluded that this was due to the images being too racially ambiguous for the children to interpret,[37] discounting several other possible explanations: that the children lacked Asian or Native American identity and self-realization; that they were unaware of the possibility of an Asian or Native American racial identity; or that they were aware of but unwilling to claim such an identity

J. F. Shireman and P. R. Johnson sought to compare single-parent, Black-to-White transracial, and in-race adoptions, using three groups of families, with each group containing between thirty-one and forty-five families. Parents were asked to report children's behavior, to establish adjustment, and the researchers used the Clark Doll Racial Preference Selection Test to assess racial identity. As in Simon and Altstein's doll test, children were presented with differently complexioned dolls and asked to state preferences between them. The researchers reported that the three groups scored similarly on adjustment, but that the transracial adoptees developed Black racial identities later than in-race adopted Black children.[38] Shireman interpreted this as further support for the idea that transracial adoption is an acceptable solution when Black homes are not available for Black orphans.[39] Another author, Watson, interpreted the findings differently, suggesting that the adoptees' parents had lessened emphasis on positive Black identity for their children, leading to the difference in the transracial and in-race adoptees' responses.[40]

Ruth G. McRoy and Louis A. Zurcher Jr.'s *Transracial and Inracial Adoptees* presented the results of a study comparing African American adolescent and young adult transracial adoptees to in-race African American adoptees. The researchers described their methodology as being based on "symbolic interaction theory, which assumes a person's self-definition develops from interpersonal relations in a social world,"[41] Parents and adoptees were interviewed separately from one another. Adoptees were between ten and twenty-six years of age, with a mean age just under fourteen. Three-quarters were male. McRoy and Zurcher found that the two groups of families were similar in many ways, but that Black adoptive parents were more likely to instruct children about Black heritage and pride, while White parents tended to emphasize that "all humans are alike."[42] Many White parents "exhibited stereotypical role expectations and perceptions of Blacks. Those parents expressed delight in raising their Black adoptee but were apprehensive about the adoptee's association with other Black children and about . . . living in a racially mixed neighborhood."[43] In addition, the researchers found that the in-race adoptees were more likely to tell their parents about racist incidents. The transracial adoptees were more likely than the in-racial adoptees to have White friends and dating partners. They were also more likely to attend predominantly White schools, which

McRoy and Zurcher judged affected self-identity negatively for these children.[44] The authors also noted that, although "the majority of in-race adoptive parents were raising their black children to live in a black and white society; most of the transracial adoptive parents were raising their black children to live in a white society."[45] They observed that children who had minimal contact with other African Americans "tended to develop stereotyped impressions of blacks and were likely to feel that they were 'better off' in a white adoptive family."[46]

Unlike most other research of the period, McRoy and Zurcher's work brought to the fore an explicit concern with the prevalence of racist ideologies in dominant White society. The authors' decision to compare in-race and transracial African American adoptees, instead of comparing transracial adoptees to White in-race adoptees or to biological children, as was done in past research, was critical, in light of their findings. The results suggested that African American parents are better equipped than White parents to prepare African American children to live in a racist world, and that White parents' love for their adopted children cannot cancel out the effects of deeply ingrained racism in American society.

Social and cultural theories of race, power, class, and gender have achieved wide acceptance across the social sciences and humanities in recent decades, influencing both the questions researchers ask and the methods they use. During the period that seminal studies of transracial and transnational adoption were being carried out, however, much of this theory was nascent, not widely accepted, or entirely undeveloped. In hindsight, the consequences of unacknowledged White racial privilege are clear in the lived reality of transracial and transnational adoption; policy and dominant narratives that fail to see problems for racially and otherwise minoritized populations in new reproductive technologies tends to reproduce and even expand power imbalances. Research design clearly influences study outcomes, and research findings that described successful "colorblind" placements and well-adjusted adoptees served to support the expansion of transracial and transnational adoption—even when the practice has faced controversy among the White public and opposition from communities of color.

Rita Simon and a Legacy of Transnational Adoption Expansion

Rita Simon is arguably the primary author of transracial adoption history and research during the 1970s and 1980s. She, with and without collaborator Howard Altstein, is the most prolific scholarly producer of books and articles on transracial adoption. I foreground her work as a prime example of how deeply biased transracial adoption research rooted in the 1970s and 1980s came to exert a strong influence on the development of policies which expanded transracial and transnational adoption practice. She has also positioned herself to influence national transracial adoption policy. Her pro-transracial-adoption books have found ready audiences among parents considering adoption and child welfare policymakers, and she has continued to publish on the topic from the 1970s to the present day. While she has taken a strong position in support of transracial adoption, her interests in transracial adoption, both personal and professional, have never been explicitly revealed in her work. In the preface of *Transracial Adoption* (written with Altstein), the authors openly lamented what they saw as the end of "transracial adoption" (African American and Native American-to-White adoption) in the United States because of opposition within communities of color.[47]

Simon and Altstein began their research in 1971, following the NABSW statement concerning transracial adoption. Although Simon and Altstein did not, in their early work, yet take an explicit position in support of transracial placement, they argued extensively against the NABSW position, explaining that (White adoptive) parents were the strongest proponents for transracial adoption. These parents were portrayed by Simon and Altstein at the time as not strong enough to win the fight to continue transracial adoption. Simon and Altstein summed up the endeavor of transracial adoption as "humanitarian acts, defined purely and simply by love and compassion for another human being,"[48] and cited Christian charity as one of the main reasons individuals and agencies are involved in transracial adoption. Their first book included a history of African American and Native American transracial adoption, and reported that most children adjusted well, in direct opposition to anti-transracial adoption activism within both communities of color.[49] In their view, transracial adoptions were seemingly without negative social or political consequence, and the authors emerged as strong early proponents of the practice.

In keeping with their desire to advocate in favor of transracial adoption, Simon and Altstein glossed over some of the findings in their longitudinal study while emphasizing others, and structured some quantitative assessments with possible bias toward a finding of high adjustment for adoptees. For instance, in *Transracial Adoption*, they stressed that African American transracially adopted children responded to pictures of African Americans more than non-adopted African American children, but failed to note that all children still responded more negatively to photos of Blacks than to photos of Whites. In *Transracial Adoptees and Their Families*, when assessing how emotionally close parents and children felt to one another, the researchers structured questionnaires so multiple choice options for children and parents did not match, with children's options weighted toward more closeness with parents. In the same book, Simon and Altstein emphasized that eighteen out of eighty-eight families (over 20 percent) with problems did not represent an "ordinary" experience, and even relegated them to a separate chapter called "Special Families" (as opposed to "Ordinary Families").

Simon's collected body of published work on the topic of transracial and transnational adoption is very large, with dozens of books and articles in print (though many are updates on her original longitudinal study with little new analysis). Her work is undoubtedly a top source of information for adoption agencies, policy makers, or indeed anyone with interest in research on transracial adoption outcomes. Even after research in the 1990s and 2000s began to focus more on self-reported adoptee experiences, and critiques incorporating elements of critical race studies and postcolonial theory were published in increasing numbers, Simon maintained that the findings she and Altstein had put forward in the 1970s showed that there are no significant problems in transracial placements (see chapter epigraph, from a 2002 publication). In 1998, Simon testified before the Subcommittee on Human Resources of the U.S. Congress's House Committee on Ways and Means hearing on legislation to decrease the amount of time minority children spend in foster care, in support of transracial adoption. In her testimony, she stated, "All of the major empirical research that has been done on transracial adoption have shown that these children come out healthy, aware of their identities, and committed to their adoptive families,"[50] going as far as stating that fellow adoption scholar Ruth McRoy's results supported the practice of transracial adoption, even if McRoy did not herself. Not surprisingly, many of her beliefs have become well established in the American popular understanding of transracial adoption.

Conclusion

Although social workers in the 1950s questioned the new practice of Korean adoption in regard to both the methods by which children were procured and placed, and the readiness of the American public to accept Asian children in White homes, by the 1970s, as evidenced here, few of these concerns were voiced in social work and other behavioral science research. In the 2000s, critiques similar to those launched at the beginning of the practice of Korean transnational adoption reappeared in scholarly research, though the reasoning behind those critiques had evolved to include critical race theory and postcolonial theory. Many recent studies still focus on adoptive parent experiences, but instead of allowing adoptive parents to serve as proxies for adoptee experiences, these studies are specific in querying White adoptive parents' beliefs, experiences, and practices around race and Whiteness with respect to their parenting of children of color.[51] In the larger context and history of empirical research on transracial and transnational adoption, the work I highlight in this chapter is somewhat of an anathema.

Despite these advances, popular perceptions of transnational adoption still reflect the assumptions and findings of this now outdated research quite closely. As the practice of transnational adoption has become both more popular and more expensive, transnational adopters are almost as uniformly White and even more affluent than their 1970s and 1980s counterparts, and adoptive parents have continued to occupy center stage in the transnational adoption story. These parents are still widely regarded as saviors and heroes, perhaps even more now that many Hollywood celebrities have become adoptive parents to children from around the world. The debate about transnational adoption, to the degree that it is visible in the American cultural landscape, continues to focus on the experiences of adoptive parents, whether it be on their fitness to parent or on their disillusionment with the adoption exchange.

Historian Catherine Ceniza Choy points out how stories of difficult Asian adoptee transitions into adoptive families tend to be subsumed, while stories of seamless and joyful union are embraced and repeated.[52] The assumption that people adopted from other countries are American success stories denies them any basis to protest experiences of injustice, and even leaves them open to attack if they attempt to criticize or reform transracial and transnational adoption practice and policy. Racial harassment, which transracial and transnational adoptees have always endured, now includes cyberbullying when adoptees suggest ending or reforming the practice (an anonymous online commenter once wrote about me, "Kim Park Nelson is lucky she didn't end up dead or a prostitute," sentiments I know are echoed to many transnational adoptees). And like other social debates that affect both people of color and Whites in the United States, the racial dimension of most transnational adoptions is still largely discounted.

Social work and policy research during the first few decades of transnational adoption presented itself, like all scholarly research, as objective. It is obvious in most of this research that authors have consciously or subconsciously designed studies to support the practice of transracial and transnational adoption. Many of these researchers used questionable parameters, such as racial assimilation as a measure of child adjustment, and adoptive parent experience as a proxy for adoptee experience. Researchers also ignored other important factors, such as the scholarly literature dealing with experiences of loss in adoption, and even parts of their own findings that suggest problems in adoptive placements. Researchers during this period had difficulty evaluating racial identity in adoptees, and all but ignored race-based power inequities in the adoption industry, though these are important factors when assessing the transracial adoptee experience and the overall success of transnational adoption programs. This body of research remains highly influential to the present day, however, and continues to inform policy decisions about transracial adoption, even though it fails to place transracial adoption within the social and historical context of lived racial and class hierarchies, to acknowledge the subjugation of birth mothers of color, or to debate the consequences of racial and cultural assimilation.

Understanding the transracial adoptee experience is important not only to answer the question of whether parents of one race can successfully raise children of another, but also to better understand our society and culture by illuminating the intersection between race and culture in individuals. Although the studies discussed here were never intended to provide advice on parenting, it is difficult to ignore parallels between these findings, now thirty to forty years old, and the experiences subsequently reported by adult adoptees. The willingness of researchers to de-emphasize reports of problems by sizable minorities of their study populations appears eerily similar to adoptive parents' dismissal of their children's reports of racist incidents. Equating assimilation to positive adjustment mirrors current beliefs about social colorblindness, a trend widely embraced by the public, and often reported by Korean adoptees as a parenting tactic in their adoptive homes. Disregard for the body of research dealing with loss seems to foreshadow adoptive parents' tendency to focus on their own gains rather than on the losses inherent in transnational and transracial adoption. The placement of adoptive parents as the primary subjects parallels current public understandings of adoptive parents as the only or primary actors in the story of transnational adoption, with adoptees and birth families reduced to lucky participants in the miracle of adoption.

The tendency in the research to explain away problems and disregard losses accords with the belief—still widely held—that adoption is a "win-win-win" situation in which adoptive parents get the children they want, unwanted children find families, and birth families are relieved of the burden of unwanted children. One consequence of accepting this beatific vision is that it becomes difficult to conceive of significant problems in current transnational adoption practice; in a world where everyone believes they are getting what they want, impetus for reform can be hard to find.

From a scholarly perspective, the research reviewed here has been eclipsed, to some degree, by later, more comprehensive studies. However, the empirical studies of transracial and transnational adoption in the 1970s and 1980s produced a lasting legacy in popular understanding of adoption and in the lives of adoptees. These deeply flawed studies supported the continued expansion of transracial adoption. When critiques of the practice of domestic transracial adoption emerged from communities of color, the adoption industry framed these critiques as anti-child. By the 1980s, the adoption industry turned increasingly to adoptable child populations outside the United States, bypassing criticism grounded in American minority populations' struggles for civil rights. Even though most of these studies did not consider transnational adoptees separately from domestic populations, their broad support for domestic transracial adoption could easily be extended to any kind of transracial adoption no matter the source of children. By the beginning of the twenty-first century, transnational adoptions were more common in some American states than were domestic adoptions, and today there are over a million transnational adoptees worldwide, about half of whom reside in the United States.

4

An Adoptee for Every Lake

Multiculturalism, Minnesota, and the Korean Transracial Adoptee

I didn't realize there were other Korean adoptees out there, . . . much less a bunch of them in Minnesota. I had no clue that there were . . . issues to discuss, . . . you know, a community of people.
                Fern, thirty-four, Korean adoptee living in Minnesota[1]

Throughout the 1970s and 1980s, with the growing popularity of a particular form of multiculturalism that "celebrated difference" without directly addressing racial injustice, transracial adoption came to be celebrated as a form of family building that exemplified the colorblind and inclusionary values of social liberalism. The experiences of Minnesota Korean adoptees reveal that this form of multiculturalism failed to protect them from racism and racial isolation; instead, most had to go outside their supposedly multicultural families to connect with their racial and cultural identities.

A Brief History of American Transracial Adoption

The history of Korean transnational adoption spans more than sixty years and is deeply entwined with both the Korean War and subsequent geopolitical relations between the United States and South Korea up to the present day. Equally relevant to understanding Korean transnational adoption, however, is the intersecting and overlapping history of American domestic transracial adoption. This history has been shaped by the changing social and cultural dispositions of Americans toward the practice of multiracial family building through adoption, as well as by the policies and practices that have made these adoptions more and more common since the 1950s.

    American domestic transracial adoption as a formal practice barely predates the start of Korean transnational adoption. Korean transnational adoption began in 1953—five years after the first American domestic African-American-to-White transracial adoption and five years before the initiation of the U.S. Indian Adoption Project, a national program with the goal of placing American Indian children in White American homes.[2] Until transnational adoptions began in former Eastern Bloc nations in the 1990s, transnational adoptions were almost all transracial adoptions. Roughly 15,000 transnational adoptions to the United States occurred between 1953 and 1962. The rate of transnational placements in the United States began to increase in the late 1960s and early 1970s, with 37,469 transnational adoptions from 1965 to 1976.[3] Korean and other transnational adoptions would become increasingly common in subsequent years. The annual number of U.S. transnational adoptions almost doubled between 1989 and 1998, with 15,744 transnational adoptions in 1998.[4] In 2004, transnational adoptions to the United States peaked at 22,884, but by 2010, this number had declined to 12,149.[5]

In-country adoption statistics are largely unavailable since 1977, when the U.S. government stopped collecting this information. It is known that 831 Black children were adopted into White families in 1975,[6] compared to 2,995 Korean adoptions that year.[7] An estimated 1,411 Black children were adopted into White homes in 1987.[8] The year before, Korean adoptions to the United States had peaked at 6,138.[9] The number of domestic transracial adoptions is believed to be stable, with African American adoption to White homes estimated to represent 1.2 percent of all adoptions.[10]

A Transition to Transnational, Transracial Adoption

The increase in transracial and transnational adoptions during the 1960s and 1970s has been attributed to a number of factors. The set of circumstances most cited is that the available number of adoptable White infants decreased during this time because of new access to family planning,[11] while the swelling baby boom population was just reaching the age of parenthood, creating high demand for adoptable children. The civil rights movement may have also furthered the practice of transracial adoption as more attempts to desegregate American society were made and Whites became more comfortable sharing their lives with people of other races. As the American middle class expanded following the end of the Second World War, more families were able to afford the costs of adopting. Children born to working-class parents are more often given up for adoption.[12] During the 1960s and 1970s, class division may have translated to Black and White, since the middle class was composed primarily of Whites and the working class had more African Americans. At the same time, as the number of adoptable children decreased, adoption agencies became more selective in their placement with adoptive parents, with the result that parents were required to meet certain standards of income and age and be infertile.

Some of these criteria may have restricted access to adoptable African American children by African Americans wanting to adopt, and indirectly encouraged further transracial adoption of non-Whites.[13] The North American Council on Adoptable Children determined that relatively few Black adoptive families could be found for in-race adoption because of a lack of cultural support within adoption agencies and the fact that parents were poorly recruited in Black communities.[14] Some researchers have also suggested that African Americans were less interested in adoption than White Americans, saying that "Evidence seems to suggest that the plight of adoptable black children does not rank high on the list of black adults' social priorities, even when they seem to be aware of the problem's severity,"[15] though this view is strongly contested by scholars such as Dorothy Roberts.[16]

The second half of the twentieth century was characterized by rapid advances in reproductive technologies, both scientific and sociopolitical: medical advances such as in vitro fertilization were paralleled by social changes that favored the removal of children from domestic and international communities of color, who then became available for formalized and legally regulated adoption.[17] These medical and social technologies became more popular during the 1970s and 1980s, and were considered commonplace by the 1990s. While the availability of medical interventions for infertility has steadily expanded, not all forms of adoption have increased in frequency. Domestic transracial placements have stalled since the 1970s,[18] but transnational transracial placements—first from Korea and later from many other nations—have become much more common. This has occurred because opposition to the practice of transracial domestic adoption crystallized in the early 1970s within the African American and Native American communities, and political activism from within these communities led to the implementation of within-race adoption policies for domestic adoption at most adoption agencies by 1975.

At its 1972 annual conference, the National Association of Black Social Workers (NABSW) announced its formal opposition to transracial adoption in a position paper titled "Preserving Families of African Ancestry,"[19] which predicted that transracial adoptees would have poor psychological adjustment and racial identity, and would be unable to cope with episodes of racism and discrimination without the guidance of a parent of the same color; subsequently, the organization led efforts to end out-of-race adoption of African American children, under a stated goal of protecting children and preventing cultural genocide.[20] A year earlier, a meeting of American Indian leaders had issued a statement that also identified transracial adoption as cultural genocide.[21] The year 1972 proved to be the peak of domestic transracial adoption in the United States, with 2,574 total placements.[22]

In 1978, the federal government enacted the Indian Child Welfare Act (ICWA), prohibiting the transracial placement of American Indian children outside the tribe of their birth without the consent of the tribe. This legislation was possible because Indian nations have limited rights of sovereignty with respect to the U.S. government, and thus can be granted protections and rights under federal law that are not available to other communities of color. The ICWA also represented an acknowledgment of many decades of governmental abuses against American Indian families, including forced removal of children by placement in White-run boarding schools (1878–1930s) or by adoption into White families (1958–1967).

Taken together, the NABSW statement and the passage of ICWA sent a clear message that American communities of color recognized abuses in the practice of domestic transracial adoption. As the number of domestic transracial adoptions declined throughout the 1970s, in response to these two events and the social forces surrounding them,[23] many social workers began to question the appropriateness of transracial placements. Although it is highly unlikely that the NABSW or the proponents of ICWA intended to promote adoption from other communities or countries, an increase in transnational transracial adoption was a major outcome of these twin milestones in American adoption history. The American public's hunger for adoptable children would not be easily suppressed, but would find other sources of children. Supplanting domestic populations of children of color with international populations solved the perception that White adoption of domestic children of color could be a form of racism.[24]

Opposition to transracial adoption in the 1970s focused on past and potential racism in the adoption of African Americans and American Indians, minority populations that had high visibility in civil rights movements at the time. Asian and Asian American populations, on the other hand, were relatively small in the United States during the 1970s,[25] and most were concentrated in a few small geographic areas. But, although the struggles of African Americans and American Indians were well publicized in the 1970s, those of Asian Americans were not. Compared to African Americans and Native Americans, the low visibility of Asian and Asian American populations contributed to the popular perception that these groups were (and remain) largely unaffected by racial discrimination and other forms of racism. In addition, tacit belief in a racial hierarchy that placed Asian closest to White as the "model minority" contributed to the perception that Asian Americans were not suffering the effects of racism. Since the anti-transracial-adoption positions of the NABSW and in the ICWA emphasized histories of racial discrimination against African Americans and American Indians, the perceived absence of racial discrimination against Asian

Americans made the transracial adoption of Asians into White homes appear safe in comparison to domestic transracial adoption.[26]

Unlike the African American and American Indian communities, no Asian American communities (apart from Asian adoptee communities) have produced any significant anti-adoption critique or policy. This is probably in part because the sending communities of birth parents are overseas and their populations do not participate directly in U.S. domestic policy debates. Since there is a very low incidence of domestic transracial adoption from Asian American communities, the abuses of the transnational adoption system are generally not visited on U.S. citizens, but on the least privileged communities in countries on the other side of the globe. In addition, Asian American immigrant communities appear to be largely unaware of, or unconcerned about, the issue of transnational adoption, and they generally do not embrace Asian adoptees.[27] This division is apparent when Asian adoptees encounter Asian American groups and organizations. When I addressed the National Association for Korean Schools National Conference in 2008 and reported that Korean adoptees constitute 10 percent of the Korean American population overall and up to 50 percent in my home state of Minnesota, an audible gasp of shock arose from the audience, most of whom had never realized that such a large number of Korean adoptees were in their midst. In addition, until recently, Asian adoptees have been virtually ignored within Asian American Studies as a group with a distinct social, cultural, or political history, and are not usually counted among Asian diasporas. To date, the fact that Asian American communities have not responded negatively to transnational Asian adoptions (though groups of birth mothers in South Korea are starting to organize with Korean adoptees living there to reform Korean adoption) serves as a tacit support for American adoptive parents in their belief that their Asian adopted children can expect a life free of negative exposure to racism.

The expansion of formalized adoption in the United States began to produce growing pains in the 1980s as adoptive families struggled for acceptance as so-called normal American families and legal dramas pitting birth parents against adoptive parents entered the public consciousness. American family law has historically privileged parents over other family members in custody disputes, and legal precedents for the rights of birth parents' ownership or guardianship of their children had been established long before legal adoption became commonplace in the mid-nineteenth century.[28] As Wayne Carp writes, "The United States has retained a pervasive cultural bias toward blood ties, and many people still view adoption as a second-rate form of kinship."[29] This attitude, supported by legal precedent in child custody law, gave rise to legal interpretations favoring the unification of biological families over adoptive placement until the passage of the Multiethnic Placement Act in 1994, the first federal statute favoring adoptive placement over family reunification.[30] Anxiety around the prospect of birth families appearing with legal claims to adopted or about-to-be-adopted children in the United States discourages many prospective parents considering domestic adoption.[31] In contrast, birth parents of foreign children in transnational adoption are largely understood to have no rights and no claims to their relinquished children. Evidence concerning any transnational adoption disputed by members of the birth family is scant and largely anecdotal, because these cases are rarely covered by the press and have generally not resulted in return of children to birth parents.[32] Adoption agencies can locate large numbers of available children in foreign countries, taking advantage of the low social and economic class positions that birth parents, especially mothers, still occupy. The extreme power differential between adoptive parents in the United States and birth families in sending countries allows adoptive parents to virtually eliminate any risk that their adoptions will be disrupted by biological relatives. Further, since the 1980s, the American child welfare system has used child removal (state removal of children from the custody and guardianship of their parents) as a supposedly child-centered remedy for a host of ills including child neglect or abuse as well as legal problems of parents, including substance abuse and incarceration. Unfortunately, these policies have been applied unevenly, with the result that children from poor, Black, and Brown homes enter the child welfare system in disproportionately high numbers.[33] While these policies have undoubtedly made more children in the American child welfare system available for adoption, ironically they have also made these children less appealing to prospective parents because the children are understood to have been damaged by abuse or neglect or by being from bad homes or born of "bad stock," recalling long-held prejudices against adopted children as "bad seeds."[34]

Because large-scale transnational adoption was established in the United States around the same time as domestic transracial adoption, and because it has not faced the same kinds of attacks as domestic adoption, it is not unreasonable that the adopting public might begin to prefer transnational adoption from Korea. By the 1970s, South Korea was the only country with an established history of overseas adoption, and it became an easy alternative to domestic adoption for American adoptive parents. Indeed, in the 1970s and 1980s, the number of transnational adoptions from Korea began to rise as American domestic transracial adoption declined.[35]

The Problem of Multiculturalism

What changes in American society permitted and encouraged the increasing prevalence of race mixing within adoptive families? By the early 1980s, two liberal movements were gaining ground in American society: social liberalism with respect to race, which gave rise to new ideals of multiculturalism; and economic liberalism, within which adoption came to operate as a form of transnational consumerism. Buoyed by these two trends, adoption—particularly adoption from outside the United States—increasingly appealed to prospective parents for whom multiculturalism became a point of entry into family building.

The liberalization of social mores around race began in the seminal civil rights movements of the 1950s that claimed equal rights for all persons regardless of race, passed through power movements that sought to affirm the distinct identities of communities of color, and ended up contributing to a colorblind conception of familial relations. This conception is commonly rendered in transracial adoption as a disregard for racial and genetic difference between White parents and non-White children, and an alternative focus on the relational bonds made through the parent-child relationship.

David Oh and Omotayo Banjo link the globalization of markets of labor, goods, and services to the popularity of ideologies of multiculturalism. They write, "the notion of 'postracialism' and 'colorblindness' was adopted because it appealed to the neoliberal shift towards privatized notions of racism as individual bigotry and toward personal rather than social responsibility, ignoring racism by ignoring race."[36] Economic neoliberalism configuring consumer choice as a key right of the individual contributed to the increase in transracial adoption; consumerism at every level allowed the marketing of adoptable children, often from economically and socially impoverished backgrounds, to more socially advantageous family positions in White America by emphasizing prospective parents' options and choices in the adoptive process. As long as they did not consider themselves racist, privileging individualism in adoption practice also meant that prospective adoptive parents were offered choices in an increasingly diversified menu of adoptable children without having to concern themselves with the problem of deep-rooted racism in society. When prospective parents were matched with an adoptable child, the exchange of adoption fees for the legal parentage of the child closely mirrored, then as now, more mundane forms of consumer behavior.

Although ideologically rooted in U.S. civil rights movements of the 1960s, the term *multiculturalism* originated in Canada and Australia in the early 1970s and began to appear in American educational policy discourse later in the decade.[37] By the 1980s, partly because of its prominence in the so-called culture wars, multiculturalism had begun to catch on as a popular ideal among socially liberal and progressive elements of American society.[38] However, with no canonical definition, the label of *multiculturalism* was quickly applied to so many different (and sometimes opposing) ideological programs that it can now be used by anyone for almost any purpose.[39] Multiculturalism today takes many forms: from the demand for recognition of minority groups to the salad-bowl concept of many distinct cultures making up a society;[40] and from the belief in a postracial society with culture but with no race,[41] to the assimilationist or "weak" multicultural agenda of accommodating difference while maintaining individualist agendas.[42] Wen Jin calls this form of multiculturalism "conciliatory," because it privileges the unity of a nation of differing cultural groups while denying the difficulty of reconciliation of those groups.[43] Indeed, multiculturalism has taken on so many definitions that it has become more a set of arguments than a unified ideology. Some forms of multiculturalism are radical, some liberal, some even conservative. But despite the potential for—even, it could be argued, the certainty of—misunderstanding and confusion, the power of multiculturalism in the public imagination keeps the term in constant use and under constant debate.

Popular contemporary understandings of multiculturalism have fallen under critique by many scholars of race and ethnicity, perhaps none more so than assimilationism, a form that drapes itself in the mantle of cultural pluralism by holding out the promise of upward mobility for all, but which critics allege "sets the fundamental conditions for full economic and social citizenship in the United States" while it "rejects racialized group consciousness [and] ignores the way supposedly neutral institutions are pro-White."[44] John Willinsky has criticized the use of assimilationist multiculturalism as a new pillar of national identity that enables the state to erase or sanitize its racist past, stating that "multiculturalism was not really about culture. Multiculturalism was a way for the state to distance itself from a history of discrimination," and in which a focus on cultural enrichment for Whites through exposure to difference was used to avoid real changes in race politics.[45] Paradoxically, the racial and cultural diversity of the modern multicultural state is a direct result of racialized oppression during periods of colonial expansion, when colonized populations were subjected to land seizure, political overthrow, forced migration, and other forms of coercion.[46]

During the 1980s, the ideal of (assimilationist) multiculturalism established itself throughout the adoption industry and was present in adoption cultures as the celebration of the "rainbow family" that includes one or more transracially and/or transnationally adopted children. Actual families were celebrated in newspaper articles, fictional ones in television sitcoms such as *Diff'rent Strokes* and *Webster*. That a family could function as a normative unit despite the lack of biological relationships between family members was broadly accepted as proof that the family—the most basic building block of community, society, and nation—could bridge race and class barriers. Kristi Brian documents the largely symbolic embrace of multiculturalism within the American transnational adoption industry's marketing of international adoption as proof of American tolerance, even though the agencies she studies appear to have used few strategies to deploy it, and virtually no critique of racist belief systems and institutional practices in American history or among prospective adoptive parents.[47]

The weak multiculturalism that became popular in the 1980s attempted to celebrate difference without acknowledging or attempting to reconcile racist American national histories and policy.[48] But even within this conciliatory framework, there were still some critical structural issues in positioning adoptive families as paragons of multiculturalism. Historically (and currently), Korean and other transracial adoption has largely been a White act, meaning the overwhelming majority of children were adopted into homes where both parents (and therefore, the extended family) were White. Jacobson documents the embrace of weak, celebratory multiculturalism constituted only by the acknowledgment of ethnic difference in the 1990s in communities of transnationally adoptive families.[49] As in other areas of American society, the embrace of weak multiculturalism within adoptive families did little to empower communities of color or to redress past racism. Instead, adoption inserted children of color into strongly assimilative situations, where their birth culture could only be dimly imagined by White family members on the basis of flawed cues from American popular culture. Barbara Yngvesson reports that this same strategy was in play in Sweden, reporting, "The multicultural challenge of the 1970s and 1980s . . . taken on by Swedish [transnationally] adoptive parents was for their children to be fully Swedish under the skin."[50] In the case of Korean adoption, most American families did not travel to Korea to obtain their children. Because South Korea was one of the only sending nations that allowed proxy adoption, most adoptive parents had never been to Korea, and few knew Korean Americans who might teach adopted children about Korean culture. When compared to the testimonies of their Korean adoptee children, Oh Myo Kim, Reed Reichwald, and Richard Lee report, adoptive parents tend to overestimate the exposure to cultural socialization to birth culture that their children experience, and tend toward extrinsic forms of socialization while avoiding discussions of discrimination and race.[51]

Despite its shortcomings as a means to address injustices faced by communities of color, the importance of multiculturalism as a gateway to identity for Korean children adopted in the 1970s and 1980s should not be underestimated. Because adoptees had been positioned as embodiments of multicultural ideals, they often embraced the ideals of multiculturalism. Because they were raised in White families and society, they quickly built cultural capital in their White communities. However, as they remained aware of their positions as racially othered, they found the limitations of conciliatory multicultural thinking. Instead of assimilating entirely, they were able to coalesce as a community and take control of their identities as both White and Asian American. This dual identity is readily evident in adoptees who grew up in the 1970s and 1980s in Minnesota, where Korean adoptees make up of half the Korean American population and are decidedly visible.

The Korean Adoptee Homeland: Why Minnesota?

I began my research—and my own Korean American adoption experience—in Minnesota, which is home to a higher concentration of Korean adoptees than any place in the United States (and the world, with the exception of Sweden). The population of Korean American adoptees in the state of Minnesota, estimated to be between ten thousand and fifteen thousand, suggests a half-joking parallel with the state motto, "The Land of 10,000 Lakes." In fact, there are about fifteen thousand lakes in Minnesota, so it would be accurate to say that there is indeed a Korean adoptee for every lake.

Between February of 2003 and December of 2006, I collected oral histories from thirty-four adoptees who lived in (or had lived or grown up in) Minnesota, most in the Twin Cities region of Minneapolis and St. Paul and the surrounding suburbs. At the time they gave their oral histories, they ranged in age from twenty-one to forty-four; most were in their late twenties to mid-thirties, with both a median and an average age of thirty-one. Only eight were men, which reflects the fact that more girls than boys had been adopted from Korea until the 1980s, and probably also my own position as a woman. Of these thirty-four, six gave their oral histories in Korea, because they had relocated to their birth county as adults; I knew two of these six before they left Minnesota for Korea. The other twenty-eight gave oral histories in Minnesota while they lived there. Seven had grown up in other states and had moved to Minnesota as adults, and the other twenty-seven were raised in Minnesota.

I have been asked many times, by people familiar with the Korean American adoptee community, why there are so many Korean adoptees in Minnesota. Minnesota is probably the only place in the United States where the practice of Korean adoption has become so normalized and commonplace that a viable and visible Korean adoptee community has developed along many different axes, including support for Korean adoptive families and children, adoptee-led networking and activism, journalism and publishing that privileges Korean adoption experiences, Korean adoptee artistic expression, participation by Korean adoptees in the Korean American community, and formal adoption research. I believe that this concentration of adoptees is the result of several historical, structural, and sociocultural factors that have worked in concert to make Minnesota an American homeland of sorts for Korean adoptees.

Minnesota has a long history of progressive social politics and policies. The radical leftist Farmer Labor party was the most successful left-wing party in the country in the 1930s and went on to merge with the state Democratic Party in 1948 to create the Democratic Farmer Labor party.[52] In addition, Minnesota has a tradition of populist engagement with state policy through civic organizations like the Citizens League.[53] This is one important factor that has led to "activist government and innovative social welfare programs [because] . . . government . . . has been viewed as a positive instrument for the betterment of society."[54] Minnesota has a strong history of liberal policies around issues like welfare reform, health care, education, and social policy, made possible (until recently) by the general economic well-being of the state coupled with high political participation among a fairly homogeneous voting population holding progressive-to-liberal political values.[55]

Minnesota's White ethnics, predominantly descended from Scandinavian and German Lutheran immigrants, have traditionally been strong supporters of the welfare state. It is notable that social conventions against adoption or nonbiological kinship are largely absent in Germany and the Scandinavian countries; Sweden has the largest population of Korean adoptees in Europe (both in absolute number and per capita). The fact that Minnesota (as well as Sweden, incidentally) has historically been racially homogeneous helped support its racially progressive policies when it came to family matters. In 1948, Minnesota was the site of the first transracial adoption of an African American child into a White family, and the state's infrastructure, social norms, and reputation as a state friendly to transracial adoption began to develop. Minnesota was also one of nine U.S. states that never enacted antimiscegenation laws, probably in no small part because few people of color resided in Minnesota during the era of antimiscegenation fervor from the mid-nineteenth to the mid-twentieth centuries. The state's high degree of racial homogeneity also meant that racial politics in the state have tended to be assimilative. Although Minnesotans may not have been threatened by small racial or cultural differences, the extreme isolation that people of color, including Korean adoptees, faced in the state encouraged assimilative adaptation; this is entirely consistent with adoption industry rhetoric from the 1950s to the 1970s that encouraged White adoptive parents to prevent their adopted children from having contact with their birth culture.

Given this social and political history, it is hardly surprising that Minnesota is home to child welfare organizations *cum* adoption agencies that have long histories of facilitating adoption. Most notable among them are Lutheran Social Services, which initiated a Korean adoption program in 1967,[56] and Children's Home Society, founded in 1889 to facilitate adoptions of poor children born in East Coast cities who arrived on the orphan trains.[57] Children's Home Society expanded its adoption program to transracial and transnational adoption in the mid-1950s during the Korean War. Children's Home is the only agency in Minnesota that still facilitates overseas Korean adoptions. Since the mid-1970s, when in-race adoptable children for White prospective parents became less available and domestic transracial adoption became less socially acceptable, both of these Minnesota adoption agencies actively promoted Korean adoption over other options because of its relative ease and predictability. By that time, Korean adoptions had been underway for over twenty years, and the agencies could offer prospective parents a reliable timeline and reasonable fee structure should they choose to adopt from Korea.

By the mid-1980s, the peak years of overseas adoption from Korea, so many Korean children were arriving in Minnesota that Korean adoption had become an obvious option for prospective parents. In fact, Korean adoption had become (and remains) normalized in Minnesota to such an extent that a snowball effect took over: adoption from Korea was no longer an act that parents felt would necessarily isolate them, but one that could actually connect them and their families with a growing community of adoptive families raising children from Korea. The size of the Korean adoptee population gave rise to a relatively large number of community resources for adoptive families and adoptees, including Korean culture camps, arts groups that teach traditional Korean music and dance, Korean-adoption-centered publications, and several Korean adoptee groups (the two earliest were Minnesota Adopted Koreans, established in 1991,[58] and AK Connection, established in 2000). As Minnesota's adoptee population grew, so did the interest of researchers (and of adoptees in other states); the large adoptee population made Minnesota a productive location for adoption research. The University of Minnesota is now one of the leading institutions in the field of transracial and transnational adoption research, with studies under way in medicine, psychology, family social science, and social work, as well as in Asian American studies and history. For Korean adoptees, even those who grew up in other states, the critical mass of adoptees living in Minnesota has made the state, especially the Twin Cities, a desirable place to live. The social and cultural climate around transracial and specifically, Korean adoption in Minnesota is complex, and adoption communities are active historically, socially, culturally, artistically, and academically.

A (Minnesota) Korean Adoptee Identity

For many Korean adoptees, configuring an identity that takes into account their experiences as Asians in families and communities that are overwhelmingly White, and as people of color whose life experiences are predominantly in White-dominated environments, is difficult, considering the culturally limited set of identity choices available to them. In addition to their culturally and socially complicated experiences, passing in between racial and cultural boundaries, many also seek identity formations that address the racism they experience as Asian Americans and the infantilization (or the tendency to always be treated and thought of as children) they experience as adoptees. For many adult adoptees now in their thirties and forties, the process of identity formation continues to be rendered using the logics of, and in response to, the climate of weak liberal multiculturalism that dominated popular discourse around race during their early lives.

The complexities of identity formation are woven through the stories of adoptees who live or have lived in my home state of Minnesota, where I began and ended the process of collecting oral histories. I have collected more oral histories from such adoptees than from those living in any other place. Many Minnesota adoptees spoke about similar topics: experiences with racism and racialization; feelings of racial and social isolation in Minnesota; encounters with other people of color, especially other Asians or Asian Americans; pilgrimages to South Korea; and connecting with other adoptees. Not every adoptee discussed all of these topics (for instance, several had not traveled back to Korea, and therefore had nothing to say about this experience), but all of my subjects covered at least one of these topics, and common themes quickly emerged as I collected more oral histories.

Moments of Realization

Within the Korean adoptee community, the process of developing, or coming to embrace, a Korean adoptee identity is often described as one's "journey." Experiences of an awakening Korean adoptee identity were highly significant for many of the Minnesota adoptees who participated in my research, most of whom defined and described their identity as "Korean adopted" (abbreviated as AK or sometimes KAD), as distinct from other identities based on culture, nation, or race such as Korean American, Asian American, or American. While they knew these other identity formations were available (in addition to White, which many say they previously considered themselves), they had chosen to define themselves as Korean adoptees. When I asked Erin, twenty-six, how she currently identified, she replied:

> Asian American, [and,] when I zero it down more, adopted Korean. . . . and I have friends who are Korean . . . Korean-Korean [this is a term many Korean adoptees use for Korean nationals], Korean Americans and I have friends who are Asian American, understanding that as an adoptee, you're always going to be in between, you're not Asian enough and you're not White enough. But even though I feel that, it's not enough to deter feeling ashamed to be adopted Korean. I'm proud to say I'm adopted Korean now, and don't have a problem so much talking about being adopted Korean.[59]

Erin went on to say that her feelings of isolation, both culturally and within her own family, contributed to her movement toward an identity with both Koreanness and her adoptive status at the core. She stated, "I always knew that I was adopted and different from my mom and my dad and my brother. And I think that has always given me the feeling of being separate. Isolated, even within my own family. Instead of going, 'Oh I'm so fortunate for having this family who loves me,' I'm like, 'Well, I'm here, they love me, but I'm really different, so I might as well pull it in to myself and work through it on my own.' ... Part of [isolation from family] is being adopted."[60] Indeed, Erin sees the isolation she feels from her family as part and parcel of being adopted and this isolation, possibly compounded by her status as a racial outsider, is a central part of her identity.

Barb, thirty-one, figured her Korean adoptee identity more as an embrace of certain characteristics and behaviors than a response to isolation. However, she did express a belief in a special relationship among Korean adoptees. She went on to say that her connection with other Korean adoptees is different from her connection with other people. She says, "I think there's more acceptance. There's similarities. And I think the conversations connect you right away, because it's in the context of being adopted. There's a connection initially, and from there you just move on to other things, you just hang out. But the initial connection is being adopted and searching for what this experience means and listening to other people's experience and finding out that you are similar...or different. But, like, that [is a] conversation you just can't have with just anybody initially."[61]

Life experiences of isolation, difference, and struggle to resolve one's own identity were common among the Korean adoptees I met. For these narrators, the development of an adoptee identity was foundational to their understandings of themselves. This process took many forms, but most narrators reported experiencing a specific awakening period before which they did not see their identity organized around their Korean adoptee status. For some, this was facilitated by education. Erin explained:

> While I was going to the [university] and taking more sociology classes, ...
> I didn't know what I wanted to do, but the more sociology classes and the more I read on prejudice and discrimination and racial identity, the more I could see how it related to me and it gave me more strength ... it gave me the vocabulary of how I felt. ... Since I'd never had a chance in the past to discuss it with another person of color, that was my first communication with what it meant to be a person of color in the United States, and it interested me, so I then chose that as my field. While doing that, I actually made a pretty good friend who was also AK, and, being friends with her, she had a different situation growing up than I do, she

had siblings adopted with her, and had gone to a lot of culture camps and whatnot, but she was my first person I could talk to about that stuff, she was also a person I could. . . . She went with me to my first AK function. . . . It was someone I could go with and introduce myself into the AK population.[62]

Some of the oral history project participants had always identified as Korean or Korean American, but several, specifically those who had previously identified as White, came to realize their non-Whiteness or their Korean-ness as adults. Many adoptees experience a profound moment of realization when they first see themselves in racial and or cultural terms, as different from their White families and communities, and these epiphanies often feature prominently in their life stories. Diane, twenty-eight, recalled realizing one day, "'Hey I am Korean, I am a minority,' and I wanted to understand how to fit this in to who I am, on a daily basis, not just in this daydreamy thoughtful sort of way, but to really understand what that means. Because it was so social-justice oriented, I think that's when I really started to develop some feelings and ideas about what racism, homophobia, and all those things mean and how it is important to me and how I wanted to affect change in the world."[63]

Kye, thirty-four, had a similar realization while in high school. After peaceably enduring racial slurs and name-calling throughout his childhood, Kye finally understood himself as racialized:

> I really noticed something, that I was actually really different, [when] a group of us guys went up to Minneapolis. . . . Somebody I knew had a car, and we all drove up there, and there was this group of Chinese guys walking by. And one of our guys is like, "Hey, look at those slant-eyed chinks!" And I kind of look at him for a second and then he's like, "Well, not you, you know, 'cause, uh, you know, you're one of us," and that was actually one of the first times where I started thinking about . . . who am I hanging out with, first of all, and what do I perceive myself as? That was one of the first times.[64]

Wendy, age thirty-one, was exposed to Asian Americans and Asian American studies for the first time in college, and suddenly realized that she, too, was Asian American:

> I was exposed to Asian Americans [at college] the first time; I still remember getting the solicitation from the Asian studies and the Asian American Student Union to come and join. It really slipped me up, because up until that point I had never seen myself as Asian American. I just considered myself, I don't know, American or whatever. Without the Asian, I kind of just disregarded that part. And all of a sudden I come to this

huge epiphany that, "Oh my god! I'm Asian American!" And then I'm like, "What the hell is that about?" . . . I just remember being in that in college campus and, especially if I would see people in large numbers, . . . I would see a group of three or four Asian people and it would freak me out! I realize now that I was like that because I was just that uncomfortable with myself and I was just projecting that onto them because I didn't know how to deal with myself.[65]

Wendy's attempt to articulate the awkwardness and tension she sometimes felt when she encountered other Asian or Asian American people is similar to reports I have heard from many other adoptees. She describes feeling curious about other Asians, but also feeling "weird" about feeling curious. I think the feelings she is describing are connected to understanding, on an intellectual level but not on a personal level, why she should be curious about other Asian people. Even though she knew she was adopted and was, through adoption, totally cut off from other Asians, she could still visually identify with other Asians when she saw them. But she didn't know anything about Asians, or what it meant for other Asians to be Asian. Therefore she understood herself to be different from other Asians, particularly because she felt curious. As an Asian who knew no other Asians, she also suspected that other Asians might not understand her, In addition to all of this, perhaps there was also the feeling of isolation, of being familiar with a racial group that one is not a part of and being excluded culturally by the racial group one is a part of. All of these thoughts and their attached emotions can make for an awkward moment, even in a wordless chance encounter with another Asian person.

Encounters with Asian America and Other People of Color

Most of the adoptees who spoke with me did engage with Asian America in some way, be it through personal relationships with Asians or Asian Americans (including other Korean adoptees) living in the United States, through intellectual discourses based in Asian American studies, or through cultural productions by adoptees or Asian Americans. Several spoke of initially connecting with Asian nationals present in the adoptees' predominantly White social settings, underlining the general lack of access so many adoptees in this research had to other Asian Americans. A few talked about having these encounters when they were still quite young; one was Gabrielle, age thirty-three, who superficially connected with Asia through a family friend. She said, "We had a friend, a family friend, . . . living in Japan during the early eighties, and she would send me stuff. . . . she would send me stuff, because she traveled from Japan to Korea, and she would, like, send me things from there that were Korean, so I would have things. My aunt, who was a social worker, in southern Minnesota—they escorted a lot of adoptees over, so they would bring stuff back for me. So I had this little tiny shelf in my room that had, like, five things on."⁶⁶ For Gabrielle, this handful of gifts from Asia constituted her connection with her Asian heritage—a scant acknowledgment, but an acknowledgment all the same.

Gabe, age twenty-nine, encountered other Asian Americans mostly through his socialization with fellow gays and lesbians. Although his gay identity was primary for him, his gay social networks brought him into contact with other Asians and Asian Americans, mostly Asian immigrants, so he considered himself lucky to not have to deal with the legal issues of immigration as did his Asian friends.

> Long Yang Club, which is this gay Asian American group, which the majority are not adopted—I probably was, the only one, now that I'm thinking about, that was adopted, but it exposed me to actually Asian people, which, before, I had really not had any exposure to at all. . . . I guess I'll say a lot of my Asian friends that are gay, that were not adopted, which would be all of them, are here on education visas, and they have to go through a ton of rigmarole to look at getting naturalized or [to get visas]. . . . Oh my God, I don't have to. . . . I'm happy that I haven't had to deal with that.⁶⁷

Most Korean adoptees who participated in my research reported coming into contact with other people of color in college or in graduate school, at least after having moved out of their parents' homes. Many first began to understand their own identities as people of color by connecting, not with other adoptees or other Asian Americans, but with foreign students attending college in the United States. Ingrid, age thirty-four, remembers:

> [I went to] the International House, where there were all these people of color and where there was also this [student group] and people were proud to be people of color, and that was the first time I really thought, "Oh, maybe it's okay to not be White. . . ." At the time though, it was just being comfortable as being a person of color. It was not being comfortable as being a Korean; it was not being comfortable as an adoptee. It was just being comfortable as a person of color. And, uh, I think that, um, . . . I didn't feel comfortable with being an adoptee until after I got out of college.⁶⁸

Amy, thirty-two, remarks:

> Grad school also opened up another chapter, because all of a sudden I was going to grad school with all these Asians—that weren't adopted, but really, I just learned so much about their culture. There were male Asians, so for the first time, I got to hang out with a whole bunch of male Asians that weren't adopted. They were from Malaysia, they were from China. They

were international students.... When they talked about their ... culture and all their traditions, I'm like, "Oh my God, that is so interesting." I remember, and I thought, "Oh my God. I know so much about [these other] cultures, and yet, I hardly know anything about Korean culture!" It was embarrassing because they would look at me and say, "You're Korean. Tell me something about that." I'm like, [tone of voice as if about to laugh] "Well, um ... okay." I had no clue. I had no clue. So then, it was just like a transition after that where I decided I'm gonna get more involved.[69]

Gabe recalls that he needed to become more comfortable around foreign students to be more comfortable being Korean, and needed to become more comfortable being Korean before he could be comfortable identifying as a Korean adoptee—as if the large distance between his identity as American and that of international students made it easier to approach these other people of color. With Amy, the ease with which international students expressed their own cultural identities normalized her approach to an Asian cultural identity. Even so, she had difficulty reciprocating in discussions about culture, because she had no grounding in an Asian culture or identity.

The inability of White students around Barb to distinguish her from international students made her feel isolated, but also encouraged her to spend more time with other Korean and Korean American students in her school's Korean student association:

So going to [college] was really hard. I started to realize that I am a minority and that I'm Asian and all these people are White and they think I'm a foreign exchange student or something very different, and I was really self-conscious, more self-conscious than ever. I think I was really lonely.... So I started looking into something Korean. So there's a Korean association at the college, and so I went there and there [were] Korean students, and that was the first time I met anyone Korean. It was, like, nine or ten people there ... international students; there were no Korean adopted students in that group.... And I think they tried to help me out, because I was adopted.... They were like, "So you don't speak Korean? Okay, well, do you want to play some games?" Of course, they were very open, but I was still having a hard time with my identity and making friends, and just being [at college]; it just ... wasn't ... good. I was very isolated.[70]

Although encountering Asians was an important first step in many of these adoptees' personal development of their own identities, it is notable that their "first Asians" were not Americans like themselves, but Asians who identified either as foreign or as immigrants (an identity few adoptees claim). In these examples, the "forever foreigner"[71] stereotype applied to Asian Americans is bizarrely visited on Korean American adoptees; they have been so segregated from other Asian American populations that their first encounters with ethnic Asians are often with foreign nationals.

Wendy, thirty-one, talked about encountering Asian and Asian American Studies in college, an experience she described as "life changing":

> I took, um, a film class, a dance class, and [an] Asian American class.... That semester ... totally changed my life. That ... was the first time that I came into contact with Asian American role models. My Korean dance professor was from Korea and my other professor was a Chinese American woman who taught my Asian American lit class. And, through the literature that I was reading about other Asian Americans and their experiences, I was all of a sudden able to literally put my finger on experiences of mine that were similar to theirs and to start unraveling and sort of decompressing and regurgitating all this stuff that I had effectively tucked away in my psychology somewhere and let sit and marinate for a while in my life.[72]

Wendy is like most Asian Americans of her generation in that her education had included no exposure to Asian American culture or history before college. Discovering Asian American literature and other forms of cultural expression was a liberating experience that allowed her to further develop her own identity as an Asian American, an identity that became very important to her afterward. Many participants described similar trajectories, from being totally dissociated from other Korean adoptees and Asian America in general, to totally embracing a Korean and Korean adoptee identity. Adam, twenty-eight, summed it up:

> I remember my freshman year of college. This guy came up to me and he was like "Yeah, you know the AA association, the Asian American association, is in our campus, you know, and we're meeting on Wednesdays, here's our little thing, you can come," and I'm like "Thanks," you know, and then I'm like "I'm not going to some damn Asian American society thing ... what the hell?" I mean, that was my mentality my freshman year. In my junior year, I was involved in Harambe, which was this multicultural group on campus.... I mean ... since there's only, like, seven Black people and, like, fifteen Asian people ... on campus, they actually gotta do something together.... So I just slowly kind of built from there, and of course it culminated when I went to Korea, and that's when you.... Not that I understand what it means to be Korean but, you know, it is definitely a culture you can be proud of, I'm Korean, and so it just seems that that country's been a success and that's something you can even be proud of.[73]

Experiences of Racism

Most of the subjects I encountered had experienced racism,[74] though I suspect that many of these subjects minimized their racialized experiences both to themselves and to me. Because injuries of a racial nature are so contentious in American society, and because the concept of a harmonious racial coexistence is so strongly emphasized in transracial adoptive families who have embraced the ideology of colorblind multiculturalism, all but the most grievous racial injuries are often considered unimportant—or worse, somehow deserved. In her study of Korean American adoptive families, Kristi Brian reports, "Parents overassumed discriminatory treatment towards their children was infrequent and harmless."[75] Most of the research participants spoke only occasionally of racism they had experienced in school or at work. Although racist slurs and remarks are only the tip of the iceberg when it comes to the racism and discrimination that adoptees face, most Korean adoptees understand that these experiences are significant. Not coincidentally, these are also the kinds of slights most likely to be interpreted by White people as racist. John, age thirty-three, remarked:

> I was little and I remember being on the bus and people calling me names, but I, I guess I wasn't one to get back in people's faces or shout back at them. I just tried to ignore them. I guess that was kind of the way I dealt with it, by, maybe, not trying to instigate it [and,] if they said something, just ignoring it. I think most people in society don't react, they usually go on and try to pick on someone else then. Then when I went to high school, then it was sports . . . It's such a small town that people knew who I was and they weren't gonna make fun of me, so the only thing I experienced at the high school was when we played opposing teams, they would make some comment, and, you know, that went all the way through college.[76]

John ignored the racism he suffered as a younger child, but dealt with it as an adolescent and young adult by engaging in sports activities, where he could build an identity based on his physical skills rather than on his race, even though insults from opposing teams still took the form of racial slurs.

Amy, age thirty-two, remembers how she dealt with childhood racist name-calling:

> In neighborhoods where the kids didn't know me, where if I went anywhere, you can really start to pick it up. The kids teasing you. I mean, name-calling, "flat nose"; I mean, everything. You know. That's when I really started picking it up, so I think at that point is when I just didn't want to be different anymore. And I think that started, you know, subconsciously, first; I just didn't want to be different. And then when you

move more into the junior high phase, is when I knew, right then and there, I just wanted to be all-American. . . . I permed my hair, you know, I had this huge, like, eighties perm."[77]

Both of these adoptees chose to internalize experiences of racism and attempt to disappear into the mainstream, through participation in sports or through changing appearance to look more White.

Adoptee participants reported, much more frequently than they reported name-calling outside the family, racist incidents that arose during family arguments or debates. Athough few adoptees described overt racism directed at them by family members, several did talk about how racism directed at others was personally hurtful to them.[78] Erin, age twenty-six, related an experience with an uncle, which has contributed to her estrangement from her family: "I was nineteen and we were talking about politics; he said, in the discussion, 'I still don't have a problem calling people gooks and niggers.' He said that to me, and I started bawling and actually I left and I still haven't talked to him since."[79]

Although there is a popular understanding that colorblindness is inherently antiracist, many of these subjects made a strong connection between their family's colorblindness and the racism they suffered in their families, in that parent commitment to the colorblind ideal prevented parents from being able to identify racism beyond superficial name-calling. Diane, age twenty-eight, remarked that she knew her father harbored racist attitudes toward other people of color, but not toward her: "I think that there is a certain element of colorblindness which unfortunately is one of the biggest downfalls that greatly negatively affects adoption, in that these parents become so colorblind that they forget that your race is part of who you are and they need to embrace that and celebrate that and help prepare you for the great big world that you're going into. I know that my parents, because of the area that they grew up in and because of the way they were raised—that they do harbor racism."[80] When I asked Diane if her parents thought of her as a person of color, she responded, "I think that were moments when I was a child and they were called because I would cry because someone had called me a chink or a gook. . . . I [did] not understand it, but I certainly knew that it was offensive, and they would do whatever they could to band-aid that situation, but I don't think they ever really recognized racism. . . . Because my parents, like a lot of other parents I've heard talk, said, 'Well, we just love you for who you are.' . . . [T]here was racism in our family."[81] Another said, "Barely. Probably not." Diane had experiences in her family that she identified as evidence of a buried racism that resulted not from her family's acknowledgment of her racial difference, but from their denial, which is identifiable as a very personalized form of colorblindness. She knew her parents knew about racist incidents in her childhood but still refused to see her as a person of color.

These stories demonstrate how parents' colorblindness allows them to harbor racist feelings toward persons or groups external to the family, seemingly without directly violating immediate family members. However, adoptees still recognized such behaviors as racism within their families, and seemed cognizant of the implications of that racism for themselves as people of color in an otherwise White family structure.

Rejection of all things Korean by family members is another form of veiled discrimination experienced by adoptees. For the adoptee subject unable to deny her own Korean origins, this sends a message that Korean-ness is shameful or disgusting. I asked Barb, age thirty-one, about her experiences of Korean culture within her adoptive family, "Did they [her parents] ever talk to you about Korean culture?" She replied, "No." I asked, "No Korean food, language? Nothing?" She responded, "No. The only mention of Korean food, I remember something came up about Korean food, and I guess I was interested. . . . Well, my father said it was terrible, just terrible. He had this *chap chae* or something and it was so gross, and I was like, 'Oh, okay, so I guess it's gross.' And that was it."[82]

Even when parents were open to hearing about the racial issues that their adopted Korean children faced, several adoptees were, they said, reluctant to tell their parents about these problems. Sara Docan-Morgan also reports that Korean adoptees tend to avoid discussing racial incidents with parents, believing their parents will not be able to help them.[83] In this study, adoptees' concerns were both for themselves, in predicting that their parents might bring embarrassing racial incidents more into public view, and also for their parents, who some adoptees felt might be emotionally traumatized if they were confronted with the racial realities of their children. Gabe recalls:

> My mom always was surprised 'cause I said, "Well, of course there were people who made fun of me because I was Asian, oh you know, just the typical picking on people sort of thing." . . . I never told them [meaning his parents], or made a big deal because I know that she [his mother] would have . . . called the school district and made a big deal out of it. I just ignored these people . . . When I tell her that this stuff happened in the past, she's like, "Well why didn't you tell me?" I was like, "Well . . . you know, I didn't want to make a bigger deal out of it, it happened, and now, you know, it's done." . . . I guess the thing [is] that I've not let it really get under my skin because I'm not a big fighting guy.[84]

Gabe connects his pacifism as "not a big fighting guy" with enduring experiences of facing childhood racism alone, without telling his parents about what was going on, though he did tell his mother eventually and found out that she had had no idea that this could have been going on right under her nose. Her response reinforced Gabe's belief that his decision not to tell her had been the correct one;

by not giving White parents the power to mismanage responses to racism, adoptees can avoid being disappointed in their parents, and avoid further trauma to themselves. Unfortunately, this also allows White adoptive parents to believe that they and their children can live in a world free of racial conflict.

In this example, Kye's mother does find out about a racial incident, and sure enough, the situation is extended instead of ended:

> I was like in [pause] fifth grade, and I was riding the school bus at the time and some of the [high school] junior and senior kids were just incessant, . . . on and on with their racial slurs, and they were pretty nasty about it. And then one day, after a couple of weeks, my [White] brother got up and just said, "Hey, just shut up. Knock it off!" And so they hit him on the head with a book. . . . My mom used to always wait for us, as we got off the bus, and saw this big ole red welt on [my brother's] head. And so the very next day, the boys and their mothers and fathers were in our living room. . . . You know, I think the guys were actually nicer to me because they felt bad for what they did rather than just because they had to.[85]

Kye also never meant for his mother to find out about the racism he was enduring, but because his brother stood up for him, and got injured in the process, their mother found out. Although it is just this kind of response many adoptees said they feared their parents would enact if they found out about racist incidents, the adoptee in the example above ended up appreciating his mother's efforts. However, his appreciation did not stem from the fact that she confronted his assailants, but because of how she did it, educating them instead of shaming them as racists. So in some ways, it was her de-racialization of the situation that he appreciated. Also of note is that even though the two brothers endured the experiences of racial attack together, they never spoke of it afterward; this shows how unable to discuss race White adoptive families can be, perhaps never having discussed it in depth before adopting.

Adoptees described a number of coping strategies to deal with racialization. Most, like Gabe and Kye above, told of how they ignored racist comments or situations, and some acknowledged that this wasn't really useful in terms of dealing with the issue of racism and discrimination. Other adoptees reacted differently. Wendy, trying to turn the racism she had experienced as an actor into something positive, tells the story of her early career. She explains how her agent worked with her to call the local entertainment and advertising industries on their racist casting practices, "She [the adoptee's agent] would get casting calls that were for, you know, women, but it wasn't anything race-specific, and she would send me on the castings. And I think sometimes it would shock the hell out of people because they weren't expecting someone who was Asian American to come and play for the part, so that was really forward-thinking for her. Because everyone else would only send you if they specifically asked for Asian, and you were cast for very stereotypical roles."[86] Wendy described becoming incensed by the racist casting she was exposed to as a beginning actor, because it prevented her from getting roles. She discovered the phenomenon of "White assumed," meaning if a role is not specifically designated racially, it is meant for a White actor, even for roles where race is in no way part of the characterization.

Adam, age twenty-eight, used the racial stereotype that all Asians know the martial arts to his benefit. Having taken an interest in Tae Kwon Do, he used this skill to short-circuit racist incidents at school:

> I think 'cause I was a smaller person, I never ever worried about getting beat up, whereas it's amazing how many guys, Asian American guys, [who] grew up in primarily Caucasian areas . . . got into fights all the time. . . . I had a speech class, and I gave a speech on how to break a brick, so I broke a brick in speech class, and that probably helped my cause, now that I think about it. . . . Of course the whole deal in high school is acceptance, so if you're the big guy and you usually pick on kids, you don't want to take a chance on a kid that can really make you look dumb.[87]

Adam wonders if perhaps he was just lucky that he was never racially harassed at school, or if it was because he was too physically small to be worth persecuting. In this example, his real luck might have been that his parents enrolled him in Tae Kwon Do classes at a young age, and that he stuck with these until he was quite accomplished.

Kye remembers his violent response to racism in high school:

> I was getting to be much more independent, basically meaning I didn't really care what my friends thought. A couple of my friends, while they thought I wasn't looking, they were joking what our [referring to Kye and his White girlfriend] babies would look like. And of course they were doing this kind of thing [makes hand motion, stretching out his eyes], and I just kinda go up to them, "What is that?" And I go, "Now if you really want to look at it," and then I was getting mean, and I said, "If you really want to look like that, let me help you." So I grabbed the guy's face, . . . and so I literally, physically grabbed this guy and I was stretching out his eyes. I'm like, "Let me help you with this then. If you want to be slant-eyed, I'll help you out." But that's where I think things really started to become more real for me, that, hey, I'm not just one of the White boys. I don't know why it took me that long to really be secure over the whole fact that I'm, you know, actually Korean and not White.[88]

This is one of the only times in all the oral histories I recorded that an adoptee talked about directly confronting an assailant in a racial incident. Although his response might seem outrageous to some, Kye was one of many of the adoptees who had recounted stories of such low-level racist incidents that had taken place throughout their childhoods, along with their polite responses. But Kye was also one of the few adoptees whose White family acknowledged and confronted the racism he had experienced as a younger child.

Even though the rarity of active responses to racism by oral history informants probably does stem from the lack of guidance adoptees get from adoptive parents, who had not been themselves the objects of racist harassment or discrimination, I could not help wondering if this was also an effect of the multicultural environment in which most of these adoptees grew up. In Minnesota, a state known for being nice ("Minnesota Nice" is a popular local expression used to evoke both Minnesotans' reputation for politeness and their supposed tendency toward insincerity for the sake of avoiding interpersonal conflict), multiculturalism is a way to "make nice" by embracing difference, but not necessarily criticizing racism or racists.

Alone in Minnesota

Most Korean adoptees grow up having little contact with other people of color. Racial isolation begins at home: the vast majority are adopted into homes where both parents are White. Of the sixty-six adoptees who participated in my research, only two were not adopted by White couples: one was adopted into a Korean American home and one into a family with a White father and a Japanese mother. Only one of the adoptees with a non-White adoptive parent grew up in Minnesota. Although Minnesota has the highest concentration of Korean adoptees in the United States, many adoptees reported having grown up in extreme racial isolation, even in cases where they were aware of the presence of other Korean adoptees in the community. These perceptions of isolation are backed up by census data; as table 1 shows, Minnesota has been a very White state throughout its history and remains so today—even though the Asian American population has increased more than fivefold since 1980 and by a factor of 28 since 1960. From the late 1960s to the mid-1980s, decades during which most of the Minnesotan Korean adoptees who are currently adults were adopted, the number of Asian Americans in Minnesota was vanishingly small.

Many adoptees spoke of being "the only one," or one of very few Asian Americans or adoptees—and in many instances, the only person of color—in a social setting, a school, the family, or even an entire town. A typical response on this topic comes from Gabrielle:

> I think there was only . . . maybe, four or five other people of color in my high school at any given time. There was one guy, . . . I'm still trying to

TABLE 1
White and Asian American Percentages of Total Minnesota Population, 1960–2000

Census Year	Percentage White	Percentage Asian American
2000	89.4%	2.8%
1990	89.4%	1.7%
1980	94.4%	0.6%
1970	96.5%	0.02%
1960	98.2%	0.01%

Source: Bureau of the Census, Historical Census, Statistics on the Foreign-Born Population of the United States: 1850 to 1990, Table 8, Race and Hispanic Origin of the Population by Nativity: 1850 to 1990.

think about whether he was an adoptee or not. I'm assuming that he was, because he was Asian, but he didn't have an Asian name. When I was a junior, um, this family moved out, and they were Vietnamese. And I actually became really good friends with the girl who was the only one . . . in school at the time, at my high school. They were my first contact of really being linked to an Asian culture.[89]

Gabrielle understood that she was racially isolated, and did her best to connect with the few other Asian Americans in her high school, but still the school's lack of racial diversity fueled her interest in getting to a place with a larger population and presumably more people of color. Gabrielle did not specifically connect her racial isolation to experiences of racism, but Barb did. She stated, "No, I don't think I knew any Korean [persons]. . . . I don't think I was even aware of it, Korean people or Asian people or White people. At all. I think, so, like some of the neighbor kids they would ride their bikes and say 'Jap,' [and] I would just say, 'They called me Jap. And that means Japanese, and I'm Korean. They are dumb. They are wrong.'"[90] Barb used her racial isolation to make moments of racial tension less hurtful. The ignorance of her adversaries, probably at least partly based on the absence of Asian Americans in her childhood community, made them assume she was a nationality that she was not; her response was to assess her adversaries as "dumb" to deflect their slurs.

In a similar recollection, Ingrid also connected her racial isolation to racist incidents:

> So growing up was really difficult in those small towns, because ... Until I moved to a town ... in the sixth grade, there were no other Asian children in the town where I grew up, and so I remember coming home and being really upset or crying because some kid made fun of me on the playground, or some kid called me a chink or a gook or adopted. And telling my mother about it, but her saying that they probably didn't really mean it. And I remember being really upset because I knew that they meant it, and I felt very betrayed by my mother for having told me that they didn't mean it, because you couldn't evade it.[91]

Richard, age thirty-one, told a story of avoiding other Asian people, even other adoptees, or at least avoiding talking about the commonality he had with them as fellow adoptees, almost as if he did not want to acknowledge that being a Korean adoptee was part of his or anyone's identity:

> Ever since I was a child, there were other adoptees, but I never saw them as other adoptees, I saw them as Asian people, and just ... maybe that's weird, but the thing was is that, if anything, I wasn't ashamed of being Korean, [yet] I certainly wasn't going to associate with other Asians, and it just wasn't natural or normal for me to grow up in ... Minnesota suburbia in a primarily White area, for me to be associated with or seen with other Asian people. ... I never knew that they were Korean, too. That's the weird thing. I even can look back to my early early childhood and my neighbors were a family of four kids, and they would always invite over this girl ... [who] was a Korean adoptee, but I swear I never knew that, and that isn't the type of conversation kids have, anyways, so ... it didn't occur to me later, when I met her again when we were practically adults, that she was a Korean adoptee. And also, a girl that I kinda dated briefly in high school, ... she was adopted, and I never knew she was an adoptee. Actually, it took me until ... we met at some, like, Minnesota conference and she attended, that I saw her again for the first time since high school, and it was like, "You're Korean?"[92]

Does racial isolation in and of itself constitute a type of broad, socially rendered racism? Based on the experiences of the Korean adoptees who participated in this research, I argue that it does. Even when racially isolated adoptees are not singled out in overt acts of racism (though they report that they often are), the experience of being isolated prevents them from being able to connect their experiences with those of others like themselves, and can cause them to assume that they have no identity as adoptees, Asian Americans, or even persons of color because they have been so cut off from cultural experiences of others who might share these identities. In Gabrielle's example, this isolation led her to leave her home town in search of a more diverse social environment; even with all the acculturation to Whiteness she had received in her White community, she still ultimately felt uncomfortable as one of the only people of color in her town. In Ingrid's example, it is clear how the social setting of racial isolation added negatively to her experience of more overt racism in the form of childhood racial teasing, because she felt more susceptible to racial attacks as the only Asian person in town; her difficulty was compounded by her mother's decision to not take the attacks seriously. A few years later, in high school, Ingrid found herself self-isolating from other adoptees, having found some comfort by this time in controlling her own racial isolation. She described her break with her only adoptee friend growing up, as arising partly because it felt somehow wrong to associate with other adoptees, and partly because her growing consciousness about her own racial identity was different than the White identity of her adoptee friend. In her own struggle in losing and then finding a racial identity as a Korean adoptee, she could not maintain a relationship with an adoptee who identified differently. In Richard's example, he denies that being Asian or adopted was important in his identity or the identities of the people around him, many of whom turned out to also be Korean adoptees. He connects this impulse, himself, saying, "I wasn't ashamed of being Korean, [but] I certainly wasn't going to associate with other Asians," saying that this felt unnatural to him. While this attitude isn't necessarily an expression of racial self-hatred, it certainly also is not an expression of the racial pride that many psychologists believe is important for the psychological health of people of color.

Conclusion

Oh and Banjo offer a telling critique of multiculturalism and its contemporary manifestations, postracialism and colorblindness, arguing that they "provid[e] an excuse for witnessed racist discrimination. Postracialism's denial [of the existence of race] means that manifestations of racism are born not from systemic injustice but from individual bigotry."[93] Even Korean adoptees raised in socially and politically conservative families were exposed to liberalizing cultural norms during the 1970s and 1980s, including multiculturalism. Not surprisingly, many Minnesota Korean adoptees followed the lead of their parents or of mainstream society. Using ideologies of multiculturalism that promote assimilation, they worked to fit in to the White majority. However, some adoptees reached the limits of the usefulness of multiculturalism, or at least of the weak multiculturalism that was beginning to permeate mainstream culture at the time, because the only remedies to racism in a multiculturalist society were individual, not societal or structural. Indeed, commitment to a colorblind worldview prevented some Korean adoptees from recognizing and coping with racist discrimination when they encountered it; many even self-isolated, refusing to see themselves or other adoptees as people of color. For others, the bluntness of the tool that they were offered in weak multiculturalism made them extra-sensitive to the institutional and more blatant racism and discrimination that they faced.

Although the socially progressive climate in Minnesota in the 1970s and 1980s certainly influenced the experiences of the large cohort of Korean adoptees coming of age during that period, the ideologies of weak multiculturalism and colorblindness have become common throughout the United States. Because popular multiculturalism and its celebration of difference in the 1970s and 1980s had no remedy for racist discrimination, it became a double bind for these adoptees. These adoptees understood that the families and communities around them had trained themselves either not to see racism, or to believe that racism was a minor problem, confined to a few overtly bigoted individuals, that could be solved with the positive attitude of inclusive multiculturalism. Even though almost every adoptee who participated in this project spoke about racist incidents they had faced, many believed that to make a claim of racist discrimination would be to break the social etiquette of colorblindness, and risk arousing resentment in their White social networks.

5

Adoptees as White Koreans

Identity, Racial Visibility, and the Politics of Passing among Korean American Adoptees

I felt very socially isolated being an adult adoptee. And always felt, a lot of times, my friends couldn't understand it, you know, they would just, pretend I was White [chuckles] or they would just say, "I don't think of you as a minority." . . . The realization that other [Korean adoptees] were . . . consciously thinking about this and connecting with one another was a huge revelation.

     Barry, forty-four, on finding other Korean adoptees[1]

Racial Visibility, Invisibility, and Authenticity

Most people of color in America must navigate racialization within dominant discourses of society and cope with stereotypes about their racial/social/cultural group. In a society with a low tolerance for multiple and intersecting identities, individual and social strategies of passing and colorblindness obscure the richness and complexity of multilayered racial and ethnic (not to mention age, ability, class, sexual, and gender) identity. In my work involving Korean adoptees, I seek to recognize these complexities, while incorporating the realities of racial passing, colorblindness, and racial visibility. In a society that continues to enforce strict boundaries among racial categories and to suppress identity formations that challenge dominant social discourses on race and ethnicity, the adoptee subjects in my research employ a variety of social and cultural tools to navigate their multifaceted identities. Among these tools is the choice to claim one or more racial and ethnic identities in order to cope with socially enforced visibility or invisibility for people of color.

  The enforcement of race-only identity in a racist and White-dominated social context has contributed to the development of multiple strategies for survival among non-White persons (or more correctly, persons identified as non-White in dominant discourses). For persons with White or almost-White phenotypes, one of these strategies is "passing" or "passing for White." Film scholar Daniel Bernardi understands all Whiteness as a performance, whether it is performed by White or non-White persons, so that the act of passing for White necessarily involves either acting or looking White.[2] By passing, an individual can use their racially ambiguous or White appearance and/or culturally ambiguous or White behavior to disappear into the White majority, escaping racialization and the disadvantages of association with their minority racial group. For persons with non-White cultural heritage, the price of passing is imagined to be high, and an accusation of racial passing is certainly pejorative.[3] For instance, in James Weldon Johnson's novel *The Autobiography of an Ex-Colored Man*, the biracial African American protagonist who passes for White ultimately despairs in his choice to trade his African American heritage and identity away, despite the fact that this choice may well have saved his life in the violently anti-Black and antimiscegenation social milieu of the American South.[4]

Although the legal structures that encouraged passing have largely disappeared, cultural penalties for race mixing and racial ambiguity remain high. The continuing racial segregation in American society ensures that interlopers who cross the color line can expect ostracism and isolation. Individuals with hybrid identities are pressured to pick a side, usually that of the most visibly obvious race (consider the widespread public rejection for Tiger Woods's claim of a mixed-race Caucasian, Black, and Asian "Cablasian" racial identity, or the constant reference to Barack Obama as America's first Black, rather than multiracial, president). Whites and non-Whites alike have taken up the politics of passing. In the current cultural moment, the practice or perception of passing or trying to pass is also often equated with a lack of cultural authenticity or pride in one's racial or ethnic identity.[5] Contemporary slurs of "apple," "oreo," or "twinkie" applied to individuals who are perceived to be racially Red, Black, or Yellow but thought to be "White inside" underscore one cultural price of supposed assimilation of non-White individuals into White-dominated society.

Currently, colorblindness, a system of race denial in which everyone is imagined to pass as White, has taken firm hold in contemporary American society and politics.[6] The ideology of colorblindness has its appeal in the seemingly benevolent repositioning of race as a social construct rather than as a biologically determined trait or set of traits, and the recognition of race itself as the act around which racism occurs. Following this line of reasoning, if we do not recognize race (which, as a social construct, can be removed from or maintained in society), there will be no racism. The appeal of colorblindness lies in reducing racism to an individual rather than a societal problem, one which can be addressed by policing individual racist infractions without having to confront racism in American institutions and in society at large. Not surprisingly, colorblindness has great appeal among Whites who have not experienced racial discrimination and seek a low-investment approach to solving America's race problems, and who perceive themselves as having been cast in the role of villain in narratives of American race relations.[7] While colorblindness frequently figures in neoliberal discourses under the guise of racial justice (often quoting Dr. Martin Luther King's "I Have a Dream" speech), the insistence that race is not real ends up concealing current and historical inequalities that are unresolved in our (still) very racist society.[8] Whereas passing involves the self-denial of a racialized identity, colorblindness denies racialized identity for anyone. The refusal to recognize race as a significant and historically grounded difference among people shifts the burden of passing from a decision of the racialized individual to an expectation enforced by family, community, or the general public.

Several theorists have articulated more nuanced formulations of colorblindness. Eduardo Bonilla-Silva articulates colorblindness in context with older forms of American racialized beliefs, pointing out that, while "Jim Crow racism served as the glue for defending a brutal and overt system of racial oppression in the pre-civil rights era, color-blind racism serves as the ideological armor for a covert and institutionalized system in the post-civil rights era,"[9] and naming it as an equally insidious contemporary form of racism. Paul Gilroy imagines a reality of "against race thinking" and Antonia Darder and Rodolfo D. Torres develop a Marxist ideology based on class rather than on race, encompassing a deracialized, but not colorblind, future.[10] Both these formulations condemn the use of race as a primary mode of identity. Like their neoliberal counterparts, these theorists argue that the use of race as a category of identity only further reifies race as a real, rather than a socially constructed, state, and tends to ignore other bases for discrimination, such as class. On the one hand, these theorists do account for historical and institutional racisms, and differentiate their approaches from weak or liberal multiculturalism, by acknowledging the continuing importance of equality and social justice in light of these historical injustices. On the other hand, they ignore the question of how this type of "against race thinking" intersects with Whiteness as a dominant discourse and with the neoliberal concept of colorblindness—which, as a popular, dominant ideology of racelessness, is also an artifact of White privilege.

Authentic Visibility, Real Invisibility

Paradoxically, two of the main problems facing racialized groups of people are hypervisibility and total invisibility. For the hypervisible, racial stereotypes associated with negative characteristics (such as supposed inassimilability, stupidity, laziness, deviousness, etc.) prevail. For the invisible, society discriminates through ignorance by not noticing difference at all, and by ignoring the needs of communities with culture-specific practices, desires, and requirements. I argue that these racisms are linked and operate in tandem. The racism of hypervisibility operates within the racism of invisibility by insisting that visible characteristics of individuals can be used to determine cultural knowledge and group identity/loyalty while ignoring the actual cultural nuances and lived characteristics of specific groups of people. The ignored, or invisible, elements of cultures of peoples of color make visible elements, based on stereotypes, hypervisible, as complicated realities of real people are overlooked. The persistent and general invisibility of Asian Americans peoples in American culture is one such example.[11]

American society's tendency toward absolute racial categorization (with no real possibility of hybridity) along with the persistence of racial stereotypes in popular culture limits the choices available to people of color in expressing their racial and ethnic identities. Racism is not only the condition of having no choices, but also of having only bad choices. The absence of meaningful options has given rise to argumentation for and against both racial visibility and invisibility as liberatory. But it is only by understanding racial visibility and invisibility as two sides of a single oppressive ideology that it becomes possible to see that neither is necessarily a good choice.

Ostracism among one's so-called real racial group notwithstanding (though I certainly do not consider this reality to be trivial), passing carries many social benefits that often translate to economic advantages. Certainly, one does not have to look hard to realize the many advantages of Whiteness in a society dominated culturally, socially, and economically by Whites. We know all too well the advantages in earnings, lifespan, and increased access to benefits like education and health that are associated with Whiteness. In his seminal research on stereotype threat (the psychological internalization of perceived dominant stereotypes against persons in the stereotyped group), Claude Steele acknowledges that one way to escape stereotype threat is to dissociate oneself from the stereotyped group.[12] Historically, this option is especially feasible for persons with hybridized identities, whether they be racially, ethnically, or culturally mixed. In the strictest sense, passing is only possible for those with phenotypes close enough to a norm of Whiteness that their appearance does not arouse suspicion. Incidentally, as the American historical understanding of Whiteness has become inclusive of darker phenotypes (with the inclusion of Irish, Southern, and Eastern Europeans), this type of passing has become possible for darker-skinned mixed-race people. However, passing also requires sufficient proficiency in the cultural practices of the dominant society to camouflage one's own differences. In exchange for passing, one can expect entry into dominant societal discourses, freedom from minoritization, and presumably, freedom from acts of discrimination.

As American dominant society becomes both racially more hybridized and socially more committed to ignoring racial differences, passing has become possible even for those who do not appear to be White. Racial colorblindness has become a legal and moral imperative for many Americans.[13] As passing becomes easier for people of color, and more widely accepted in dominant society, both the expectation to pass and the benefits of passing have increased. Hudson argues that the trend toward colorblindness in American culture has deemphasized race-based identities in favor of national identity and nationalized American values of "individualism, consumerism, patriotism, ahistoricism—that sustain foundational myths of 'America' as a 'nation of immigrants,' 'land of opportunity,' and 'democracy.'"[14] Thus, passing invisibly into dominant American society has potentially become part of a nationalizing project whereby subjects' primary identification is with the American nation rather than with a specific racial or cultural group.

In addition to giving rise to neoliberal understandings of racial unity and justice-through-colorblindness, civil rights movements of the 1960s and 1970s also gave rise to racial identity movements. Among other goals, these movements sought to heighten the visibility of people of color beyond negative racial stereotypes.[15] Identity-based activisms had—and continue to have—enormous positive impacts on American society, transforming the social, political, and academic landscapes. Despite the rise of colorblind agendas, these struggles continue. These historical and contemporary movements of self-defined racial visibility give communities of color platforms from which to demand equality, justice, and recognition of difference.

Mechanisms for defining what constitutes a race or ethnicity—including unambiguous ways of demarcating identity boundaries—are integral to the establishment of racial or ethnic identity. The act of claiming racial or ethnic identity is only possible through the dialectical process of defining who or what is outside the boundaries of that identity. Often, these considerations are based on the concept of authenticity, but the question of who determines authenticity is also complicated. Ironically, by seeking acceptance in dominant culture through heightened visibility, identity-based movements can themselves risk excluding people whose right to identify as members of the minority group is susceptible to challenge on the grounds of inauthenticity. As we seek to define ourselves, we draw lines that leave others out. We are cautioned by scholars such as Vincent J. Cheng to have a thorough understanding of the historical and cultural contexts of claims on cultural authenticity because "the search for genuine or authentic native voices will serve only to provide us with a feel-good liberal and multicultural glow—while in actuality merely recycling tokenism and nostalgia."[16]

Although the politics of passing, visibility, and racial identity are very real, I focus instead on another equally potent reality: heterogeneity and the authenticity of complicated identities. While Korean American adoptees are often depicted in absolutely racial terms (as "Asians") or in absolutely raceless terms (as "Americans" or as "humans") I approach them as people who navigate multiple identities and engage in complicated conversations with the dominant discourses that would seek to categorize them neatly within their so-called real identities.

American Racial Hierarchy and Identity: Ethnic Choices?

Escaping the constraints of racial hierarchies and negative racialization is a lifelong challenge for many people of color. For Whites, arguably at the top of the American racial hierarchy and without significant negative racialization, escape from trappings of racial identity is less imperative. For White ethnics, racial Whiteness allows for ethnic exploration, experimentation, and choice. In *Ethnic Options* (1990), Mary Waters establishes that White American ethnics often choose to identify with one part of their ethnic heritage over other parts. By exploring parallels between how White ethnics see ethnicity and how non-White Americans see race, Waters shows that many White Americans see their ethnicities as simultaneously defining and unimportant, but most of all, as unrestricting. Waters subjects' view their ethnicities as pleasant accessories, not as essential parts of their daily lives.[17] Although Waters reports that her subjects both participated in and were subject to ethnic stereotyping, and the subjects agree that this may have created difficulties for earlier generations, they do not feel that their ethnic identities are problematic in the present day.

Because of these beliefs, Waters' multiethnic White subjects seem to have many options in choosing from a menu of ethnicities (often equated to ancestral nationality) and from the behaviors that subjects linked to each or several of their chosen ethnic identities, without real social consequence. The more mixed a White person's ancestry, the larger the menu of ethnic choices available to them. Although the multiethnic heritages of White Americans are allowed to operate both as concurrent ("I am French, Scottish, and Swedish") or divergent (the same person identifying as Swedish only), identity formations depending on social context, there is much less social tolerance for hybridity in ethnic (and sometimes therefore racial) identity formation among people of color. Despite the belief among Waters's White subjects that their ethnicity operates similarly to race for people of color,[18] processes of racialization in America ensure that people of color are identified in dominant discourses by their race alone (Black/African American, Yellow/Asian American, Brown/Latina or Hispanic Americans, Red/American Indian) without regard to ethnic heritage or national/cultural identity. Therefore, as Miri Song suggests, "The actual range of ethnic identities available to individuals and the groups to which they belong may not be wholly under their control" because "the ethnic identities asserted by groups need to be recognized and validated by the wider society."[19] American historical and legal traditions have tended instead to enforce race-only identification for non-White Americans though practices ranging from the "one-drop rule" legal definition of Blackness to the creation of census categories such as "Asian Pacific Islander" or "Hispanic" that lump together people of different cultures, ethnicities, and nationalities who are racialized similarly. These practices have proven problematic throughout the histories of these groups, considering the heterogeneity of national and cultural affiliation within all of these racial categories as well as the miscegenation and exogamy that have been present in all racial and ethnic sectors of American society throughout history.

Korean American adoptees are exposed to the practice of ethnic choice because they are raised into families headed by White ethnics, and it is not uncommon for them to choose among ethnic identifications that may include both their parents' ethnicities and their own. However Korean adoptees are also like other American people of color in choosing their race. Since race is an identifier enforced by others, no matter how individuals may perceive themselves, this process is much more contested.

Asian American Racializations

The racialization of Asian Americans began as an experience of heightened visibility for a population perceived as foreigners and interlopers. In *Forever Foreigners or Honorary Whites*, Mia Tuan articulates the positioning of Asian Americans between Black and White, and describes the unique racialization of Asian Americans, including the need to closely attend to one's Asian image because of high visibility: the high social cost paid as Asian ethnics who are therefore non-American (or "forever foreigners").[20] More recently, Asian Americans have also been rendered legally and socially invisible through the "model minority" image and the reclassification of Asian Americans as "over-represented minorities" ineligible for affirmative action admissions or scholarships and fellowship programs geared toward underrepresented populations.[21]

At the same time, social discourses that privilege the binary racial construction of Black and White often completely exclude Asian Americas, American Indians, Latinos, mixed-race persons, and members of other minority groups, as numerous studies by scholars including Matthew Frye Jacobson, James W. Loewen, and Aiwha Ong, have documented.[22] Ong's treatment of the racialized position of Asian Americans between Black and White traces both the social Whitening of Chinese cosmopolitan transnationals in *Flexible Citizenship* and the social Blackening of Southeast Asian immigrants in *Buddha Is Hiding*. This Blackening is enacted through the social and cultural positioning of Southeast Asians, in this case Khmer, as victims, welfare recipients, unfit parents, and a population given to superstition over intellect. In a deepening of analysis around the Black/White binary, Ong also positions Khmer in relation to Asian Americans positioned as Whiter, such as Chinese or Japanese, or even Vietnamese. In their anthology *Model Minority Myth Revisited*, Guofang Li and Lihshing Wang explore the implications of Ong's work, writing that "increasingly, underachieving and/or 'misbehaving' Asian American[s] . . . who do not fit the 'model minority' image are ideologically Blackened while those who do fit are whitened."[23]

Within the limited framework of Black/White binaries, Korean adoptees exist with a Whitened racialization in the United States as adoptees, but as less White in the context of their birth nation as parentless orphans. As orphaned infants or children,[24] adoptees are saddled with the patronizing racialization as a result of what Ong refers to as "compassionate love." In her discussion of compassionate love, Ong outlines her ideas about "paternalism toward subordinated populations" built around the well-intentioned but denigrating guiding principal of "uplift."[25] As Kit Myers's analysis shows, the reification of adoption as an exclusively loving act erases the violence leading up to and including child removal from transnational adoption discourse.[26] In the absence of any awareness of its imperialist implications, adoptive agents deploy the motivation of saving babies from poor countries, destitute mothers, and sexist cultures to give adoptive parents a mission of salvation through adoption equated with love.

Tuan's title, *Forever Foreigners or Honorary Whites*, also alludes to the Whitening of Asian Americans with the advent of the model minority image in the 1980s.[27] However, concerns about Asians "out-Whiting the Whites" reveal that White dominance in American racial hierarchies is not so easily relinquished. High academic performance and economic attainment in some sectors of Asian American communities feeds long-held American apprehensions about Asian cultural domination in a contemporary version of "Asian horde" anxieties.

As a result of the location of Asian Americans so close to Whites at the top of the hierarchy of American racialization, privileged social roles have been created for Asian Americans, based on stereotypical perceptions and on Asian American internalization of these roles.[28] Stereotypes of Asian Americans as naturally smart, musically gifted, or hard working prevail. These perceptions, though they are often described as positive stereotypes, are ultimately harmful to Asian Americans: the stereotype of Asian Americans as naturally high achieving prevents high-achieving Asian Americans from getting credit for their work; instead, they are viewed as average performers within a population that is expected to excel. The high incidence of depression and suicide among Asian Americans—especially college-age Asian American women—is a stark reminder that the consequences of so-called positive stereotypes can be devastating.[29]

The just-about-White perception of Asian Americans, who make up only 5 percent of the United States population,[30] has also affected that group's experience when it comes to higher education. For instance, many institutions of higher learning consider Asian Americans overrepresented in relation to White students rather than underrepresented with other people of color if their share of enrolment exceeds their share of the general population, and do not actively recruit them.[31] In fact, despite a high degree of media attention paid to Asian American enrollment in elite institutions, most Asian American students (like other students of color) attend less prestigious public two- and four-year colleges.[32] Although Asian American students are becoming more common in American colleges and universities than in the past, they still have life experiences that include racialization and discrimination. Aggregating all peoples of Asian or Pacific descent also creates a false picture of the Asian American access to education: populations derived from recent Asian immigrant groups, particularly Southeast Asian Americans, are extremely underrepresented in American colleges and universities.[33]

The demographics of college and university faculty are often difficult to interpret, largely because of the general lack of differentiation between Asian and Asian American faculty.[34] The National Center for Education Statistics estimated that Asians and Asian Americans made up 5.7 percent of American college and university faculty in 2007.[35] However, the center did not disaggregate foreign-born Asian from Asian American faculty (though the center does separate out nonresident alien faculty). In 1993, William Wei found that Asian faculty outnumbered Asian American faculty in American colleges and universities by ten to one;[36] in 1995, Eugenia Escueta and Eileen O'Brien estimated only 40 percent of Asian faculty were foreign born.[37] If Wei's ratio is still accurate, only about one-half of one percent of American post-secondary faculty are Asian American; if Escueta and O'Brien's estimate still holds, the proportion is 3.4 percent.[38] These low numbers may be partially explained by the fact that Asian American PhD holders are less likely to enter the academic workforce than their White counterparts, and in the late 1980s, had one of the lowest rates of academic tenure among minority groups.[39]

Racial Roles of Korean Adoptees

The model minority phenomenon is well described in Asian American studies research and is succinctly summarized by Tuan, who states that Asian Americans "remain 'model minorities,' the best of the 'other' bunch but not 'real' Americans."[40] Because the insidious nature of the model minority myth has yet to be well understood within mainstream and adoption circles, it is sometimes embraced as a form of acceptance into dominant society.[41] Some published

Asian adoptee research even takes a celebratory view of this position of racialization for Asian adoptees. Chinese adoption scholars Richard C. Tessler and Gail Gamache write that the Asian American model minority image, "sets a positive example for socially responsible and achieving behavior.... It is possible that children adopted from China will gain from these positive images. On the other hand, they may suffer if negative images predominate."[42] The research of transnational adoption scholars Sara Dorow, Heather Jacobson, and Kristi Brian show the perception of Asians as the "model minority" is one reason adoptive parents choose Asian children over other children of color.[43]

Currently, Korean American adoptees constitute a little less than one percent of the Asian American population (approximately 7 percent of Korean Americans, who are themselves approximately 10 percent of the Asian American population).[44] In addition, most Korean adoptees have been or are being raised in non-Asian homes, largely in isolation from Korean American or other Asian American cultural influences. Because of their acculturation separate from other Asian Americans, and the general racial segregation still common in the United States, they might not be considered or might not consider themselves a part of Asian American communities. So, in many ways, Korean adoptees cannot be considered representative of Asian Americans numerically or culturally. However, despite their minority status within Asian America, Korean adoptees epitomize what it means to be Asian American, in several different ways. These include Korean adoptees' positions as colonial subjects, created by acts of war in the quest for imperial domination; as Asian Americans acculturated to embody the ideals of colorblindness; as examples of a hybrid Asian American identity, Asian by birth and American by acculturation; and as persons subject to model minority expectations to assimilate willingly and quickly into dominant society.

Korean adoptees experience many of the same issues of identity and positionality at an individual scale that other Asian Americans experience at a familial or community scale, though the personal histories of Korean adoptees are often different from those of other Asian American populations. In their American families and communities, Korean adoptees are subject to a Whitened racialization. Other second- and third-generation Asian Americans experience a similar Whitening through acculturation, where Whiteness is seen as analogous to American-ness,[45] but for adoptees this process is accelerated. The Whitening of adoptees, technically first-generation immigrants, is achieved through assimilative processes in (usually) predominantly White families, processes that include colorblindness as a common parenting strategy.[46]

Korean adoptees are generally accepted as "culturally White" and often assume roles as racial and cultural bridge-makers that are remarkably similar to the social roles of Asian Americans described by Henry Yu in *Thinking Orientals*.

Yu explains how early sociological research of the Chicago School produced scholarship that cast Asian Americans in roles that they still occupy today. Themes of the Asian American "caught between two worlds" and the role of the "marginal man"[47] are reproduced among Korean adoptees in my research, even though they are largely isolated from much of the rest of Asian America. Adoptees are imagined by adoptive parents as providing the adoptive family with an entrée into communities of color, and positioned as ambassadors by the Korean government; though I recognize these roles as disempowering for Asian Americans, my own research indicates that they still obtain. The racialized position of Asian Americans in general, and of Korean adoptees in particular, between Black and White (or at least between White and non-White), with responsibilities to act as racial and cultural mediators, is certainly problematic, perhaps especially because of how fully many adoptees have embraced this role.

"Passing" for White: Korean Adoptees in Colorblind America—White Family, White Community

In her essay "Brown-Skinned White Girls," about women of African descent who self-identify as White, France Winddance Twine summarizes four necessary conditions for the construction of a White identity among a population visibly coded as non-White: 1) isolation from other non-Whites;[48] 2) "racially neutral" environments that enforce colorblind interpretations of family and community; 3) an ethic that privileges individualism; and 4) high priority placed on the material achievements of a middle-class existence.[49] In many ways, Twine's theories can be applied to Korean adoptees as well; most are in family and social environments that fulfill Twine's conditions. In their White American families, the Korean adoptees I interviewed tended to be "raised White,"[50] possibly because the adoptive parents were not interested in the birth culture of the adoptee, certainly because of the lack of availability of parenting models that privileged the modeling of another culture over the parents' own.

Korean adoptees' assimilation into the family is followed by assimilation into racial and cultural identities of Whiteness. Many adoptees remarked that the only people they saw, growing up, were White. Because of acculturation to Whiteness through rearing, many Korean adoptees find easy access to White privileges and life options, because of both a general support for White identities and a lack of support for non-White ones.

The practice of transracial adoption both highlights and erases race in adoptees. While most adoptees can never escape the reality and the heightened racial visibility that they are one of the few persons—if not the only person—of color in their adoptive families (and often in their communities), White parents and even entire communities often work to lower adoptee racial visibility and erase racial differences using a number of strategies, including instilling the values of a "weak" multiculturalism (which, as noted in chapter 4, celebrates difference but does not address a history of racism and imperial injustice), downplaying racial incidents, and enacting racially homogenizing ideologies.

For Korean adoptees, the ambiguity of Asian American racialization is compounded by racial ambiguity within adoptive families that use colorblindness to smooth over racial differences and conform to a normative construct of family that includes blood ties and physical resemblance between parents and children.[51] Twila L. Perry calls this tendency "colorblind individualism," and argues that it includes a belief that transracial adoption "constitutes a positive step towards a more integrated, nonracist society."[52] Paradoxically, although a colorblind ideology seems to have become a norm for adoptive parents in raising their transracially and transnationally adopted children, that the process of searching for a child to adopt is, recent research reveals, typically highly racialized and full of race-based selection preferences.[53] Most adoptive families continue to acknowledge racial differences, but these differences can be wiped away by the claiming of a single culture and national identity (usually White-dominated American culture). Recent studies of the tendency to conflate culture and race in mainstream American society have illuminated this privileging of cultural sameness over racial difference in adoptive families.[54]

Individualism is highly valued in mainstream American society, and especially, perhaps, in adoptive families, in which parents have approached child acquisition with much decision-making and deliberation.[55] It is the experience of choosing, described by transnational adoption scholar Sara Dorow as "the discursive power of the 'chosen child,'"[56] that is deployed to compensate for the lack of normativity in family building by adoption. Many adoptive parents tell their adopted children, "I chose *you*!" in order to make adopted children feel special despite their lack of biological relation to the family, a practice Kristi Brian attributes to the emphasis on choice for prospective adoptive parents in the transnational adoption industry.[57] Although there are surely good intentions in this particular parenting strategy, unbeknownst to parents, this can be construed by adoptees as a very one-sided choice; most adoptees understand very well that they had absolutely no choice in their family placement, certainly no more than biological children have in being born into a family.

The conditions identified by Twine for the creation of a White identity regardless of phenotype—racial isolation, a racially neutral environment, and emphasis on individualism and material attainment—are in place for most Korean adoptees. That they would develop White identities while in White families could be seen as predictable, even unavoidable. Vincent Cheng notes that, for better or for worse, interracial and intercultural "adoptions make a radical mockery of any notions of an authentic identity. Children adopted as infants . . . have almost no experience of their birth parents and of the culture of their birth parents."[58] Indeed, few of my interview subjects had any memory of their family or lives in Korea. Although the Korean adoptees who spoke with me described many different axes of identity, for most, a White identity was as much or more a part of their personal histories as their Asian, Korean, or adoptee identities.[59]

Although they experience constant pressure to choose one identity over the other, and though many see a conflict between their White and non-White/adoptee identities, adoptees have many choices from a multiplicity of ethnic and cultural options. For some, acknowledging their White cultural background is essential and phenotype alone is insufficient for how they would like to be characterized.[60] For others, building up an Asian American, Korean American, or Korean identity is more important. Still others understand their identities to be a product of the many complicated cultural and racial processes of being Korean, American, Asian, and adopted.

Flexible Racial Boundaries, Mobile Racial Hierarchies: Korean Adoptees as White Koreans

Many participants in my research reported that they had identified as White or had wanted to be White while growing up, which seems hardly surprising in light of the racial makeup of most adoptive families, the assimilationist ideology that prevails in White American society, and the colorblind mindset within which many were raised. While issues around White identities were not the most prominent topic among the participants, several emphasized Whiteness in their social and family histories; many (of both genders and in all locations where I collected oral histories) said that, when they started dating, they had only considered White partners.[61] Gabe simply stated, "I wasn't happy with myself being Asian . . . or, for that matter, I wasn't happy with myself . . . not being Caucasian."[62] The majority of adoptees who participated in my research had, at some point, thought of themselves as White, mostly before they moved out of their parents' homes; part of thinking of themselves as White was self-consciousness about their visible non-Whiteness, their Asianness. As a result, many adoptees, like John, thirty-three, experienced a great desire to be White, and a rejection of their Asian racial identity and racial characteristics. He stated, "I wish I didn't stand out so much . . . I mean, I think, growing up, I didn't wan[t to] be Korean; I wanted to be more Caucasian because, what this society values as beautiful, is more the Caucasian [ideal]. Seems like that [was] being bombarded when I was growing up. I think maybe that's a little better now, but back then every commercial, every advertisement, definitely pictured blue-eyed people."[63] Beatrice, age thirty-seven, remarked, similarly:

Now looking back, I remember that feeling always being in the back of my head. And, growing up, I struggled, you know. I used to think I was the ugliest girl in the world. I didn't like my eyes, I didn't understand my, uh, identity, I didn't understand, you know, why I looked different compared to other people around me; I always wished that I was a blonde, with blue eyes or brown hair, or blue eyes like my best friend . . . all White. I grew up in an all-White world. So, I remember, I wanted to be a White girl. I remember that being one of my goals. But of course it was impossible. And I didn't understand it at the time. I denied myself as a Korean individual. There were a lot of things that I did wrong because I wanted to please people around me, like my friends. . . . And, you know, I [was] Korean in an all-White community in an all-White world, as far as I knew.[64]

Although some found it easy to understand themselves as American (in many cases, a euphemism for White), others considered working toward Whiteness more solemnly. Henry, age thirty-two, spoke first of how he initially found it easy to fit into an all-White family and community: "My parents didn't put any expectations on me. They didn't put any pressures on me. But I've always put pressure on myself to do the best I could, whether in school or in athletics. . . . So that was, I guess, my elementary, high school years. Going to college, I surrounded myself. . . . You know, obviously growing up in a small town there weren't any minorities, so, you know, all my friends were Caucasians, or whatever you want to call them. And that was the normal; you know, that was the norm."[65] Later in his oral history, Henry discussed the conflict he felt later in life because his identity as an American didn't leave any room for his Korean or adoptee identity. In the end, he directly connected his inability to accept himself as Korean to the shame of not knowing who or what he was because he didn't know anything about his own birthplace; he eventually returned to Korea and is now married to a Korean national. Many participants believed that it was necessary for adoptees to dissociate with Korea and Korean-ness in order to become American and to fit into the White world.

The drive to dissociate from other Asians in order to fit in to White communities can be very strong among adoptees. Diane, twenty-eight, talked about her own racism directed at other Asians as she grew up:

I went to a small Catholic school . . . , so we had very few students of color, which I think would have been different if I had been at a bigger public school. I know that, at that time, that my town was getting a larger population of Vietnamese refugee families, and I knew that I had to do whatever I could to distance myself from these, you know . . . [Immigrants] . . . I mean, God forbid! They couldn't speak English! And that was just horrifying, that I could be categorized that way. I remember, I was a cashier at [a grocery store] when I was in high school and I would do these weird things: if I thought somebody thought I was one of those kind of immigrants, I would start talking really loud so they could tell that I didn't have an accent.[66]

While Diane's reaction to Asian refugees appears to be a form of internalized racism, it operates differently than the self-hatred or self-doubt that the concept of internalized racism generally describes. Caught in the paradox of being Asian but having a White gaze and socialization, Diane believed that it was important to create social distance between herself and Asians who bore the cultural signifiers of foreignness. Diane's story also shows the pressure to assimilate, as she worried that the Vietnamese immigrants were "blowing her cover" because Whites might consider her a foreigner instead of an assimilated, English-speaking American.

For most of my informants, White identity decreased after leaving home and becoming independent as adults, though this process is often complicated and difficult. Many found that the development of a non-White identity, though culturally rewarding, carried a high price, including coming to terms with one's own lack of Korean cultural knowledge, and experiencing rejection or dislocation within the family. An Asian or Korean identity emerging after adolescence seems to be common among Korean adoptees; many participants only began to question or reject their White identity in their late twenties and early thirties.

Many Korean adoptees who identified as White throughout childhood encountered social pressure to re-identify as non-White after they began dating, and during their college years. This corroborates Twine's findings; her subjects experienced breakdown of White identities as a result of "reality checks" with dating and immersion in a more racially diverse environment in college.[67] Many adoptees who experience this realignment of identity are traumatized by the change, but also see its benefits in terms of their sense of ethnic pride.[68] However, it is important to note that Korean adoptees who self-identify as White do not necessarily ever stop using this identifier; my analysis is not meant to suggest that all Korean adoptees develop White identities.

An emerging Asian or Asian American identity can be particularly risky for adoptees who have previously expressed a White or culturally White identity. For many, changing identities is a painful and confusing process that family may not be able to understand. Gail, thirty-two, stated:

> The sad thing about it is that, once you take the lid off it, you can't go back. It's a can of worms. In some ways I wish I could be so ignorant again; you know, that ignorance is bliss. My mom knows that there is something terribly wrong in our relationship, on a gut level, but she

doesn't know what. She's blinded by her privilege. I try to engage her and [I] understand that Whiteness is about being totally blocked off and not having to look at anything you don't want to, and I keep bumping my head against this, and it's impermeable. It's an obstruction I can't get through.[69]

In this example, Gail feels that her exploration of an Asian identity as she has matured has isolated her from her mother. One of the major contradictions for Korean adoptees is their tendency to be raised White, but then be told they are not White by those inside or outside the family, upon reaching adulthood. Gail continued:

I did identify as White. I remember asking my mom when I filled out my college form what to put. She said, "Well you're *Asian.*" But that totally flies in the face of what I've been told. . . . If I'm raised White, then I'm supposed to be White. As a good liberal college student, than race doesn't matter, and I'm going to mark White. But then I found out that other people didn't know that I was White [laughs]. . . . It gets complicated because other people actually look at you. So then I have to think about what I'm marking on those boxes, and I started changing it every semester, and that does not sit well with people.[70]

Here, Gail pays a social price for making choices about racial identity and then changing her mind. Identity switching presents more practical difficulties for Korean adoptees than for White ethnics because race is a more powerful social signifier than ethnicity in American society. Even though Korean adoptees are well versed in enacting Whiteness, they are sometimes reminded that they are not White, at least not biologically or visibly, by those around them.

This contradiction has been named the Transracial Adoptee Paradox by research counseling psychologist Richard Lee, whose research queries the psychosocial development of transracial adoptees, with particular attention to identity building and psychological adjustment to the adoption experience. He describes the paradox as the contradiction felt by non-White persons adopted by White parents, "racial/ethnic minorities in society . . . perceived and treated by others [inside the family] . . . as if they are members of the majority culture."[71] This paradox may become a problem when adoptees have to transition from racial invisibility within White families and communities that do not recognize a racial element of their identities, to the visibility of the "real world" where race is recognized and adoptees must cope with more explicit forms of racialization, as Barb, age thirty-one, recounted:

Going to college, I was getting really depressed. Just not dealing with my emotions and all the anxieties I had, it was all happening at the same time. I'd called home and said, "I don't know what to do. I feel like I want to kill myself, I'm so depressed right now. I've been crying for all day long and I don't know what to do. I think I need to leave or something." I said, "Mom, I feel really suicidal and I'm so depressed." I just remember the conversation was really short. She said, "Oh, you'll figure it out, it will work out, you'll figure it out, it's okay." . . . We just said 'bye; I called my brother and said, "I just don't know what to do." He listened. But I decided I just needed to drop out. I came back home. I started trying to explain to my parents that I feel like I'm having issues with being Asian. People look at me like I'm Asian. People look at me like I'm a foreign exchange student. I don't know. There's a lot of issues; that's when I started realizing that I was very very different and people saw me and they didn't see who I really was.[72]

In the complex racial reality of transracial adoptees, the real world means a racist dominant society where transracial adoptees encounter racist language or forms of racial discrimination among strangers or peers, or in institutional settings such as work or school. The racial rules of the real world are also enforced by the racializing tendency to consider race as a set of discrete, bounded categories; the transracial adoption paradox operates within a paradigm of identity in which the adoptee can be either White or non-White. In her work on how strangers intrusively interact with Korean adoptees and their adoptive families, Sara Docan-Morgan points out that racial remarks from those outside the family can disrupt adoptees' self-proclaimed White identities.[73] The dissonance of claiming an identity not supported by others (the social consequences of being wrong about your own identity, such as in the example above, if a person checks "White" when he or she is "really" Asian) is of primary concern to many adoption researchers, who fear that a White acculturation may not prepare transracial adoptees to live in a racist society, and that these survival skills are best learned from parents of the same race as the child.[74]

Just as the incentive to accept a White identity in a White family can be strong, the consequences of rejecting such an identity can be grave; I have found that adoptees find that challenging this White identity threatens their inclusion in their White families. This is consistent with the racial ambiguities enforced within many adoptive families to achieve normative familial sameness by deemphasizing racial differences. If adoptees are raised to believe that race doesn't matter, in order to maintain family harmony, the insistence that racial difference does matter can upset this balance, sometimes in extreme ways.

At the same time, pressure to be more Asian within Asian American communities, the Korean adoptee community included, can be high for Korean adopted adults. So many Korean adoptees have the experience of being raised White that one mark of maturity among adoptees is to revert or discover one's roots. This journey of discovery often includes travel back to Korea, searching for birthparents, self-education about Korea, Asia, and/or Asian America, and sometimes the rejection of White family and friends. Korean adoptees may be responding to these pressures if they seek to move away from culturally White identities as they mature. Transracial adoptees may face social pressure from people of color to take on a strictly non-White identity, backed by the suggestion that a White identity is a denial of one's "true" self. Even if well-intentioned, these renderings of the "real" racial identity of transracial adoptees are often just as ignorant of transracial adoptee life experience as are those of White families and society. For many adoptees, the wholesale rejection of White identity and culture is no more satisfying an option than the denial of their Korean identity. Diane, age twenty-eight, recalled her response to an invitation to a social event that excluded Whites, including her White fiancé:

> There is something that happened not too long ago, with someone [a person of color], . . . somewhat out of our group, [who] was throwing a party and had made the comment, "I'm having this party with such-and-such and let's try to keep it to folks of color, because I don't think my nerves can handle anyone else." And I was really offended by that. Because I have spent most of my life trying to feel comfortable with people who are Asian, and there is absolutely no way in hell that I am going to start feeling uncomfortable because there are White people in my life. And I really resent that sentiment. I get it on a sociological level, I get it, but I don't agree with it. It's hurtful. I'm sure the same way it's hurtful for you sometimes. I feel like, as a person and as a couple, we're above that. The person inviting me was not the person who wrote that, so I told that person. I said, "Anyplace my partner's not welcome to, I'm not welcome to. That's offensive to me and that's just the same as me sending around an email saying don't bring any people of color."[75]

When speaking about racism she's experienced as a Korean American adoptee, Abigail, age thirty-two, had more complaints about other Koreans in her life than about her White friends and family:

> I'd have to say that I think I experienced more racism from other Koreans than I did from Caucasians, for example. Most Caucasian people that I knew and were friends with, they were pretty accepting of my family situation. But, I think, the—the recurring theme for me was running into a lot of Korean Americans and Korean families who had a strong bias against adoptees. . . . I ran into that numerous times growing up. . . . For

example, all through grade school, middle school, and high school, there was a group of Korean Americans who kind of teased me and called me "twinkie" and, you know, "banana," and things like that. I think I always tried to laugh it off and, you know, just pretend like it didn't bother me. But I think, inside, I did internalize a lot of that. I did really think about what—what it is to be a "real" Korean and what it is to be a "fake" Korean, which is the other term that was used quite often.[76]

Madeline, age thirty-six, compared the racialization she experienced in Korea, for being "White inside," to that in the United States:

[When] I came to Korea, . . . people were like, "Oh, you're a White person inside," and . . . when I was in the U.S, they'd be like, "Oh, you're . . ." umm, what is the, "You're a banana," and I never really understood, completely, that concept. I mean, I understood, yeah, you're a White person on the inside, Asian person on the outside, and I really did understand that, but . . . they'd just be like [pause], "Well, you know, you, you're a wannabe White person." And I'm like, "No, [pause] I don't think I'm a wannabe White person. I, I think I am what I am, because I didn't have a choice. So, does that make me a banana?" An Asian person who comes . . . I think a banana is an example of an Asian person who goes to America, and starts [pause] just completely disses his culture, his or her culture, and then starts acting like a White person. . . . That would be an example of a banana. However, because I'm placed in that society does not, I don't think, really [pause] say that I'm a banana, because [pause] I don't think I follow that example. So, do I think more White? Do I think more Asian? I don't know if I, if I think more White, because . . . I think more Western. I definitely don't think Korean . . . so, if you differentiate . . . maybe I think more Asian if I go to America, and when I go to America . . . go to Korea then I think more White. So, [pause] I don't know. It's such a hard question.[77]

Diane, Abigail, and Madeline are caught between a rock and a hard place: on the one hand, they are connecting with other Asians and Asian Americans, either because they want to while in the United States or, in Madeline's case, at her workplace in Seoul. Although none see themselves as racial-cultural curiosities, they are treated as such, or at least each is asked to choose a single racial-cultural identity by the Asians and Asian Americans with whom she comes in contact. Diane is not willing to abandon her White friends and partner in order to be in with an Asian American friend who seems to not want White people in his life (or at least in his presence). Abigail's experience of abuse by Koreans and Korean Americans puts her on guard against those communities, but it also makes her question if she is really Korean, or only a "fake" Korean (which she takes as meaning Korean in body only, but not culturally). Madeline rejects the suggestion that she is a "banana" because she does not feel she should be held responsible for a cultural identity that she did not choose. Although she feels that the description of "yellow on the outside, White on the inside" may be accurate in one way, she does not see herself as having rejected Korean culture of her own volition; instead she claims "I am what I am, because I didn't have a choice."

In contrast to the race-neutral positions cast for Korean adoptees by parents, or the race-positive positions cast by some adoption researchers and communities of color, many of the Korean adoptees I spoke with expressed a profound sense of racial in-between-ness. Considering the competing social pressures to identify as White (usually within the family and close friends) and as Asian (in larger social contexts among groups that do not identify the adoptee as Asian and adopted), it is not surprising that Korean adoptees feel divided.

Adoptee Identity between Races

Recent studies of Korean American adoptee identity corroborate this work in their complication of racial binaries among adoptees. Grace Kim, Karen Suyemoto, and Castellano Turner identify "Korean adoptee" as an important identifier among some adoptees, as well as the recognition of separate racial (Asian) and cultural (American) identities among their Korean adoptee subjects.[78] Jiannbin Shiao and Mia Tuan, in their study of sixty adult Korean adoptees, separated their subjects into four groups, rating them according to their degree of self-identification with either Asian American or White American identity.[79] However, the life histories of Korean adoptees in this research suggest that these classification schemes are not entirely adequate to describe Korean adoptee-identified individuals. First, identity formation for many of the participants in this work has been fluid throughout the lives of the adoptees; many reported that their racial identities had changed over the course of their lives. Similarly, Dani Meier found that most of the Korean adoptees in his study "opted out of Korean cultural experiences" as children.[80] So how have adoptees who exhibit strong Korean adoptee identity developed this identity over time? Most of the participants in this research who elected to express a Korean adoptee identity reported that the decision to do so grew out of experiences of marginalization that were difficult to reconcile in White or nonadopted circles, or out of meeting other adoptees with whom they felt a meaningful connection. Through these common experiences, an adoptee identity is formulated.

David, age fifty-two, told how connecting with other Korean adoptees changed his life and helped him heal from many years of racial discrimination, abuse, and depression:

> I had this pain inside of me, and I didn't know what it was. You know. Several years after I played sports, I just quit and started taking drugs, you know, just to kill that pain. And I went kind of crazy . . . in fact two years ago at [work] I was sitting there and putting on this big dinner, and there was some maintenance people kind of sitting down there, and somebody had said some offhand remark about a gook or something like that, which, you know, of course my ears pick up right away. Kind of like, and it's like in a moment's time, I was transferred from being a forty-nine-year-old man or whatever. It felt like I was five years old again. I was sitting at the table, I was kicking my leg, and it felt like I was so little and they were so big. So you know, I mean it's amazing how, after all those years, people can say things and trigger— triggers. And it can take you back in time. . . . And three months later I joined AAAW [his local adult Korean adoptee organization], and I met everybody there. And my life really started to change. I started doing activities there, and it felt so good because, you know, we all had something in common. You didn't have to worry about saying anything. "Were you adopted? When did you come?" You know. "Did you find your mother?" . . . It just felt so good. [81]

Finding other adoptees represented more than just social enrichment for David. Even though he did not realize it at the time, spending a lifetime in racial isolation had prevented him from being able to deal with the discrimination he experienced. In connecting with a community of Korean adoptees, David felt that he was surrounded by people who understood him, for the first time in his life.

Just making these types of connections is significant for some adoptees; some also spoke about consciously or subconsciously avoiding other adoptees. Diane, age twenty-eight, said she did make friends with other adoptees as a teenager. Although their status as adoptees was not a comfortable topic of conversation, physical commonalities were a source of comfort:

> There were a couple of other Korean adoptees. There was one girl for a short time I was friends with, she was a few years older than me, but it was still one of those things where you kind of didn't talk about being adopted . . . it was too weird. The only thing that we ever really touched on that was really ironic and funny was that, we were looking at magazines, and there was this magazine that was talking about putting makeup on and about putting eye shadow in your crease, we were laughing, because we didn't have a crease! [Laughs] It was the first time where I remember where I joked about, in a lighthearted way, my ethnicity and my shared background with somebody who was coming from the same background. That was maybe, like, sixteen-ish.[82]

John, age thirty-three, said that avoiding other adoptees was part of his own frustration with his problems around being an adoptee himself:

> There was a girl a year younger than me that was a Korean adoptee, but I did not hang out with her at all. I mean, growing up in high school, I mean, definitely being a Korean adoptee was not something I wanted to be. I mean, I think, like a lot of people, I just wanted to fit in, I mean Caucasians, you know. . . . Non-Caucasian children, I mean, you know, everyone wants to fit in. For me, you know, to be so much more different, I remember people saying "You should go out with her because you are both Korean adoptees," and it's like, you know, that was the last thing I wanted to do was to, so there would be two of us together to, you know, stand out. [83]

Having a strong desire to fit in motivated John to avoid other adoptees, since he believed that being seen with another adoptee would visibly confirm his own differences, presumably from the White majority. He also avoided other adoptees because his peers would expect him to connect with other adoptees, again highlighting the racialized status as an Asian American that he wished to escape, or at least to conceal.

The accounts noted reflect a range of experiences around Korean adoptee identity, and many also reflect changes in identity that take place over adoptees' lifetimes. In her work on mixed-race identities, Maria Root finds that many mixed-race individuals change their self-identity over their lifetimes.[84] Researchers Cookie White Stephan and Walter G. Stephan make similar findings in their research on mixed-race Japanese Americans: identity is often based on the particular social context each person is in, and the social pressure for mixed-race persons to only have a single ethnic identity is psychologically harmful.[85] Although most of the Korean adoptee informants with whom I spoke were not of mixed race, transracial adoptees are in many ways culturally mixed in their cultural identities of White, Asian, American, Korean, and/or adopted, and many identified as White earlier in life, while living with parents, and had an epiphany of sorts sometime during adulthood where their racial designation changed from White.

In their study of Korean adoptee college students, Joy Hoffman and Edlun Vallejo Peña note that "adoptees assumed two identities—one being Asian and/or Korean, and one of being White."[86] Some experienced this as adolescents, some as young adults, some not until they were in their thirties. Not surprisingly, I found ambivalence in adoptees as they were transitioning and questioning their racial and cultural identities. For many, the price of changing racial and cultural identities (from White to Korean or Asian) was high. Most eventually chose identities as Asian or Asian American. However, many remarked that even this identity did not entirely fit their life experiences. One subject said that "as an adoptee, you're always going to be in between; you're not Asian enough and you're not White enough."[87] In a more complicated rendering of this idea, Gail remarked on the stark contrasts between her White and Korean identities, "Minnesota is profoundly White; it doesn't get any Whiter than this, except North Dakota, and I'm from a town near the North Dakota border. The population and the ignorance and the White privilege that comes with that. But then I think what is the alternative. I can move to California or Hawaii. . . . but . . . I can't even make it to the grocery store . . . I can't even make it to King's [a local Korean restaurant], because then I have to be profoundly Korean."[88] Later she continued with these thoughts about being "in between":

> I really struggle with feeling fraudulent . . . That's a thing . . . I have a really hard time hanging out with people who were raised Korean, because I have such tremendous feelings of insecurity about that. I get in these situations of racial starkness . . . if everyone is starkly Korean, then I feel really White. If I'm with my family, I feel really not White. It goes in degrees, depending on the cultural consequence, because if I'm not White, then I must be Korean, and that doesn't take me very far either. Right now I feel very not White and very White at the same time. . . . That has to do with cultural competence, and it's the chameleon thing, like who am I standing next to. . . . These days, the only people I feel completely comfortable being around are my Korean adoptee friends, because I don't feel fraudulent.[89]

Korean adoptees often expressed context-based identity shifting as an experience of in-between-ness,[90] and like Gail, often mentioned the "chameleon effect" where they felt they could or had to adapt to whatever identity was dominant or expected of them in any given social situation. Like White Stephan and Stephan's findings in mixed-race communities, dominant ideologies outside adoptee communities seek to regulate Korean adoptee identity more rigidly. Resistance to any Korean adoptee self-concept that complicates simple identity categories takes many forms, all of which attempt to pigeonhole adoptee identity into either "White" or "Asian/Korean" categories. Miri Song suggests that, within mainstream society, the act of opting out of one racial or cultural group can only be accomplished by opting in to another group, with little space between groups. She goes as far as to cite research that suggests mixed-race people have to suffer with identity issues and low self-esteem.[91] Korean adoptees have much in common with both groups, as highly assimilated immigrants because of their immersion in White American society at a young age, and as individuals who are often mixed in their cultural and national identification.

Because of their age and their awareness about Whiteness as a problematic identity in their lives, many adoptees expressed some rejection of the Whiteness that they had embraced as younger people. These rejections were filled with painful realizations of what was lost to gain their Whiteness, and what is lost now in rejecting Whiteness. Many equated Whiteness with a deeply held ignorance in relation to non-White people and about difference in general. Some reported experiencing a profound sense of internal conflict because, although they understood well how such ignorance was produced and maintained, it was painful for them to confront.

When they spoke about what Whiteness means to them today, as adults, Korean adoptees had a variety of perspectives, including explanations of a contradictory access to White privilege, equating Whiteness with ignorance, and a rejection of Whiteness altogether. Although the adoptees who shared their thoughts about Whiteness acknowledged that they had some access to the advantages that come with a White identity in American society, their experiences with White privilege were complicated by encounters with racism and experiences of partial rather than complete access to the privileges of being considered White.

In navigating Asian American roles, the role of the model minority member has special appeal to Korean adoptees. Some adoptees see the position of "best of the worst" as a way for adoptees, as people of color, to be allowed to coexist in their largely White world. The racially neutral position of many White families and social circles do not allow adoptees to acknowledge that a model minority position enacts an inferior racialization, but only to acknowledge that it is far better than a negative Asian racialization, or the racialization of other groups of people of color.

The ambivalence about racial identity that some Korean adoptees expressed in their conversations with me appeared related to the pressure many felt to pick a side. Limiting adoptees to the choice of a White or an Asian identity leads many to search for a third space where the complex realities of adoptee racial and cultural identity can be more fully rendered. This space of racial ambiguity expresses itself in two major sites: Korean adoptee communities and race-neutral communities (often of or around adoptive families).

Richard Lee's concept of the transracial adoptee paradox describes a familial space where race is not recognized, and a space outside the family where the rules of racial engagement are much stricter.[92] Adoptive families develop race-neutral values to minimize the obvious biological differences within their families, but in contemporary American society, where colorblindness has become the ruling racial etiquette, many transracial adoptees can increasingly choose to stay within spaces imagined to be race-neutral, even outside their adoptive family spaces. Expanding on Lee's concept of the race-neutral family, which he applies to the individual adoptee subject, I suggest that the practice of transracial adoption has contributed significantly to the development of race-neutrality, practiced as colorblindness, as a moral imperative extending beyond families to their communities, becoming significant even on a national scale.[93] For example, many adoptees who contributed oral histories discussed their extended families, churches, schools, and towns as having similar race-neutral values.

Conclusion: Neutralizing Racial Etiquettes for Korean Adoption

Omi and Winant's concept of racial etiquette, in which "everybody learns some combination, some version, of the rules of racial classification.... Race becomes 'common sense'—a way of comprehending, explaining, an acting in the world,"[94] is one way to usefully examine the racial attitudes and identities Korean adoptees have about themselves. Legal scholar Janis McDonald also describes a contemporary racial etiquette of "polite Whites" who prefer not to engage in dialogue about race that is too challenging to themselves or others, and who tend to respond to racial queries with polite silence.[95] I suggest that there is a specific racial etiquette to transracial adoption, wherein the White communities tend to politely overlook the racial difference between the White majority and the adoptees themselves. Some Korean adoptees may follow this racial etiquette of denial of racial difference out of a sense of obligation to adoptive families who enforce a enforcing a race-neutral ethic within the family sphere. Some may have overarching beliefs in the importance of colorblindness as a solution to America's race relations problems. Either way, I argue that transracial adoptees can remain racially invisible even outside their adoptive families.

Because of high acculturation into White society and comprehensive understanding of White social and racial rules, adoptees often make it easy for those around them to look past their race, which in turn enforces the correctness of colorblind racial etiquette among nonadoptees in their communities. Many adoptees see any acknowledgment of their race as racist or at least uncouth. These cultural demands of adoptees and adoptive families to maintain color-blind perspectives feed back into their communities and help to maintain the racial invisibility preferred by some adoptees. In one example, Amy, age thirty-two, told how she learned that her White fiancé, early in their dating lives, was unable or unwilling to see the racial difference between them:

> That summer, late on a Sunday when they had that National Night Out, where they have block parties—we started dating in April, so this is August and I came over—he invited me over to do the block party [laughing]. And the neighbors right down the street [pauses to suppress laughter], this woman, this wife, of this couple comes up to [her fiancé] and says,

"Oh my God! I'm so glad you moved in. . . . Another interracial couple on the block, I'm so happy." 'Cause she sees us standing there. And he says—and I wasn't there when she said that—he was, you know, helping her husband grill. And I wasn't there, and he's telling me this, and he's like, "I couldn't for the life of me understand what she was talking about." He goes, "I had no clue what she was talking about." He goes, "My mouth just opened," and I'm like—he said he just sat there, "Interracial couple? Well I'm Irish and she's Norwegian." He said, "I couldn't figure it out!"[96]

Some Korean adoptees have found that communities of other Korean adoptees can offer a more comfortable environment. Fellow adoptees are able to readily recognize adoptee differences from both the White racial majority and from Asian and Korean American communities. It is in these adoptee-centered communities that many adoptees are able to express cultural and racial hybridity without feeling pressured to pick a single racial identity. Gail remarked, "The other day when I was feeling really in despair about the whole Whiteness thing, I think it has to do with identifying myself in terms of negations: . . . you're not White, you're not Korean, and that's how it always is. That's why it's so affirming to be around other adoptees, because for one time you can refer to yourself in the positive, you know, linguistically. Because I'm always negating myself otherwise."[97]

Other adoptees echoed Gail's experience of being at home around other adoptees. The development of a Korean adoptee identity, which is neither culturally Korean nor culturally White, functions for these adoptees as a remedy to feelings of in-between-ness. Unfortunately, Korean adoptee communities almost always exist outside mainstream communities and other adoptive communities. Adoptees seem to recognize that the identification with the third space of Korean adoptee communities sometimes feels too Korean for colorblind communities. Referencing the precarious position adoptees find themselves in when trying to break free of White identities, another adoptee stated, "We know not to congregate [with other Korean adoptees]. It's too conspicuous," as if the mere act of being seen with other adoptees or other Asians would be threatening to White family and friends, or to the adoptee's own sense of identity.

Consistent with assimilationist understandings of Korean adoptee adjustment, designations of "well adjusted" or "happy" are sometimes conflated with "White" while opposite designations of "bitter" or "angry" are associated with "Asian." Although racial unrest is not always articulated as the primary reason for feelings of dissatisfaction with being adopted, it is often inferred. Consider the example of Gabrielle:

> I started taking language classes, Korean language classes. I think that's when I really started to sort of meet a lot of adoptees and make big connections.... It was interesting because I had this woman in class that was the first woman I met who was super angry about being adopted. Like really, really, really angry. She had two other siblings that were adopted from Korea, and, her parents weren't very educated, and she would tell them every day how she couldn't believe that they were able to adopt children. So it was really an intense experience. And I presented with her at this conference, and I, I think I adopted a little bit of that anger.... [It was] the mid-nineties ... and that's when I started having big conversations with my parents and they were getting really defensive with me.... Like, I would tell them all the facts.... Like, "Did you know that people would go around to families and ask them to give up their kids? Did you know that? Like, did you know that that's what you were sort of perpetuating by adopting me?" And they were all freaked out, because you know, in their minds that was, that was not connected to the reason they were doing it. And I asked them all these questions, and first accused them like, "Why didn't you send me to culture camp?" [laughs] and all those things.[98]

Meeting other adoptees expanded Gabrielle's consciousness; through contact with an "angry adoptee," she eventually developed a critique of adoption practice, and confronted her very surprised parents with what she was learning. In stories such as this, it is easy to see how high consciousness around being a person of color, an Asian American, or a Korean adoptee, could be perceived as ingratitude, poor adjustment, or even mental instability.

Unfortunately, the binary understanding of Korean adoptee identity politics has been used to mobilize adoptees against one another. A striking example of the polarizing tendency in Korean adoptee communities took place in 2006, when an American adoption agency, which has a long history of facilitating Korean adoptions, responded to a legislative proposal in South Korea which advocated for the end of transnational adoption from Korea. The agency initiated a letter-writing campaign directed at South Korean legislators, soliciting Korean adoptees to express support for continuing transnational adoption from South Korea. A letter addressed to Korean American adoptees stated:

> "Some of you may have already heard about this proposed legislation.... One of the driving forces behind this legislation is the fact that Korean officials are only hearing from adopted Korean adults living in Korea currently who had negative adoption experiences and who support

ending international adoption in Korea. We felt that there was a need for Korean officials to hear from voices of other adopted adults when the timing was right. . . . Many [Korean] officials see adopted Koreans still as "poor orphans," as one put it, and continue to apologize for the fact that they were adopted, when in fact they are leading productive and satisfied lives."[99]

The letter, which was written by an agency director who is not a Korean adoptee, was signed by agency workers who are Korean adoptees, presumably in order to use their personal appeal to other adoptees to further the cause of the agency. That the agency, which has both a financial and an ideological stake in the continuation and success of Korean adoption to the United States, opposes the end of transnational adoption from Korea is not surprising. However, the tactics it chose to create a binary trope of the race-aware (those adoptees living in Korea) versus the race-neutral ("concerned friends" of the agency who are living in the United States) script onto adoptees as happy versus angry and uses divisive techniques to pit so-called happy adoptees (those who are "productive and satisfied") against so-called angry adoptees (those with "negative adoption experiences").[100]

Gratitude has always been a prerequisite for people of color to be admitted into White American society; non-Whites accepted and loved by Whites are expected to be grateful for this privilege. Embedded in the demand for gratitude is the strong maintenance of White as hierarchically superior to all other races. Using this logic, any non-White person elevated to a position of Whiteness should be grateful.[101] The accusation of ingratitude is both common and disturbing when launched at Korean adoptees. This charge almost always refers to adoptees' failure to appreciate the benefits afforded them through adoption. Inferred here is the ethnocentric assumption that any person adopted from Korea (or any poor country that sends its children to rich White countries for adoption) should be grateful for their adoption, since the quality of life as an American is obviously higher than that of a Korean. Those who accuse adoptees of ingratitude are attempting to enforce the colorblind racial etiquette of transracial adoption by accusing the adoptees of breaking the rules of etiquette. Any adoptee who is ungrateful, especially if racial difference is seen as the basis for personal problems experienced by individual adoptees, is disrupting the more harmonious norm of colorblindness—a norm that denies racialization as potentially divisive and threatening for people of color in America.

Ingratitude among Korean adoptees potentially threatens adoptive family systems and relationships, the multimillion-dollar transnational adoption industry, and paternalistic relations between the United States and the nations that supply adoptable children. So, for grateful Korean adoptees, becoming and remaining White (equated with becoming and remaining American) fulfills an important nation-building function of transnational adoption. With the stakes so high, there is little tolerance for adoptees who express interest in Asian, Korean, or in-between identities.

Despite efforts to regulate Korean adoptee identity by setting up a dichotomy of angry Asian or grateful White, many Korean adoptees respond to being placed in the either/or position by staking a claim to the in-between space. Although adoptees do express frustration at being neither here nor there, neither American nor Korean, neither White nor Asian, Korean adoptee identity occupies any and all of these identities as well as any number of hybridized identities between and outside them.

As I both conduct research on and engage personally with Korean adoptee populations, I observe firsthand the difficulties caused by identity pigeonholing. Korean adoptees use different ways to define their identities and to dissent against the identities imposed on them; these ways are diverse, but the will to self-define, and the dissent against dominant definitions of identity based on common racializations, is clearly evident. Korean adoptees are resisting racial assumptions, socializations, and categorization thrust on them through dominant discourses of law, policy, media representation, and family. This group, pressured into incomplete identity binaries (Asian or White, Korean or American) that often collapse into identities of no choice (as in, "You think you are Asian or White, but clearly, you are not!"), undermine this process of forced racialization by constantly using strategies that subvert racial categorization to reinvent their images as infinitely more complex.

6

Uri Nara, Our Country

Korean American Adoptees in the Global Age

I think I look Korean and I go back to Korea and people think, you know, I am Korean 'til I open my mouth. But no, I definitely don't feel Korean. I felt comfortable in Korea, but, I mean, I don't feel Korean.

John, thirty-three, on being a Korean adoptee in Korea[1]

It's always good to have friends where you travel, and I am lucky enough to have a few close friends who live in Korea full-time. So in the summer of 2006 when I was collecting oral histories from Korean adoptees who had returned to live and work in Seoul, I had the opportunity to spend a lot of time with my friends, who are all also Korean adoptees. There is an active open-air-market life in Seoul, where one can bargain for all manner of goods and services. Korean people, as well as tourists and visitors like myself, make good use of Seoul's many markets, and, for me, a market visit is mandatory on a trip to Seoul. On a trip to one of these markets, I was with a Korean resident friend, also an adoptee. As we made our way through narrow streets crammed with sheets, quilts, and *yo* (sleeping mats that look like thick quilts), merchants called out to us in hopes of making a sale. A central part of my experience in Korea as a Korean American adoptee is that Koreans seem to be able to tell I am not one of them (a perception I know to be shared by many other adoptees who visit Korea). This is certainly because of my lack of Korean language skills, but even without making a sound, I know, I stick out. Perhaps it is because of the way I dress, or my body language. In any case, I am used to being read as not-Korean in Korea. I guess this is true for my friend, too, because the one market merchant yelled out to us, "Where are you from?" in English. I don't speak enough Korean to feel comfortable engaging in conversation with most Koreans, and certainly not in marketplace banter, but my friend is much more accomplished than I. She looked the merchant squarely in the eye and replied, "*Uri nara.*" I'm from our country.

One of the differences between the Korean language and English is the Korean tendency to use the plural possessive pronoun *uri*, "our" where an

English speaker would use the singular possessive "my." In Korean, one refers to our family, our government, our school, rather than my family, my government, or my school. Thus, Koreans refer to Korea as "our country," *uri nara*. However, this formation is generally reserved for use among Koreans; a Korean speaking to a foreigner does not use *uri nara*, but the country's proper name, Korea. So the use of *uri nara* signifies shared nationality with other Koreans, and the shared possession of the nation of Korea among Korean people.

For Korean adoptees, the use of *uri nara* has additional meaning. Because of the common use of *uri nara* among Koreans, the term also separates Koreans from foreigners. Korean people can be fiercely nationalistic, and the divide for Koreans between *us* and *them* seems ever-present. Therefore, I wondered if it was a bit gauche for foreigners to use *uri nara;* how can a foreigner refer to Korea as "our country"? When I asked native speakers of Korean what the use of *uri nara* by a non-Korean would signify, they answered that a Korean assumes that the foreigner was speaking about their own country, not about Korea. The use of *uri nara* by Korean adoptees in a Korean context might be confusing for Koreans in Korea, further underlining the national confusion about transnational adoption in Korea and the spectacle of Korean adoptees returning to Korean soil. Nonetheless, this speech act of referring to Korea as *uri nara* signifies a claim on the part of the speaker to shared possession of the nation of Korea and its history—a claim of Korean-ness in the heart of the Korean motherland.

After this incident, my friend explained to me, "They think we are Japanese. I tell them I am from *uri nara* so they know we are Korean too. Adoptees are Koreans too." When I got to the home of another adoptee friend with whom I was staying while in Seoul, I told her about this incident. She laughed and remarked, "That's right. *Uri nara*, motherfucker." It was then that I knew many of the adoptees living in Korea were trying to assert themselves, trying to determine if Korea is indeed our country.

Although Korean adoptees are similar to other diasporic returnees to home nations in terms of their experience of Americanization, they also have key differences. Identification with birth country culture may be obscured by adoptees' experiences of growing up not just in dominant American society and culture, but also in (usually) White families and social contexts, cut off from family and community experiences of immigration. Instead, Korean adoptee identity is often shaped by connections to fellow adoptees and by feelings of cultural and racial in-betweenness, which forms the basis for much of Korean adoptee networking and activism today. I see Korean adoptees as transnational subjects, but, in many ways, the Korean adoptee experience defies current explanations of the transnational in Asian American studies, because adoption complicates our current understandings of diasporas and transnationalism.

Transnationality and the Korean Adoptee

The use of the term *transnational* is much debated, and I use Nina Glick Schiller's basic definition (as cited in Lee and Shibusawa): "refers to 'political, economic, social and cultural processes that extend beyond the borders of a particular state, include actors that are not states, but are shaped by the policies and institutional practices of states.'"[2] Using this definition, Korean American adoptees are inherently transnational, in that their life experiences are shaped by state policies of at least two countries, policies that have led them across borders at least once, though many cross and re-cross these borders again and again. In *Nations Unbound*, Linda Basch, Glick Schiller, and Christina Blanc-Szanton define a framework of transnationality. The authors, while acknowledging that categories of national identity continue to be in common use, offer a strong critique of approaches to transnational study that employ the category of the nation-state as a primary element. Their critique is based on the significance of race in the establishment of nation, emphasizing the key role of race in nation-building and the identification of a racial order or hierarchy within national identities. They also point out the forced transnationality of immigrants who become identified as racial minorities in receiving countries where they are classified as subordinated people, making them more likely to maintain national and cultural adherence to another home, the place from which the migration took place. Although Basch, Glick Schiller, and Blanc-Szanton were not writing about transnational adoptees, their framework of transnationality fits the transnational adoptee experience well. The Korean American adoptee population exhibits all of the characteristics that make it impossible to understand them in a single-nation framework, like many other migrant groups and individuals, although they rarely self-identify as transnational. Although, in 1994, Basch, Glick Schiller, and Blanc-Szanton pointed to literature as the primary venue for the expression of in-between identity, I have found that Korean adoptees constantly and commonly identify this way in their daily lives.[3]

The understanding of Korean adoptees as transnational subjects in my work begs the question of who is native in a transnational population. This query is in effect a variation on the question posed by Wanni Anderson and Robert Lee in their study of so-called displaced Asian Americans—"Where is 'home?'"[4]—as they attempt to qualify what could constitute "home" for diasporic Asians politically, socially, and spatially. Superficially, the answer might seem easy: those native to more than one place, or perhaps native to no single place, are, by default, native to transnational experience. Of course, this is something of a trick question, in that to theorize about transnationality is implicitly to problematize the concept of exclusively rendered nation-based identity. Are

Asian transnational adoptees displaced? I am not sure if I can assert that they do not belong in America or in Asia, but it is impossible to ignore their own articulations, in the oral history setting, of displacement and in-betweenness.

Understandably, transnationalist theory has often been applied to immigrant populations, or has used them as examples. For instance, Inderpal Grewal uses the example of South Asian H-1B visa migrants—highly skilled tech workers chasing the American Dream of unlimited upward economic and social mobility in Silicon Valley—who are using their new economic access to "consumer cultures."[5] Technically speaking, transnational adoptees are immigrants, but they differ from members of other immigrant groups in important ways. What if the American Dream is unlimited family building not by immigrants but through immigrants, acquired as children through transnational adoption? In the context of Asian transnational adoption, Grewal's American Dream, "linked . . . to American discourses of multiculturalism and diversity through proliferating target markets and diverse lifestyles,"[6] is achieved not through the acquisition of material goods, but through the acquisition of the adoptee immigrant. The transnational adoptee, raised within, and assimilated into, the White family, might be the ultimate expression of Grewal's American Dream, since this dream, as articulated by Grewal, also includes the achievement of equivalent-to-White social status such as that enjoyed by many Asian adoptees.

Foremost among the differences that further separate transnational adoptee immigrants from other transnational immigrants is the lack of cultural connection to the adoptee's sending or birth country. Although many groups of immigrants to the United States become isolated or disconnected from a motherland, and/or acculturated into the United States, adoptees often experience this as the sole immigrant (or perhaps one of two or three other transnational adoptees in the family) in their immediate surroundings. It may be true that most adoptive families have immigrants in their family histories, but the demographics of transnational adoption are such that transracially adopted children will almost always be the only recent immigrants in their adoptive families. The isolation-as-immigrant that transnational adoptees face is often compounded by their additional isolation as the only person of color in the family. Transnational adoptees, unlike children in other immigrant families, often are exposed to native country culture, when it is addressed at all, through dominant culture interpretations, without any adoptee, immigrant, or person-of-color perspective. Power differentials in American society between immigrants and nonimmigrants, and between Whites and people of color, increase the potential for isolation for transnational adoptees. I believe that it is this very potential that creates such urgency around the erasure (legally, and often culturally) of any vestige of immigrant identity for adoptees in order to acculturate them into American family and society. It is as if the possibility that a Korean adoptee might slip into a Korean immigrant identity threatens the primacy of (adoptive) family.

The cultures and politics of both South Korea and the United States have influenced the lives of Korean American transnational adoptees throughout the history of transnational adoption. The very existence of over one hundred thousand Korean American adoptees is based in the American Cold War policy decision to support a program of Korean transnational adoption after the Korean War. Against the backdrop of American political involvement in Asia during and after the Cold War, South Korea has responded to American demand for adoptable Asian children by developing the longest-running and most successful transnational adoption program in the world, while the United States has adapted its immigration policies to grant Asian adoptees preferential status and to extend the privileges of White adoptive parents to their soon-to-be children born to foreign parents.

It is important that South Korea has also recently enacted special visa legislation that makes most of the privileges of Korean citizenship available to adoptees. The Korean position of welcoming adoptees' return is particularly important for Korean adoptees who choose to return to South Korea to live and work, though it also impacts those who visit Korea.

Even during the period of Asian exclusion, the exceptional privileges afforded Korean American adoptees when arriving as immigrants, and in naturalizing as American citizens, paved the way for them to transfer their national and familial allegiances from South Korea to the United States. Since 2000, special immigration provisions for transnational adoptees make them the least restricted group of immigrants in the United States. But Korean adoptees become truly transnational when they return to claim Korean family and a place in Korean society, recognizing the persistence of blood ties to Korean family and ethnic ties to the Korean nation. Although the legal processes of transnational adoption are designed to sever all connections between adoptees and their birth families and countries, some continue to be drawn to Korea; for many adoptees who return for extended or permanent residence, living in Korea is part of exercising a Korean identity. While this group of repatriates is small,[7] the fact that return immigration is taking place within the largest global group of adult transnational adoptees may be a sign of things to come for the growing population of transnational adoptees. There are an estimated million transnational adoptees born in at least twenty-two countries in Asia, Africa, Latin America, and Eastern Europe, and adopted in at least fifteen countries in North America, Europe, and Australia. This is a population currently growing at an estimated rate of twenty-nine thousand per year.[8]

Adoptee Business on a Tourist Visa

Many more adoptees visit Korea than live there. For many adoptees, a trip to Korea was foundational to their personal understanding and formation of a Korean adoptee community, since connections between adoptees take on heightened importance during birth country visits. Of the sixty-five adoptees who participated in my research, forty-eight had been back to Korea—a huge proportion, considering this is a trip that the majority of Korean adoptees do not make, and indicative of strong participant self-selection. Many participants seemed to consider a journey to Korea a rite of passage that legitimized their Korean adoptee identities. Travel to Korea also appeared to be almost a prerequisite for entry into adoptee leadership circles.

The South Korean government's Overseas Koreans Foundation (OKF) reports that 38,712 Korean adoptees visited South Korea between 1982 and 2005,[9] though it is unlikely that this is accurate, since it is based on information from four South Korean adoption agencies that offer post-adoption services to overseas adoptees; many more adoptees are likely to have visited the country without contacting their adoption agencies. It is also possible that the agencies may have counted individual adoptees who visit an agency multiple times, over the years, more than once. Although most adoptees who have traveled to Korea have done so since 1982, some did make the trip earlier. For instance, one of the participants in this oral history project told me that Holt Children's Services in Korea started motherland tours in 1975 (this is corroborated in the research of Tobias Hübinette, though other sources claim motherland tours began in 1983),[10] and that he went to Korea for the first time in 1977. However, in the absence of better data, I use the figure published by the OKF, which implies that roughly one-fifth of the more than two hundred thousand Korean adoptees worldwide have returned to Korea, meaning that most adoptees never make the trip back.

An examination of one's adoption story and identity is almost unavoidable when returning to Korea. The trip is a transformative experience for many adoptees who visit Korea as adults, in terms of how they see themselves as Asian Americans, as Koreans, and as adoptees. The specific meaning of the experience varies greatly: some adoptees ponder what might have been, some find or grieve for lost family, some recover childhood memories, and some encounter other adoptees making pilgrimages. Some experience racial invisibility for the first time while in Korea, because they look like everyone else for the first time in their memories, though most say that language and cultural barriers keep them from feeling like "real Koreans."[11]

Not surprisingly, many adoptees experience a new interest in, or reconnection to, Korean identity when they first visit Korea as adults. Many participants in my research talked about what it felt like to be among so many other Asians for the first time. Some reported feeling deeply self-consciousness while in Korea, because they looked Korean but were unfamiliar with Korean language and cultural norms. These responses, verging on embarrassment about their adoptive status when immersed in Korean society, seem to go beyond the typical tourist's culture shock and anxieties about being in a strange country where people speak an unknown language. Adam, age twenty-eight, explained:

> I took Korean Air there, which was kind of painful but it kind of preps you for what it was really going to be like, and it was. . . . I mean, you can talk to everyone about the culture shock but it was scary for me, and, in going alone, I think it was an interesting. . . . I mean, I got off the plane and they were all speaking Korean to me. I went to customs; that was painful, you know, I couldn't get a taxi. I mean, I can't speak Korean. I don't know anything. . . . I mean, I think it sounds stupid. . . . I mean, the signs were like so, they weren't even, I mean people in Europe . . . well, at least the characters are recognizable. . . . I mean, I think I'd be embarrassed to tell you that.[12]

For Adam, even the plane trip over was 'kind of painful,' because he took Korean Air, and many of the passengers were presumably Korean nationals. However, his pain stemmed from feeling inadequate in his own country of birth, and being unable to hide this in front of other Koreans who would not necessarily know that he had been adopted when they saw him. Being read as non-Korean in Korea as soon as one opened one's mouth was commonly reported by other adoptees who had traveled to Korea. Of course, the irony of the situation is that Korea, the place where they were born and where they could visually blend in most easily, was also a place where they absolutely could not blend in, because most did not speak the Korean language or understand everyday Korean social norms very well.

The experiences of affirmation and/or displacement upon returning to Korea are common enough among adoptee returnees that they serve to bond disparate individuals in the community to one another. Sometimes, however, meeting other adoptees who have been back to Korea can divide individual adoptees from the larger community. Edward, age fifty-two, visited Korea for the first time when he attended an international Korean adoptee conference in Seoul, and immediately met many other Korean adoptees. During a group discussion that was part of the conference, he realized that his experience and his attitude about his adoption were very different from those of the adoptees whom he listened to. Instead of feeling more a part of a larger group of Korean adoptees, this experience made him see that there were deep differences between his and other adoptees' understandings of adoption:

> I was silent the whole time in our group. And I found very little in common with many of the people who spoke. . . . I guess because I didn't feel like my experience, was the same and maybe there [were] more of us like me, . . . but the ones who were more verbal were the ones that, in at least our group, were kinda angry. Yeah, and they were upset. They were adopted, they were, . . . a number of them . . . uh of the. . . . ladies were, were very resentful. They didn't get to grow up in Korea. . . . They said their experiences weren't happy. . . . especially the ones from Europe. And I didn't have anything to say. And it was difficult for me to relate to what they were talking about. Because, that wasn't my experience. So I was very fortunate . . . beyond what I deserved.[13]

However, many adoptees also experienced a return to Korea as a healing experience that helped them address experiences of racism in the United States.

For most adoptees who travel to Korea, the experience is an important one in initially developing or furthering their adoptee identities, though the effects for different individuals vary widely. Many experience the double-edged sword of relief and anxiety in this foreign environment, which often feels like displacement since tensions around increasingly multicultural society exist in both United States and South Korea[14]—relief because they are not in the racial minority for the first time in their memory, but also anxiety and self-consciousness because they know they are being judged by Korean nationals. Some also relive the trauma of their relinquishment as they go through though birth family searches or make contact with children currently in Korean orphanages. However, return to Korea is an important marker for most adoptees with a high degree of Korean adoptee identity, and many, like myself, find themselves traveling to Korea many times.

Searching in Korea

Contrary to popular belief, not all Korean adoptees journey back to Korea to conduct a birth search, a search for Korean family. However, many do make some effort to find Korean family. According to the Overseas Koreans Foundation, 19,599 birth searches were conducted between 2000 and 2005 through the four Korean adoption agencies that facilitated overseas adoptions.[15] In that same period, the agencies only recorded 15,637 birth country visits,[16] so it appears that some who searched were doing so by e-mail, letter, or phone. For those who search, the process can be fairly straightforward, or very complicated and difficult; some adoptees have enough identifying information in their adoption records to find birth family quickly, while others must follow up on a few clues that may or may not lead to family identity. Most adoptees who search do so through their adoption agencies, through soliciting information about themselves in the Korean media (in newspapers or on television), or both. Although I have spoken to some adoptees who did not search through their adoption agencies, most chose to use this resource, even though it is often a source of great frustration and pain.

Many adoptees start with one of their two adoption agencies—either their agency in the United States or their agency in Korea. Korean adoptees have reported quite a bit of difficulty getting reliable information from agencies: records often appear incomplete, different agency officials give different or contradictory information, and some charge high fees (US $50 to US $400) to supply files that adoptees may already possess. There are many stories of adoption agencies in Korea allowing adoptees to see their adoption files but not to make copies, making the pursuit of any important information all but impossible for the vast majority of adoptees who do not read Korean fluently. The difficulty and frustration that adoptees experience with their agencies when looking for their birth and adoption histories has been well documented in Korean adoptee memoirs and documentaries. For adoptees like these writers and filmmakers, birth search and reunion with Korean family becomes a central part of their adoptee identities. In addition, some adoptees have searched using online or print media, or through Korean television shows, to get themselves and their stories to the Korean public.[17]

Although reliable statistics on the number of adoptees who search over the course of their lives are lacking, it is clear that most adoptees do not undertake a search. Some are satisfied with their identities without knowing more about their Korean families. Other participants in my research had not made a final decision about whether or not to search, but had not ruled it out. Still others had been discouraged from searching by the difficult experiences with both adoption agencies and with Korean family (in many reunions) reported in adoptee memoirs and through word of mouth. According to the Overseas Koreans Foundation, only 8.3 percent of Korean adoptees who searched for Korean family between 2000 and 2005 found relatives.[18] Although this statistic, as such, is probably not well known among adoptees who search, word of mouth is perhaps the most important source of information about birth search for adoptees, and the high incidence of adoptees who search and find nothing, even after exhaustive (and exhausting) search efforts, is well known among the searchers. Among the many reasons adoptees choose not to search, the low rate of success when searching is probably what motivates many adoptees to be emotionally cautious, even ambivalent, if they do choose to.

Ambivalence in searching is reflected in the stories of adoptees like Henry, who returned to Korea for the first time at age thirty; he made a cursory search starting at his American agency, but decided not to pursue it once both American and Korean agencies told him there was nothing to find:

> When I went over for the first time in 2003, I did contact the adoption agency here [in the United States]; and they didn't have much, they just gave me their sister agency, over there, and a contact person. . . . They didn't have much information. . . . I could have stopped over there [in Korea], but . . . they looked my case number and they didn't have anything. . . . [The] story is that the record-keeping back in the seventies were just crappy. . . . I have a life, and that's part of the reason maybe why I kind of distanced myself, maybe, back in my younger years, from—my, from the culture, from my culture. . . . I got a great family, and there was probably a reason why my biological parents, you know, put me up for adoption. . . . So I'm saying, I have a hell of a good life here, I got a roof over my head, I got a job, you know, and—who knows what I'd be over there? . . . I made that . . . one call, and it's like, "There really isn't much," you know, and [my Korean host], she said, "We can drive there," it's like, fuck, screw it, you know. We stopped. . . . But I don't feel abandoned . . . You know, I got a great situation here, and . . . I don't feel unloved. I don't feel like I need to find my parents and ask them why, you know.[19]

Here, Henry's ambivalence about searching is clearly bound up with his identity, not just as an adoptee but also as an American son and as an adult satisfied with his life. Caleb, forty-eight, had been to Korea several times throughout his adult life, but never attempted a search until the birth of his daughter, many years after his first return trip to Korea. Caleb has helped many Korean adoptees with birth family searches, and when I asked him if he ever searched himself, he said:

> I guess I just haven't been that interested. Once [my daughter] was born, I was suddenly curious. Gotta be somebody else out there. But, all along, I've never been interested in birth parents, more interested in siblings. . . . But part of it, too, I think, back then I mentioned it to my adoptive parents, and they had known I'd been involved in this stuff all along; my dad was pretty supportive and said, if I wanted to search and if I found something, that would be pretty cool, from his standpoint. And my mom was so quiet and said, "Haven't I been a good enough mom to you?" . . . So I've been sort of halfheartedly trying to think about it, not really doing anything about it. But I know that kind of hurt, because the first time we helped somebody find birth family, I just went in the other room and just bawled. Because here someone was so lucky to find something, and, you know, I had nothing back there.[20]

Although Caleb reports a very positive relationship with his American parents, his desires to search were quashed by his mother, who was hurt that he would consider trying to find another set of parents. The possibility of this response from American parents seems to factor into many adoptees' decisions not to search. In a society where a person can only have one mother and one father, and the legal apparatus around adoption totally obliterates the legal relationship between biological parents and children, it is understandable that adoptive parents might feel threatened by an adoptee's search for birth family. However, most adoptees who search are not seeking to replace their adoptive families, but to reconnect with their own histories and their own lost pasts.

Barb, age thirty-one, told of her experience searching for Korean family, none of whom she ever found. She felt her search was exhaustive, and did not search further after this attempt:

> I always wanted to search but it was such a big . . . effort. To get started. But I started it and I don't think I had a lot of expectations, but I thought I'd give it my best shot. [I got my records] . . . I connected with both organizations. It was another opportunity, and I thought, I just gotta do it. It was a chance. . . . [T]hey [the agency staff] are with you every step of the way. . . . They used every resource, newspaper, television, magazine. . . . I did a documentary when I was there, I told my story. . . . And they aired it during that week. Everything was like boom, boom, boom, boom. . . . I did get my hopes up a little bit. . . . After it had aired, a few people had called, but there was no match. . . . I didn't find anything. I was very sad. I think that . . . it was kind of strange, it was very emotional, and I started to accept that I was not going to find anything. . . . The last night was . . . what I say about that trip after I came back, was I think I left all my sadness and all my fears in Korea. I did my best and I did it and I didn't find anything. I cried, I thought about it and dealt with it, and I left all that in Korea. . . . All said, it was my very last night in Korea, and I cried so hard, I never cried that hard in all my life. That was completely an emotional release. It was another dream. Every time you go to Korea, it's like a dream. It's completely another world. Afterward, it's back to reality. That's just what it's like. A dream.[21]

Barb's goal was to try every method available to her to find her Korean mother before giving up. Most striking about her story is her description of Korea as otherworldly, "like a dream." She searched because she felt that she had to at least try, no matter what she found. Still, finding nothing was heartbreaking, even though she decided to "leave all her sadness and all her fears in Korea." This was possible for her because she had made every effort to find her Korean family; no stone, in her mind, was left unturned. During the course of our conversation, Barb expressed surprise that all adoptees don't search, as if searching and being adopted were inseparable.

Richard, thirty-one, who went to Korea for the first time at age twenty-nine, described reuniting with his Korean mother as a matter-of-course operation.

> I was just visiting . . . really just to visit Korea for the first time. And . . . I, um, . . . had the opportunity to meet my mom on that very trip. . . . By the time we made it to Korea, I was pretty confident, even though I really wasn't that excited, that I was probably gonna have a chance to meet my mom, or at least learn something about her. . . . Coming into it, I was a little bit curious and a little bit excited, but I wasn't overly enthusiastic about the whole thing. . . . And, it wasn't . . . a surprisingly, or incredibly, emotional time for me, and it wasn't shock either, because I've had plenty of time to think about it, to relive that . . . since, and my emotions haven't changed. . . . [I]t was really, really unusually anticlimactic when I got there. . . . She just sat there and cried and kept on saying in Korean, "I'm sorry, I'm sorry, I'm sorry." . . . I guess . . . most adoptees might be under the impression that you can just carry a baby to term and . . . give him or her up for adoption . . . but in her case . . . her conscience got the best of her and . . . she'd gone through several bouts of depression . . . trying to commit suicide. . . . From there, we kept in loose contact . . . nothing really exciting . . . nothing really amazing had changed, the way that I viewed life. And I think that it's kind of disappointing, because for me to take for granted what had happened, versus so many adoptees going looking for their parents and who would really give next to anything to meet them, it's kinda sad that it happened to me.[22]

Richard acknowledges that searching and finding Korean family is extremely important to some adoptees, expressing some regret that it happened to him instead of someone who really wanted to find family. Richard was interested in his own past and wanted to explore it by learning more about his Korean mother, but he did not express an emotional response to her at, or since, their meeting.

Korean adoptees choose to visit Korea, or not, for many reasons, and they have just as many reasons to search for Korean family, or not to search. While search and reunion are central to most memoirs and fictional stories about adoptees, in fact most Korean adoptees do not return to Korea and do not search for birth family.[23] The broad understanding of searching for Korean family as a symptom of an adoptee's dissatisfaction with his or her current family or social situation may be one reason why more do not search, though there are many other practical and psychological reasons.

Whether because of lost or destroyed records, or reluctance on the part of adoption agencies to release complete and truthful records to adoptees, or because Korean families are unaware of or unwilling to meet Korean adoptees, most searches for birth family end in failure. Unfortunately for adoptees who do seek reunion with Korean families, the transnational adoption system is structured not to help adoptees find birth families, but to create legal ties between adoptees and adoptive parents, often by permanently erasing records of the very existence of Korean families related to adoptees.

For Korean adoptees, visiting Korea can be a vacation, an opportunity to search for Korean family or to encounter other Korean adoptees, or a way to connect to their Korean-ness. This is not lost on the South Korean government and media, which have embraced Korean adoptees as ambassadors to the West and as Korean subjects living in the West.[24]

Korean Nationalization of Transnational Adoption: Korean American Adoptees in Seoul

For Korean adoptees who do choose to live in Korea on a more permanent basis, the South Korean F-4 visa and dual citizenship can make them Korean again, at least for as long as they stay in South Korea. South Korean F-4 visas are specifically for "overseas Koreans," meaning those with traceable and verifiable South Korean past citizenship or nationality.[25] The special visa for overseas Koreans was established in 1999 by the Act on the Immigration and Legal Status of Overseas Koreans, partially in response to appeals by Korean adoptees living in Korea for permanent legal status as Koreans.[26] The F-4 visa is the least restrictive of any residence visa in Korea, conferring on the holder all the rights of native Koreans except voting, including unlimited entry and exit privileges, the right to own property and businesses, and the right to reside in Korea without a work-related sponsor. Although the F-4 has a two-year term, unlimited renewals are possible. An F-4 visa is as close to citizenship as a noncitizen can have. It carries such comprehensive and flexible rights that, when I asked Patrick, a twenty-eight-year-old adoptee businessman living in Seoul, if he would want dual citizenship if it were an option, he responded:

> No... I pretty much do right now, with the F-4 visa. Like, I got my business license for free. Most foreigners that want to get a business license here, they have to prove they have at least $50,000 in an off-shore account. I can work here wherever I want to. I actually pay less taxes.... I get pretty much all my money here, and I don't get stuck with jobs, like they're in control maybe because they have control of my visa. So I'm like, you know what, if you screw me over, and I don't like you, I'm leaving! And go and do the next thing.[27]

There has been some controversy in Korea over the F-4 visa since its introduction. Because it only applies to overseas Koreans who were once South

Korean nationals (along with their descendants), it is restricted to those who left Korea after South Korea became a nation in 1948, meaning that it mostly applies to diasporic migrants who reside in Western countries and excludes 5.65 million ethnic Koreans, descended from people who left before 1948, almost half of whom live in China, Russia, and Japan.[28] For this reason, the act has been attacked as discriminatory against the ethnic Koreans in these locations, especially the Korean-Chinese. Criticism has also been directed at the promotion of unity among ethnic Koreans over persons of other ethnicities who live and work in Korea.[29]

Since 2011, Korean adoptees who have permanent residence status in Korea (most commonly with an F-4 visa) can also apply for dual South Korean citizenship. In addition to the privileges afforded by the F-4 visa, adoptees who become dual citizens may also vote and have similar political and economic rights to other South Korean citizens. Adoptee dual citizens are exempt from the compulsory military service required for male citizens, and are not required to relinquish the citizenship of their adoptive countries. While the option of dual citizenship has considerable symbolic value for adoptees who wish to reclaim political belonging while in Korea (and South Korean citizenship for overseas Korean adoptees literally only applies while the adoptee is in Korea; Korean adoptee dual citizens cannot access Korean citizenship while outside Korea), few adoptees have completed the process to become dual citizens.

Since Korean adoption did not formally begin until 1953, all Korean adoptees are eligible for the F-4 visa (and dual citizenship), though the application process can be onerous. Since the F-4 visa is for those with foreign citizenship only, to obtain one, an adoptee wishing to live in Korea must provide documentation of onetime Korean citizenship, as well as documentation of the loss of Korean citizenship. Proving current American citizenship is not difficult, but to obtain proof of Korean ancestry, adoptees must obtain their family registry, or *hojeok*. The hojeok lists the entire known patrilineal family; since these records are generally accurate and complete genealogies, they are the basis on which claims of citizenship can be made. Adoptees who have no information on birth family must obtain an orphan hojeok (which lists only themselves, with no other family members) from their Korean adoption agency in order to fulfill the requirement for proof of onetime Korean citizenship.

Even for adoptees who have found members of their Korean birth family, an orphan hojeok has many practical advantages. Many adoptees were never entered into their birth family hojeok, or were removed when they left the family. Even if the adoptee is on their birth family hojeok, since important personal details like birthdates, parental identities, and family circumstances were often changed by adoption agencies in the adoption process, the orphan hojeok can better match the adoptee's American identity papers, removing the possibility of conflicts of information within the visa application materials. Additionally, since adoptees' legal identities are completely changed through the adoption process, an adoptee who gains access to their birth family records may have no way to legally establish that he or she is the person listed on their birth family hojeok.[30]

For adoptees who seek the F-4 visa or dual citizenship, there is considerable irony in claiming legal orphan status in order to reconnect with Korea, Korean people, and possibly Korean birth family. Unlike other overseas Koreans, who must document their own Korean citizenship by showing a direct familial connection to other Koreans to obtain an F-4 visa, adoptees usually must obtain it through formalized documentation that the adoptee has no relationship with anyone of Korean citizenship—or in the Korean context, with anyone at all. It is exclusively by acknowledging the practice of removing the identities of Koreans who become overseas adoptees that these adoptees regain legal status as Koreans.

Nonetheless, does the legal opportunity afforded by the F-4 visa or dual citizenship make Korean adoptee ethnic return migrants to South Korea feel Korean to the extent that they more fully identify with other Koreans? Certainly, permanent residency or citizenship gives adoptees a legal toehold in South Korea, where they can live and work among Korean people. However, I have not found that adoptees really feel like they become Korean just because the South Korean government has removed barriers to their return. Instead, many of the adoptees who live in Korea find little acceptance in Korean society at large, but are deeply folded into adoptee communities, where they can connect with others whose experiences are similar to their own. Most Korean adoptee ethnic return migrants plan to stay in Korea for periods ranging from one to five years and do not consider a permanent move to Korea to be a viable option.

Making Korean Adoptees American

Few Korean adoptees see themselves as immigrants, though Korean adoptees share many characteristics with immigrant populations, including the phenomenon of return migration to the land of their birth. Return migration is one of several characteristics the Korean adoptee population shares with immigrant populations. Politically, Korean adoptees are born in a country that is under the influence of nations with greater geopolitical power. As children of Korean citizens, they are born with national membership in an Asian nation (though their social membership there is less certain).[31] They migrate to nations that have diplomatic (and, historically, imperial, in the case of the United States) relations with South Korea. They are perceived to have better economic and social opportunities as a result of their migration. The primary difference between Korean adoptees and other immigrants is the relative political ease with which adoptees can make their migratory transition—their immigration aided, sponsored, and advocated by (usually) White adoptive parents, citizens of some of the richest and most powerful nations in the world. However, few Korean adoptees see themselves as immigrants.

Why are Korean American adoptees disinclined to identify as immigrants? Writing about transnational adoptees in Spain (which currently has the second highest rates of both international immigration and international adoption after the United States), Diana Marre notes that Spanish adoptive families draw a clear distinction between adopted children and immigrant children. These distinctions are largely based on class and other social advantages Spanish families can confer on their foreign adopted children to protect them from the racism they might otherwise suffer as immigrants.[32] A similar dynamic exists among Korean adoptee families in the United States. Adoptive parents, usually White, often middle class, always U.S. citizens, are not traditionally a politically or socially marginalized group within the United States. Parents' treatment, as agents of adoptee immigration, by the federal government through the United States Citizenship and Immigration Services (USCIS),[33] as well as by state governments, appears to differ from the treatment of nonadoptee immigrants, who are often neither White nor middle class, and are obviously not citizens. Although adoptive parents have to go through lengthy legal and immigration procedures as part of the adoption process, the procedures are different from those required of other immigrants. Adoptive families can avoid contact with immigrants (and, therefore, any association of their children with immigrants) if they wish, in their dealings with the USCIS. In short, Korean adoptees, from the moment of their adoption, are considered by their adoptive parents and by the government of the United States as the children of U.S. nationals.

This policy stands in stark contrast to both historical and contemporary immigration policies for most other Asians. Of particular note is Chinese exclusion, whereby Chinese peoples were the first and only group to be excluded purely on the basis of nationality from immigration to the United States. In *At America's Gates: Chinese Immigration during the Exclusion Era, 1882–1943*, Erika Lee explains how the codification of Chinese exclusion marked the federal sanction of anti-Asian discrimination, support for which was created and maintained by popular anti-Asian sentiment prior to, and during, the period of exclusion. Lee establishes anti-Chinese immigration legislation as a starting point for all anti-immigration and immigrant-restrictive legislation and sentiment since then. The criminalization of immigration to the United States began with Chinese exclusion, and the current state of anti-immigration legislation and immigrant suspicion is deeply rooted in this history. Not surprisingly, many of the strategies used by Chinese migrants to undercut immigration law are still in use today by new groups of scrutinized immigrants. The United States continues its assault on immigration, currently focusing on Latinos and people of Middle Eastern descent, using tactics which continue to undermine the civil liberties and human rights of targeted groups.[34] Even though the general public might prefer to historicize the period of Chinese exclusion as a relic of our racist past, Lee's research reveals that the context in which these acts of racist exclusion occurred have disturbing echoes in present anti-immigrant and anti-foreigner sentiments.

Historically, immigration status has greatly influenced the differing American racializations of immigrants in the United States. Asian immigrants have been subject to racialization and placement within class hierarchy through unequal access to legal and cultural citizenship. As Lee's work demonstrates, it is the U.S. government that has taken on the role of gatekeeper and enforcer of who is prevented from migrating into the United States, who is allowed in, and on what basis. Since 1965, immigration has been liberalized (through formal deracialization) to a system that restricts access for most immigrants, but makes exception for "special" admission of foreign professionals such as participants in the Exchange Visitor Program or H-1 visa holders, grants liberal admissions of elite immigrants on student or professional visas, and privileges family reunification—a clause through which adoptees are able to easily enter the United States as children of American citizens. If Asian exclusion and other anti-immigrant policies are on one end of the immigration spectrum of restriction, transnational adoption is on the other, with a remarkable ease of access for America's most desired immigrants, child adoptees.

Since the passage of the Child Citizenship Act in 2000,[35] transnationally adopted children of U.S. citizens even have access to automatic citizenship, without the legal necessity of a naturalization process. Even after the general tightening of immigration restrictions following September 11, 2001, this extreme liberalization in immigration and citizenship policy has never been questioned, even though it privileges nationals of countries who are people of color, who have otherwise been regarded with great suspicion by immigration authorities. The Asian, African, or Latino child migrant, adopted by American citizens and entrusted to the nationalizing influence of an American family, is so far from arousing the suspicions of American immigration authorities, that even my suggestion of it here probably seems outlandish. My point is not to encourage additional policing of adoptee migrants, but to underline the almost total disregard for the adoptee migrant as an immigrant at all. As transnational adoption has become more common as a family-building strategy in the United States, understanding adoptees as deracialized members of American families (not as racialized threats in the form of alienimmigrants) has come to be seen as a matter of supporting American families, and is never criticized as evidence of leniency in immigration and naturalization law, even in these xenophobic times.

Before February 27, 2001, parents had to submit several forms for naturalization of their transracial adoptee children, following a process specific to transnational adoptees, with no exam or residence requirement for minor children, and with the explicit requirement that at least one parent had to be a citizen of the United States. Even though this process was considerably easier for adoptive parents than for nonadoptee immigrants, legislation concerning the naturalization of transnational adoptees has changed since then to make the naturalization process even simpler. Now, under the Child Citizenship Act of 2000, transnational adoptees whose adoption has been finalized before they reach the age of eighteen and who live in the legal and physical custody of a citizen parent automatically receive citizenship.[36] The Child Citizenship Act, lobbied for by U.S. adoptive parents,[37] does not even appear to share the same goals as other immigration or naturalization reform legislation; rather, it was positioned as an act of corrective justice for White American citizens and their children. Through such legislation, parents have been successful in positioning these adoptee immigrants higher on the immigration hierarchy than other immigrants. Of course, parents' beliefs that transnational adoptees are deserving of exceptions to regular immigration policy are also reinforced by permissive naturalization policies of the USCIS concerning transnational adoptees compared to other immigrants.

One of the reasons cited for enacting this legislation was that many parents were unaware that their transnationally adopted children are not already automatically receiving citizenship[38] and that transnational adoptees who slip through the cracks, like other noncitizens, are in danger of deportation if convicted of a felony. The act of deportation in these circumstances is especially outlandish because most transnational adoptees have no cultural ties to the country of their birth. This legislation is not without gaps; parents who have not physically seen their adopted children before adoption (this is true in many cases where parents do not travel to the birth country to pick up their adopted children) are not considered to have a finalized adoption and must re-adopt their children in their home states before citizenship will be granted.[39]

Since September 11, 2001, American immigration policy has become more restrictive, with fewer visas issued and higher rates of deportation.[40] In sharp contrast, transnational adoptees and their families enjoy extremely liberal immigration and naturalization policies, as well as a special new office, the Office of Children's Issues at the U.S. Department of State, established in 2008, with staff who "are dedicated to assisting parents as they seek to provide a home to orphans abroad."[41] Parents, perceived as the primary agents of transnational adoption, are privileged through their high cultural capital and as citizens in the naturalization process; their adoptees children have an advantage as secondary beneficiaries.

Assimilationism is the ruling paradigm within federal naturalization law, with applicants required to demonstrate high American cultural competency through English language proficiency, knowledge of American history and culture, and long-term residence, before citizenship can be considered. Many researchers theorize that citizenship allows some access to political agency desirable to immigrants who are minorities, in both their naturalization and racial status. Bill Ong Hing advocates for a broadening and strengthening of Americanism through a reconception of American "core values."[42] Noah Pickus argues that this same ideal should be reflected in the process of naturalization where naturalization processes would be even more constructive of a nationalized citizen than they are currently.[43] Alejandro Portes and Ruben Rumbaut see naturalization as the first stop for "any foreign minority that wishes to make itself heard" within the political processes of the United States.[44]

Immigrants are generally acknowledged as having families in the nation of emigration, from which they may be separated by citizenship. This condition is more complicated in the case of transnational adoption, because adoptees are physically and legally separated from family in their countries of birth, and are often encouraged to sever emotional ties to birth nation and family, or prevented from developing these ties in the first place. In exchange, they are granted entry into American families (and to imagined American genealogies). Through the easy access to citizenship that transnational adoptees enjoy, the adoptive family and national relationship trumps previous categories of national membership. In this example, family and nation is solidified as family units are used as foundational building blocks of nation.

Among participants in this research, most of those who chose to address the issue of immigration did not see themselves as immigrants, and in fact sought to deny any similarities between themselves and other immigrants. In my observations, the use of the pejorative "FOB" ("fresh off the boat;" i.e., a recent immigrant) is common among Korean adoptees who want to be differentiated from immigrant Asians. Some adoptees in my research remarked on the arrival of other Asian immigrants, including Vietnamese and Hmong people, in their communities as they were growing up, and recalled fearing that they might be mistaken for members of immigrant groups that were seen as far more differentiated and racialized than the adoptees wanted to see themselves. If adoptees hope to develop positive racial identities, contempt for similarly racialized individuals is clearly problematic. It is apparent that many adoptees do have a sense of racial justice, no doubt as a result of growing up a person of color in predominantly White communities. These adoptees' statements about

Asian immigrants betray some internalized racism, but they also are sensitive to anti-immigrant sentiment within their families. Some adoptees I interviewed talked about their difficulties with the racism and xenophobia of their parents against Mexicans or Middle Eastern immigrants and their parents' failure to acknowledge that their own children were immigrants and people of color.

All of the adoptees in this research were adopted before the Child Citizenship Act became law, so all had to go through the naturalization process to become U.S. citizens. However, for the most part, the adoptees with whom I spoke did not consider stories about their naturalization to be an important part of their narratives, and most did not even mention it, though I know all were naturalized before the age of eighteen. When I asked one adoptee about her naturalization, she told me that the most remarkable thing she remembered was that it was her first elevator ride (she was raised in a rural area and the naturalization took place in a federal courthouse in "the big city"). The lack of importance attached to the naturalization process is particularly striking in how closely it resembles the attitudes of Americans born into their citizenship. It is as if the citizenship process is only important to immigrants, from whom transnational adoptees understand themselves to be different. Not surprisingly, the attitudes of Korean adoptees are consistent with their placement in families and society by their parents, their government, and their societies. Designated as pre-assimilated by those around them,[45] these adoptees have occupied the positions and created identities as nonimmigrant citizens—though I would argue—not without conflict.

The immigration of transnational adoptees blurs the distinction between immigrant and citizen in the eyes of the USCIS, the community of transnationally adoptive families, and transnational adoptees themselves. Even though transnational adoptees have a different migrant story than nonadoptee immigrants, they still are immigrants and, though their experiences may differ from those of other immigrants, they have many of the issues that other immigrants face. For adoptees who have been removed from contact with birth country and family, the experience of immigration to the United States could become an important foundation of a new American identity. However, the erasure of adoptees' immigrant pasts, like the erasure of many of their other pre-adoptive experiences, separates them (and their adoptive families) socially and culturally from important potential bases of identity in the United States by preventing them from identifying with other American people of color and/or other immigrant populations whom they might benefit from knowing and understanding. Instead, adoptees and their adoptive families are insulated from contact with other immigrant communities. It comes as no surprise, then, that Korean adoptees, as they become adults, often choose to further distance themselves from other Asians by avoiding contact with Asian immigrants.

Travel abroad to Korea, like travel to other parts of the world, is a marker of American privilege; for Korean American adoptees returning to South Korea to live can be seen as a marker of both American and South Korean privilege, or as a rejection of both.

The Adoptee Bubble in Seoul

I traveled to Seoul in the summer of 2006 to collect oral histories from Korean American adoptees who have chosen to return to Korea to live and work. Estimates of the size of the transnational Korean adoptee population in South Korea range up to several hundred repatriates from adoptive countries in North America, Europe, and Australia. I collected oral histories from sixteen Korean American adoptees in Seoul that summer, augmenting the five oral histories I had previously collected in the United States from American adoptees who had lived in Korea as adults but had returned the United States. All twenty-one of these participants had lived in Korea for one year or longer, and most had lived primarily or entirely in Seoul. Nine were men, twelve were women, and all were under age forty.

No reliable or official statistics exist that would reveal demographic information about adoptees who reside in Korea; those that do rely on adoptee voluntary contact with adoptee help organizations, such as the Global Overseas Adoptees' Link (GOAL). However, it is commonly believed in the community that the numbers of male and female returnees are roughly equal and that most are young (under forty) and unmarried. It is very possible that adoptees outside this general demographic have returned to Korea and are unknown within larger adoptee social circles because they do not associate with other adoptees or contact organizations like GOAL. I made several attempts to connect with adoptees who were living in Korea because they were stationed there either with the American military or with the U.S. State Department, but none of them ever returned my calls or e-mails. I suspected that these individuals might have very different experiences, in terms both of their reasons and and their preparation for coming to Korea, and of their daily lives in Korea, than others with whom I connected, but I was left not knowing about this group. This made me wonder if the adoptees I did see were more invested in developing social connections with other adoptees simply because they were professionally isolated since adoptees who had stronger professional ties (for instance, with the U.S. government) seemed less interested in spending time with other adoptees or participating in research about adoptee identity. My methodology for collecting oral histories depends on volunteerism among the subjects; while I did not hear of many adoptees in Korea who were not single adults between twenty and forty, this does not mean that these demographics are not represented there.

The adoptee population living in Korea, like the overall Korean adoptee population, is difficult to characterize in any kind of absolute terms; if Korean adoptees most resemble each other in having been adopted from Korea to the West, then the repatriate group in Korea are most similar in that all have made the decision to leave their adoptive countries and live back in Korea. Some stay for a year or two, some indefinitely, and they describe a wide range of reasons for returning. In other words, while their circumstances might tie these adoptees together, not much else necessarily does.

I also want to note that a large proportion (perhaps half) of Korean adoptees living in Korea are not American, but European, having been adopted to one of several European countries that participated as receiving countries in Korean adoption. This is consistent with the proportion of Korean adoptees worldwide, roughly half of whom came to the United States while the other half went mainly to European nations. Although there did appear to be considerable cross-socialization among American and European adoptees I encountered in Korea, I also noticed some separation based on nationality, mostly because of differences in language and/or cultural preferences. There is a professional separation between English-speaking and non-English-speaking adoptees because the default profession for the English speakers, teaching English, is not open to the non-English speakers. Although the entire community of Korean adoptee returnees to Korea interests me, because of time constraints and my interest in American-Korean relations through adoption, I limited myself to collecting oral histories from American adoptees; nevertheless, I want to acknowledge that the population of adoptees in Korea is diverse in terms of adoptive nationality. All the adoptees I contacted in Korea seemed to understand that the community of adoptees in Seoul is quite international, consisting of Americans, Scandinavians, Francophones, and a few Australians and Italians.

Being Korean I: Moving to Korea

Before I arrived in Seoul, I had made a couple of assumptions about the adoptee community there, both of which were subsequently proved wrong. The first was that adoptees living in Korea would all articulate some sort of deep and meaningful connection to the Korean nation, Korean culture, or Korean people. As the motherland for Korean adoptees, I thought, Korea would have a special draw for adoptees that they would discuss as the reason they decided to move back. I also assumed that adoptees would say that they were in Korea mostly to connect (or reconnect) with Korean culture and language, and that most would be fluent, or quickly becoming fluent, in the Korean language

Instead, the adoptees I spoke to articulated much more mundane and pragmatic reasons for moving to Korea. A few said they wanted to be in Korea to maintain relationships with birth family or with other individuals who also lived in Korea, but many more said the main reason they came or decided to stay was because nothing much was happening at home. Many mentioned that they had left behind uninspiring or nonexistent careers in the United States or that they had experienced recent personal breaks with family or long-term partners. Nate, thirty-one, explained how a difficult year in the United States led him to decide to move to Korea:

> What started it off with me was . . . losing my job . . . as a computer programmer. And . . . losing my house . . . losing my car . . . 'cause I got in a car accident. My parents were going through a divorce . . . I know my brother was starting to get into some legal troubles . . . But it was just like a series of things . . . being involved with a . . . girl that . . . screwed me over financially. But I remember going through a period of . . . close to a . . . year where it was just like one thing after another happened to me . . . [it] just kind of all multiplied and, like, you know . . . losing myself throughout the whole thing; my personal identity.[46]

Although Nate's story was unusually dramatic, many, like him, did not mention the pull of Korea as much as the lack of a pull to stay in the United States. Larry, twenty-six, told how, after he dropped out of college, he made the seemingly random decision to move to Korea:

> I didn't know anyone Korean, I didn't talk [speak Korean], I never had Korean food, nothing. But I was just, like, why not? You know, I got nothing else going on, I got nothing else to really lose at this point, so I'll just do it. So I just booked a plane ticket, and when I got here I arranged for, like, a homestay thing. I just stayed with a homestay family, or a host family, whatever, . . . and when I was here I got to know a lot of people, and I really liked it, so I didn't really have anything to go back to in America at that point. I couldn't go get a job because the economy was sort of bad at the point, and I wasn't going to go back asking for my old job back, so I was just, like, well, I'll stay here and see what happens.[47]

So, more than the inescapable pull of Korea that I thought adoptees would cite as the reason for returning, the issue for those I spoke to was being unanchored or unencumbered in the United States, with Korea coming up as a viable possibility as they reviewed their options. To be sure, becoming familiar with Korean culture and learning the Korean language were still important for adoptees living in Korea, but as necessities for surviving in Korea, rather than as primary reasons for being there in the first place. Ingrid, thirty-four, described a search for identity that brought her to live in Korea, including an acknowledgment that her search could not be fulfilled in the United States:

I think that what made me know that I had to come back was . . . I think you know, part of what has really influenced me has been my interest in racism and my interest in Asian American experience. From there I started to become interested in adoptee experience just because I had this growing awareness of myself as an adoptee and knowing there were some things I hadn't really dealt with when I was younger, and I knew that I still had a lot of anger for never having talked . . . about it. So I think it was reading adoptee stories and reading about adoption that helped me to understand that I really needed to make peace with my identity as an adoptee, not just as a person of color living in America, but as an adoptee. And that there was some piece of me in Korea that I needed to get that I would not get just living in the United States, so I don't really feel like I had a choice.[48]

Being Korean II: Learning Korean, Teaching English

To my surprise, most adoptees living in Korea, even those who had lived there for an extended time, were not fluent in Korean—even though (not surprisingly) most cited this lack of language proficiency as a major barrier to their ability to live comfortably there. Lack of Korean language skills was also the biggest reason why adoptees said they would never be able to be truly Korean or pass as Koreans in Korea, a major frustration for returnees. Linguistic research has generally found that acquiring a second language in an immersion environment such as a study abroad experience is faster and more effective than classroom studies in a native language location.[49] Given this finding, in addition to the high degree of motivation Korean adoptees living in Korea reported, I was surprised that so few were functionally fluent; even those who had been living in Korea for several years had only rudimentary language skills, such as the ability to navigate the city, make simple purchases, or order food in a restaurant.

Although most of the repatriate adoptees who participated in my research had studied the Korean language in the United States, in Korea, or both, most had stopped Korean language studies in Korea because it was so difficult for them. Only one of the twenty-one claimed to be fluent enough to read and understand a Korean newspaper or to participate fully in street conversation. Many talked about being tormented by the Korean language, and said this was compounded by the everyday social pressure of Korean people who did not understand why the adoptee did not speak and understand Korean, and who often shamed them for their lack of language skills. Adoptees reported that this was in contrast to how they see other (White) westerners treated by native Koreans, where even the slightest Korean language ability is effusively praised. In addition, adoptees reported feelings of guilt, anger, and shame at their lack of

Korean language abilities. Some adoptees refused to work on Korean language skills, for these reasons. Ingrid remarked,

> I had this attitude that, "Oh I can learn language fairly easily, and learning other languages hasn't been a problem for me, learning Korean should be fine." I took my first class in Korean maybe a month after I got here, and it was really hard! At that time I started to talk to other adoptees about their experiences learning Korean and started to hear things like, you know, it's more, it's more difficult for adoptees to learn Korean, and we have other emotional issues attached to learning language. . . . The longer I was in that Korean class, the more I started to feel myself having emotional issues from Korean . . . because here was this language I was supposed to know and now . . . I have to learn it as if it's this new language I have no connection to, and that was, it was really frustrating, and it made me at times not want to learn Korean, and it made me want to just only speak in English.[50]

Ingrid's story points to a hardship associated with a perceived loss of Koreanness that adoptees, especially those living in Korea, seem to feel. Similar feelings of inadequacy and fraudulence have also been described in Chinese American (not adopted) returnees to China after a generation or more of acculturation in the United States,[51] but the situation is somewhat different for adoptees. Being in Korea can cause adoptees to reflect on many aspects of their adoption experience, and this is one of them: being immersed in Korean society reminds adoptees that they might well have grown up there, in which case they would not have to struggle to learn Korean. The irony for adoptees in their struggle to learn Korean is palpable (and this is true even for adoptees who were adopted in early to middle childhood, not as infants, and who know they came to the United States speaking Korean fluently), and their frustration with learning the Korean language is almost universal.

However, adoptees are highly motivated to learn and/or improve their Korean language skills; though many adoptees came to Korea wanting to pass in Korean society based on their physical appearances, their poor language skills give them away as foreigners. Adoptees struggle with this contradiction and equate their language skills with their level of "Korean-ness." Rebecca, thirty-one, who had been living in Korea for several years, said,

> I don't think I could ever live in Korea forever . . .'cause Korea also drives me crazy. It annoys me. [Laughs] Sometimes I think language is a big thing. I don't think I'll ever be able to speak Korean fluently. . . . I studied, like, for a few months, just, like, part time. I never did like a full-time program. I think if I studied a lot, and actually spoke it a lot, then I could

be at a decent level but I would never sound like a Korean person. I will always have some sort of accent. . . . I think the longer I've been here, the more I've gotten used to being here, but I actually hated it when I first arrived.[52]

When I asked Richard, age thirty-one, if he felt more Korean living in Korea than he did living in the United States, he replied, "I don't think that I feel any more Korean than I did and especially, even though I met my birth family, I don't feel any more Korean, because I'm reminded that I'm a foreigner every day, and the biggest part is the language barrier. If I could communicate with my peers in their native tongue, then it would be no problem, but otherwise I'll just continue to be a foreigner, and it will just always be that apparent."[53]

Adding further to the irony of adoptee existence in Korea, most adoptees living in Korea must teach English to Koreans in order to make a living. Because of their lack of Korean language proficiency, the only marketable skill most Korean American adoptees have to offer is their English-language skills as native speakers. Korea's ongoing efforts to enter the global marketplace, where English is the dominant language of business, have made English-language ability a valuable skill; English teaching positions are well paid and fairly easy to obtain. Most adoptees teach at *hagwons*, cram schools where Korean students take supplemental courses.

Unfortunately, teaching English in a hagwon does not contribute to a recognizable career path in Korea or back in the United States; adoptees teach in the hagwons because this is the only employment available to most while in Korea. Many adoptees also complained about the discriminatory hiring practices in many hagwons, noting with surprise that there is a marked preference for White teachers even in Korea. Nate recalled, "Most of these people that they do hire that are White, they can't speak better English, . . . but worse English, than I do. With the accents. And people in here from, like, . . . Russian countries that can barely speak a lick of English, but they're hired as English teachers. Because they're White."[54]

This racism and discrimination parallels that which adoptees face in the United States, because they are discriminated against for being Asian in appearance. The assumption that native speakers of English must be White creates a barrier for adoptees who seek to benefit from their native speaker status as a way to earn a living and stay in Korea. Some adoptees complained that they had seen situations in hagwons where non-native speakers who spoke English, but were White (such as Europeans who speak English as a second language) received preferential hiring or payment, presumably just for being White. Even though most adoptees would not argue that Korea is somehow more racist in labor and hiring practices than the United States, these complaints about discriminatory treatment toward adoptees in Korea illuminate several racial realities for adoptees. When I asked Nate if he feels like a minority in Korea, he explained:

> In Korea, sometimes.... That's strange to say that, 'cause I look Korean and I fit the profile of a Korean ... but, yeah, sometimes I do. I've been in situations where I'm the only English speaker there, you know, and, like, running around ... trying to figure out how to say what, or try to draw on a piece of paper (laughs). [But it's] different [from being a minority in the United States] because [there] you kinda know you're a minority, ... I mean, physically ... your guard is always up. Here it throws you off guard. And the reason why I say that is 'cause when you start to feel the most comfortable is when you start to lose yourself in the fact that [you are still different]. Then, I start to realize, "Wait ... yep ... I'm still a minority here at this point," you know. You know.[55]

Many adoptees remarked that teaching English makes it more difficult to learn Korean, and fully recognized the irony of being in the position of representing America because they are teaching English in Korea, even though they themselves were born in Korea. Adoptees also recognize the class differences that their English language education of Korean nationals supports, especially because so many Koreans see acquisition of English as a way out of Korea. Victor, age twenty-eight, remarked,

> Teaching these rich kids, like all these rich families' kids, English. It's just such a weird, ironic little ... fucked-up thing, you know. Especially like during this summer camp where it's very, like, all specialized around American learning, right? And so ... I'm teaching American history and stuff, like social studies, American social studies, right now in the classes.... Considering all the circumstances leading up to this moment, it's like, oh man, these kids, they just come from these rich privileged ... I mean in Korea if you have money you're ... like gods here, right? I mean, like, you get everything. So it's like in some ways I prefer teaching the blue collar, because where I was working before was more like blue collar kids. In some ways, I prefer that.[56]

In contexts where phenotypic Whiteness is valued, broad contexts such as dominant American society or more specific contexts like the English language hagwon scene in Seoul, non-White persons often experience racial discrimination. Adoptees are understandably angry when they find themselves subject to discrimination in Korea. In the United States, such treatment is illegal and increasingly socially unacceptable; social mores that discourage the acknowledgement of race have likely reduced the incidence of individual-to-individual racist interaction in contemporary America (though I would argue that institutional racism continues to be common). In addition, many adoptees imagine that racial discrimination could not exist in Korea, certainly not against themselves as ethnic Koreans. As a result, many adoptees are caught off guard by racist hiring practices in Korea.

The few adoptees who find employment outside the hagwons and English-tutoring scene have vastly different experiences at work. One adoptee talked about the advantages of having a corporate job in Korea, where his America-ness, not just his English language skills, are valued and rewarded, despite his Korean appearance. However, the valorization of Western-ness is the same as in hagwons; Richard, who has the privileges of being a corporate employee (and probably because he has the privileges of being male in Korean society), compared his daily life to that of adoptees who teach in hagwons.

> In Korea, there are a lot of professions that are time-honored here, and one of them happens to be mine. And, if I tell them the company that I work for, anyone here will just know, and lots of people are really impressed, and it carries a lot of weight. And it's not just in social circles, it makes a difference when I go to the bank, when I do any types of transactions, if I present them my business card and they see the company that I work for and the position that I do, then it makes all the difference in the world. And it's bad because, then, other friends that don't do what I do will try to get, maybe, similar things that I get, maybe, like, just going out to buy a cell phone or getting a credit card or something, they'll get completely different responses than I'll get. So, I know that it makes a difference, and Korea is just that shallow, they're focused on payment and status, education and other things. . . . Pretty much, the profession I'm in is ruled by America. Pretty much all the precedents, all the rules, regulations, all the laws, everything eventually streams down from America. . . . And, so, even though I'm reminded that I'm American almost every day, at least in the environment that I spend the majority of my time in, and I'm in contact with Koreans, it's totally a benefit. Because, my advantage is to be American. And, they listen to me, and the things that I talk about, the models we use at the American firm, the resources available, and they're nothing but envious, and they should be, because we're not at the global standard in this [Korean] office.[57]

It is difficult to discern whether the discrimination that adoptees (and other overseas Koreans who wish to teach English in Korea) face on the job market stems from internalized racism against Korean foreigners within Korea as a country colonized by the United States, the fierce nationalism present in Korean culture and subsequent distrust of "non-Korean" Koreans, or a Korean popular understanding that Whiteness is naturally associated with superior

English language skills. Certainly, there is considerable irony in adoptees' experiences of discrimination in the workplace, given that they are generally trying to fit into Korean society by learning Korean while many of their students are learning English in order to leave Korea. Although some may see this as an even exchange (much like many see the entire process of transnational adoption as an even exchange between birth countries who seek a solution for overburdened child welfare systems and economically disadvantaged birth parents, and receiving countries who seek a solution for a shortage of adoptable infants), adoptees do not report even exchanges in their experiences, but tilted toward Korean social needs and expectations and against them as adoptees.

Being Korean III: Eating Korean

There is a primacy about eating that is especially telling about how people identify, though this same primacy makes many take the act of eating as a cultural statement for granted. As the most basic form of consumption, we can eat culturally significant foods in order to assert a shared identity with others who engage in the same culinary customs,[58] or we can eat these same foods in order to engage in culinary tourism where history, culture, and politics disappear as we eat to have a literal taste of a place or culture as well as to satisfy our physical hunger. Historian Hasia Diner writes that "preparing and consuming food together solidifies social bonds. . . . The notion of the common table connecting people exists in many cultures as an embodiment of communal trust."[59] For Korean adoptees not raised on Korean food (and some are never exposed to Korean food until adulthood), eating Korean food at a (culturally) Korean table is a way of connecting to other Korean adoptees or connecting back to Korean culture. Several adoptees with whom I spoke mentioned Korean food and the frequency with which they eat or do not eat it in the United States as evidence of how Korean they felt they were; the consumption of Korean food seemed to be evidence of Koreanness for adoptees, as understood by themselves, and sometimes by Koreans or Korean Americans around them. Two of the adoptees I talked with in Seoul had worked at Korean restaurants in the United States and considered these experiences points of entry into Korean culture. Victor remembered, "I was working at this Korean deli restaurant, called Grandma Chung's. In a sense, I think I was just doing it to prepare me to come to Korea. I just wanted to be around Korean people and eat Korean food. Just me and this grandma cutting vegetables and cooking food and stuff."[60]

For Paula, age thirty-one, whether she ate bread or kimchi was the primary signifier to her Korean American employer of whether she was Korean or American.[61] She recalled, "I worked in a Korean restaurant, so that was a nice introduction to Korean food, and the lady, the owner, [when I first started working there,] . . . was trying to place my identity; I think she figured I was American. But she would ask me . . . 'Do you eat bread, or do you eat kimchi?' And I was like, 'Well . . . I do eat bread, and I really, I just started eating kimchi,' so I was, like, 'both.'"[62] Although she was successful in claiming both Korean and American identity by saying she ate both bread and kimchi, later she remembered how her lack of familiarity with Korean dining customs revealed her as more American than Korean: "I made a lot of mistakes. I remember one time, the owner's friends came in, they were in their fifties, an older couple. And then only thing that was missing was the kimchi. And they were like, 'How could she forget the kimchi?' I learned that was a big mistake [laughs]. Like, 'She's not Korean!'"[63]

Alternately, not consuming Korean food signified an absence of Korean identity. One adoptee remarked, "At that time I was like, 'I don't even have anything in the Korean community. I don't do anything in the Korean community. I don't even eat Korean food.'"[64]

Many of these adoptees also talked about what they ate in Korea as a significant part of their past and present identities. Eating in restaurants is very common in Korea, and can be done very inexpensively by Western standards. Even among the adoptees who spoke very little Korean, many remarked that they had favorite Korean dishes and knew enough Korean to order them in restaurants. Eating Korean food evoked powerful taste memories for other adoptees, like Patrick, who had been adopted as children (instead of as infants), even if they had no other memories of Korea. He stated, "When I ate first . . . when I was back in Korea, I was like, 'Holy shit, I tasted this when I was little!' It was like one of those flavors that I remembered; it was like all this rush of memories and whatever, [it] was a very distinct flavor, and it's like, OK I know I had this before, and I was like, I know where I had it. I had it in Korea."[65] Victor had a similar recollection:

> I was four years old when I was adopted, and actually I have . . . I have no memories of being in Korea or living in Korea, but I do remember certain things since I've been back. I've, like, realized that there are some things that I remember. Not like visually, but more like taste things and these, smells. Like a. . . . I remember, . . . when I first came to Korea on vacation in 2003, I had some of the grapes, the black grapes with the seeds, and you don't eat the skin, some of those. I was just eating them, because they always had fruit on the table. . . . I put one in my mouth and, you know, we're just talking and I was like, whoa, I, like, had this moment of *This is kind of strange, because this is so familiar,* and I think—I don't remember for sure, but I think—I said something right then and there: *This tastes familiar.* [The Korean there said,] "Yeah, this is a very famous fruit, parents will give this to their children at birthdays, or a special holiday." So

> they say if you've lived here in Korea, there's a good chance that you've probably ate it. So that, and also . . . the seaweed, kelp soup . . . that tasted familiar and . . . some smells, you know, like some random Korean smells you smell on the street. . . . some of those smelled familiar. . . . I wanted to get it on tape.[66]

In both of these examples, the memories evoked by taste served to connect the adoptee in a physical way to Korea, even though their other memories of themselves in Korea had been lost. Both relished their moments of realization that they could remember eating food in Korea from their childhoods, perhaps because this is a piece of evidence about their pasts that they could recall themselves instead of having to rely on others to fill in the blank spaces of their memories. The essentialization of their Korean identities through eating Korean food may also be directed towards adoptees by Koreans, as reported by Elise Prébin.[67] In my own experience, my enjoyment of Korean foods is proof to many Korean nationals and ethnics I've encountered that I am "still Korean."

Food-based nostalgias can work in multiple directions; Nate relied on the Americanization of chain restaurants in Seoul to keep from getting too homesick for the United States. He remarked,

> I think I came at the right time . . . Americana here is not so much an exotic thing anymore, and it's almost part of the norm. And you got a McDonald's on every corner, you got a Baskin Robbins . . . every third store there's a lot of American restaurants. . . . So, I eat pretty much the same food [as in America]. . . . I do enjoy Korean food, but I do have the occasional McDonald's and Burger King and . . . you know, if I want to order pizza, I can order a pizza, or get fried chicken. I mean, what I'm getting at is, the comfort food is there, a lot of the same kinda things are there, you know?[68]

The visible globalization in the emerging fast food market in Korea, besides being a comfort for transnational adoptees raised in the West, also serves as a powerful symbol of the investment by global economies in Korea. Korean national interest in westernized globalization extents to overseas Koreans, including adoptees, who have Western educations and cultural currency to contribute to Korean society and the growing and increasingly globalized Korean economy. Perhaps it is not a coincidence, then, that Nate perceives himself as having got to Korea "at the right time," since the F-4 visa that makes his move to Korea possible also happens to have been created during the time period that saw a huge increase in the availability of American-style fast food.

Being Korean IV: Loving Korea

Diner writes, "Food, like sex, intensifies group identity."[69] In many ways, the personal, political, and cultural significance of eating and sex are similar. Both are intimate bodily acts, and depending on what we do and with whom we do it, we use both to assert our identities. And both are acts which most people understand to be personal (based on taste or preference), rather than culturally conditioned. In their research on Korean adoptees in the American Pacific Northwest, Jiannbin Shiao and Mia Tuan found that the majority of adult adoptees in their study dated and married White partners, and that most adoptees considered Whites to be their "natural" partners. Shiao and Tuan interpreted this finding as consistent with the culturally White upbringing of most of their adoptee subjects.[70] However, the pattern among Korean adoptees I contacted in Seoul was very different: all those who were actively dating reported that they exclusively dated either fellow Korean adoptees, Korean nationals, or nationals of other Asian countries.

Most of the adoptees I encountered living in Korea were single and all identified as heterosexual at the time they were interviewed. Gender differences between the experiences of heterosexual women and men in the project seemed heavily focused on dating experiences. In the United States, gendered racialization of Asian Americans creates dating opportunities for adoptee women as objects of orientalized desire. Men, on the other hand, more often talked about their invisibility as dating partners in the States, consistent with Asian American racializations of men as emasculated. In Korea, roles are reversed: men seemed more likely to use the party atmosphere in the adoptee community to date many different people, while women reported more problems with the party scene and the promiscuous dating patterns that seemed more common among the men. These problems were marked enough that women cited the lack of suitable partners as a major reason for leaving Korea; many of the adoptee women I interviewed were dating no one. Paula remarked, "I feel like it's kind of hard to date in Korea; [most of] the older guys are . . . married. Dating Korean guys, . . . there are so many . . . differences . . . language, cultural. . . . For Korean adoptees and Korean American guys, maybe if they're in the States, they would date Korean Americans or Korean adoptees, but in Korea, I feel like they're more interested in dating native Korean girls. . . . That's part of my . . . reason for going back to the States; I find it hard to date in Korea—or, not date, but to have a relationship."[71] In this example, Paula gives a good reason why it might be so difficult to find men to date in Korea for adoptee women. Korean men are more interested in Korean nationals as dating partners, and many adoptee women consider Korean men to be too traditional and unlikely to accept the level of equality that a Western-raised woman would expect in a dating relationship.

Women living in Korea rarely discussed dating in their oral histories, except to remark that they were not dating. Men, on the other hand, extensively discussed the party life in Seoul for adoptees, the dating opportunities that resulted, the women they had been with since arriving in Korea, and what type of women who interested them. Nate discussed how accessible the adoptee party scene was for him (and, in his estimation, for other adoptees) because of the relatively high pay adoptees could earn by teaching English:

> I mean, the cost of living here is relatively decent, where I can get by . . . and then be able to pay my living expenses, and then pay off extras. . . . I've told the other adoptees that . . . and they'll complain and bitch and moan about their jobs, and like . . . there's nothing you should be complaining about. 'Cause you kinda live like rock stars out here, you know? These are people that can go around, party all night . . . sleep until three o'clock, start their private tutoring until ten o'clock, and then, go back to a night of all drinking, and then be able, yet, to pay off their bills back home, and . . . keep the cost of living the same here.[72]

Victor attempted to count his many Korean lovers since his arrival not two years previous:

> Okay, yeah . . . sex . . . let's say seven or eight, and a little bit less than sex, seven or eight to ten. And then like making out with it you include just like heavy kissing, probably fifteen. That's a lot I guess . . . maybe twelve or thirteen because I think, every almost every girl that I've made out with and kissed, I've done more with . . . , but I definitely had my heyday, oh I would say from last . . . it would have been from, like December, 2004 December to about . . . March or April 2005. So just like four or five months I was really, like, I felt like, if I liked a girl and I tried hard, I could get her.[73]

Sam, twenty-seven, had not dated as extensively as Victor, but did still have a pointed interest in the datable population of women in Korea. For him, Korea was a place where he could find his ideal wife, and he described what she would be like and how he might meet her:

> I want to meet a lot of people and if I can meet up with somebody who's Korean American, that would be great. You know, and I feel like the best place to do that would be . . . probably here. It's probably the best place to do that. . . . I mean a Korean who spoke English and who had been exposed to American culture. That would also be someone who I would be compatible with, you know. And I feel like I have to be really realistic about this. Is that if I marry somebody who wasn't Korean or Korean

American, I'd be missing out on a big part of my life, you know. I mean obviously you could share some of that with that person [74]

Men were more likely than women to date widely, and some eventually settled down with a Korean (national) woman who could help them become more established in Korea by navigating and translating the nuances of Korean society for their adoptee partners. Unlike the concern that adoptee women had with dating Korean nationals, men felt they could exert their influence as men in relationships with Korean women to make them more Americanized in order to adapt their Korean partners to their own American cultural preferences. Nate, who had a serious Korean girlfriend, said, "I think with my girlfriend and I . . . she's becoming more Americanized than I am . . . Koreanized . . .'cause she's following . . . my mannerisms, versus me following her mannerisms. 'Cause, you know, we speak English, we watch American TV, stuff like that."[75]

Adoptees of both genders were interested in dating other Koreans while living in Korea, but, whereas women saw mostly barriers, men perceived a tantalizing menu of options and opportunities. Because adoptees of both sexes understood Korean women to be more open and adaptable to Americanization than Korean men, adoptee men were interested in dating Korean women more than adoptee women were interested in dating Korean men. Since adoptee women were just one of several options for adoptee men, some found it difficult to compete with nonadopted women and tended to date less as a result.

A Transnational Korean American Adoptee Identity

Korean adoptees living in Korea commonly express a profound sense of in-between-ness in their identities, straddling divides in symbolic representations in popular discourses that divide the West and the East: rich nations and (supposedly) poor nations, and White and Asian racial identities. While many adoptees refer to and borrow some elements of these polarized and opposite identities, most do not dichotomize their own identities within these frameworks, and choose instead to articulate national, cultural, and racial duality or multiplicity. Korean adoptees have access to easy permanent residence or dual citizenship in Korea and their ease of immigration to the United States. They have privileges as American citizens and as native English speakers, but they also have access to Korean citizenship through their Korean heritage and because of Korea's economic and cultural interest in Western countries. However, because of language and cultural barriers, most say they never feel truly Korean.

Korean adoptees living in Korea are reminded daily that they are simultaneously Korean and not Korean. Wendy, age thirty-one, described her neither-and-both identity as a Korean adoptee:

[Being in Korea] made me feel more American, at first, definitely. Which is the opposite of what you'd think it would. There were those typical first experiences from when you first jump off the plane and you're in a pool of Koreans it's kind of overwhelming and kind of like elation, my god, there's so many of us, and you're trying to pick out your face and see who looks like you, and trying to listen to all of this chatter, and it's almost overwhelming. . . . And there are these moments were you're like, this is super super cool, and you can't even describe being able to just blend, and be a part of this whole country of people, or be connected to this whole country of people and you didn't have any real sense that they were there, kind of, so all of a sudden there's all these things manifesting that you didn't know about, kind of. But then there's this big slap in the head, and your head goes the other way because you can't communicate and you don't understand the culture and the culture class and you're unable to assimilate immediately to the community so it's like you're ethnically Korean but you're not that obviously.[76]

Other adoptees made similar remarks, and noted that a sense of being Korean has been part of their identities for longer than they have lived in Korea. They also said that living in Korea opened their sense of being Korean further than when they were in the United States. Paula said:

From when I was little, I've had this strong feeling like, deep down I was Korean, but I couldn't explain it . . . and, after, I learned that I was Korean. . . . Now I . . . identify myself as being Korean American. I could never be a native Korean. I don't think I can be totally American. . . . My parents or my relatives, they, they told me, "You're American. Don't forget you're American." But, I do feel American, but I feel I do want to recognize my ethnic identity too. . . . I still I feel like sometimes it's hard to balance the two, because sometimes you're marginalized, sometimes you're in different situations, and who you're with, sometimes you feel more American, or feel the pressure to be Americanized, or American, or Korean. It can be stressful, it really can be stressful, but I try not to let that pressure get to me too much. . . . Ever since I was little, I've felt like, in a way I did belong in the States, but not really. And, then, in Korea, I also feel like I kinda made it my own, my own . . . place. . . . Even if I found my birth family, or married a Korean, I still feel like it wouldn't be totally—unless, unless I grew up here. Even after eight years, I felt like I'd be fluent in Korean, I'd understand myself more, I'd know—have a clear idea of my identity.[77]

Rebecca remarked:

I've never felt fully American. Um, I was a bit more radical when I was younger, especially in college, and I was totally anti-American and I hated America and I thought, you know, America was responsible for so many awful things. . . . And now, since I've been in Korea, my feelings have kind of mellowed out a bit, because, or not mellowed out—evened out a bit—because I think Korea, Korean society, is really messed up in a lot of ways as well and definitely needs to change. There's the adoption issue, but there's so many other problems as well among Korean society, the way they treat people. . . . For a while here, I felt more American than I ever did back in the States. But when I was in the States I never felt like I was American, so it's hard to say. It's a mixture of both, so partly Korean, partly American. And I know [that] inside, I am that way as well. . . . I really can't say whether I'm American or Korean but—both.[78]

These adoptees express their in-between-ness, but also the stress caused by this state of belonging neither to Korea nor to the United States. Sometimes this stress is underlined by the experience in America as Asian Americans who are culturally White and racially Asian, and by American family and friends who insist on American-ness over other identities for the adoptee. Ironically, the experiences of discrimination that these adoptees face are transnational—for being Asian in appearance in the United States and for not being culturally Korean enough in Korea. Since most adoptee returnees do not articulate a preference for how and where they are discriminated against, these social pressures do not push them toward a less complicated identity.

Even the way adoptees are perceived in Korean society is different than in American society; this was one of the most unsettling cultural differences I noted the first time I traveled to Korea. In the United States, the perception is generally how lucky adoptees are to have been adopted in the first place, and to have been taken into loving American homes. Implicit here is the assumption that the economic and social circumstances of being adopted to America are far superior those they would have had from staying in Korea, a place most Americans have never visited, and do not understand in any real way. In Korea, I realized shortly after the first time I returned as an adult, Koreans often pity adoptees. They claim to have a connection to adoptees because we are Korean, like them. But they feel sorry for the fact that adoptees were not raised in Korea as Koreans. And sometimes they seem to feel ashamed that they couldn't raise adoptees themselves. Being an object of pity as an adoptee was a new experience for me, because this is so different from what I am used to when Americans learn that I am adopted. Korean adoptees who live in Korea live with this cultural mismatch every day; some talk about it, some exploit it, some just sidestep it.

Adoptees living in Korea as privileged Westerners often find it difficult to imagine themselves as objects of pity because adoptive societies have always impressed on them that it is the Korean nation that should be pitied, and that adoptees are the lucky ones, not the pitiful ones. The use of adoptees as pitiful symbols of South Korea's past mistakes in this mobilization of political will among Korean nationals can feel strange and unexpected for adoptees. An additional irony is that adoptees are also understood in Korea as being born of the lowest and most shameful circumstances, shrouded in poverty, and stained with an uncertainty of lineage. Korean understanding of adoptees as simultaneously Korean and Western makes it possible for adoptees to participate in Korean social and political interaction without the requisite scorn that adoptees would have received had they not been adopted. Although Koreans still commonly express pity toward adoptees, the Western quality of adoptee upbringings trumps the imagined lowly circumstance of their births; it is as if the act of adoption raises adoptees from near-untouchables to socially acceptable by transforming them from Koreans to Westerners. For some Koreans, adoptees may even come to symbolize an escape from Korean poverty or social stigma to Western success and prosperity, in a Korean version of the American Dream.

The sense of duality and of being in between two races or nations seems more pronounced for the adoptees I encountered in Korea than for participants in the United States; this may be because adoptees living in Korea have more access to everyday examples of what constitutes Korean-ness though observations of so-called real Koreans. Many of these repatriate adoptees say it is difficult for them when they return to the United States because of the racism they experience as return culture shock, though most do not cite this as a reason to stay in Korea. This tension of the in-between or divided self is further exacerbated by the very nature of the Korean and American mechanisms that make adoptee transnationalism possible. The United States privileges the entry of adoptees as minor children and Korea does so for adoptees as Westernized adults. Both nations are specific in their valuing adoptee immigrants as either children or as adults, revealing national interests in child adoptees in America, and adult adoptees in Korea.

Conclusion

Unlike other groups of transnationals, Korean adoptees generally lack the cultural fluidity that comes from being fully bilingual and bicultural, but they do have considerable legal fluidity when crossing borders. Korean adoptees benefit from unusual immigration privileges in both the United States (as children of American citizens who are usually White) and in South Korea (as Western-educated adults who belong to the imagined global family of the Korean diaspora), which move to the front of immigration queues. Adoptees who live in Korea especially feel this transnationalism-on-paper in which access to legal residence in Korea is a matter of filling out the correct paperwork, as adoptees are only rarely denied the Korean F-4 visa. Of course the opportunity to return to the United States never disappears, since naturalization of Korean adoptees (if this process takes place before the adoptee turns eighteen) was also just a matter of paperwork, and citizenship by naturalization was all but assured. Their transnational legal status enables adoptees to occupy a variety of in-between positions in a world that would have them identify as American or Korean, White or Asian. These liminal positions are not always comfortable, but they can be understood by, and shared with, other adoptees, as interview participant Ingrid articulates:

> You know, adoptees always talk about feeling like they're in between two cultures—well, it's true. . . . You're not comfortable in America or your adoptive country because you don't feel like you are Korean, and yet people look at you, and to them you are Korean. . . . And then you come to Korea and you look like you're Korean, but you're really not. And so I think I will always be in between those two worlds, and it's almost like there's this other alternative space for adoptees to be in, and it's almost like Adoptee Land. It's like we have a very specific space and it's not in Korea and it's not in America. It's in a place that I think we're going to have to create for ourselves. It's in a place I think we've already begun to create, to a certain extent, but I don't think anybody else really understands why we need to do that or where that space is for us.[79]

Although immigration rules for Korean adoptees in South Korea and the United States are very different than for other groups of immigrants, Korean adoptees leave and enter America with immigrants from all over the world, and return to South Korea with thousands of other overseas Korean ethnic return migrants. Korean American adoptees living in Korea share many characteristics of other groups of Asian American diasporic immigrants, marked by (as described by Anderson and Lee) "establishing and maintaining kinship, economic, cultural, and political networks across national boundaries, and the creation of multiple sites of 'home.'"[80] The obvious difference between the Korean adoptee returnees to Korea and the Asian American immigrants Anderson and Lee describe is location. For Anderson and Lee, the Asian American population is in exile in America, still reaching back to Asia; in this study, the diasporic Asian American population is back in the country of their birth, struggling to maintain all the same networks described by Anderson and Lee while in exile in Asia and reaching back to America.

The population of adoptees who have returned to Korea also share many characteristics with other Korean ethnic return migrants in that their return to Korea is motivated by interest in their ethnic homeland rather than by economic opportunity, and is facilitated by liberal South Korean immigration policies with respect to overseas Koreans. That the adoptee returnees maintain social relations largely segregated from Korean nationals is also consistent with the experiences of ethnic return migrants from around the world, who find cold comfort as foreigners in their supposed homelands.

Both Korean adoptees and other overseas Koreans who return to Korea face a cultural chasm that separates them from Korean nationals; but, while this separation often reflects multiple generations abroad for non-adopted Koreans, it is achieved in two or three decades of life as an adoptee. Adoptee returnees also share with other overseas Koreans the burdens of high expectations of Korean cultural competency, including understanding the Korean language and a knowledge of Korean cultural practices, because they are perceived to be Korean. Like other Korean ethnic return migrants, Korean adoptee returnees find themselves in a paradoxical position within Korean society: neither fully Korean nor completely foreign, subject to high expectations as ethnic Koreans but also to rejection as outsiders.

However, Korean adoptee ethnic return migrants also differ from other groups of returnees in several ways. Unlike other groups of emigrants, most adoptees experience racial and cultural isolation (with respect to birth culture and society) as a direct result of having been adopted not just transnationally, but also transracially into homes that are both Western and White. They identify most strongly not with Korean or American nationals living in Korea, or even with other ethnic return migrants, such as other Korean American returnees, but with other adoptees. This creates a cohesive, but sometimes claustrophobic, social reality for the small group of Korean adoptee returnees. That Korean adoptees have symbolic significance in Korean culture as the pitiful lost children of South Korea's modernization project only adds to their complicated reception as Koreans born into, but removed from, Korean society.

Conclusion

The Ends of Korean Adoption

It seems that every year that I have been engaged in research on Korean adoption, there has been at least one major news story about transnational adoption that has created widespread discussion both in adoptee communities and in the general public. In the past, these have ranged from whether or not adoption should be part of humanitarian aid to countries coping with natural disasters (Haiti after the earthquake in 2010, several Asian nations after the Indian Ocean Tsunami in 2004), notable court cases (such as the 2000–2007 custody battle for Anna Mae He between her Chinese birth parents and her American foster parents, and the 2013 Supreme Court decision denying Cherokee birth father Dusten Brown custody of his daughter under the Indian Child Welfare Act), adoption scandals (such as the return of her Russian adopted son to Russia by his American mother, Tory Hanson, in 2010, and the practice of "rehoming" of adopted children, as reported by Reuters in 2013), and, of course, a seemingly endless string of stories about celebrity adoptions.

In 2015, the *New York Times Magazine* published an article by Maggie Jones, in which Jones, an American adoptive mother, reported on a small group of Korean adoptees living in Korea who are working to reform or end Korean overseas adoption and raise awareness about legal and ethical problems within that industry.[1] I know many of the adoptees featured in the article and was interviewed at length myself by Jones for the piece, and I've spent a lot of time in Korea doing field work for this project and working on other projects. So for me, the issues raised in the article are nothing new. Although I was impressed by the depth of Jones's research and reporting for the article, I found online comments responding the articles were far more interesting (and, admittedly, disturbing) than the article itself. Many comments from readers are similar to sentiments expressed about international adoption for decades, that adoptees are lucky to have been adopted and should be ashamed to criticize either adoption practices generally or their own parenting specifically. Others chastised Jones for portraying a narrow and/or negative view of Korean adoption when (according to commenters) "happy" adoptions are much more common. However, there were just as many commenters, some who identified as adoptees, adoptive parents, or birth parents, who left nuanced articulations defending a critique of the adoption industry and of the lack of understanding about transnational and transracial adoption within adoptee-receiving cultures.

From the beginning of my scholarly interest in adoption, some twenty years ago, I have seen a huge change in how the public perceives Korean and other transnational adoption, which is well-reflected in the broad range of public comments in response to the Jones article. In the mid-1990s, most research and policy on Korean and other transnational and transracial adoption skewed heavily towards the expansion of these kinds of adoptions as generally unproblematic; most studies included adoptees only as child subjects, often spoken for by their White parents, never as authors or policymakers. Today, largely because adoptees, including scholars, activists, and artists, have inserted their critiques, life experiences, and perspectives into public debates about adoption, public views on transnational and transracial adoption have slowly shifted to allow much more nuanced understandings of the problems that cause adoptions, and of the complicated consequences of adoption for those in adoption triads. Although South Korea has now limited its overseas adoption programs to a fraction of its former numbers, as the largest, oldest, and probably most organized community of adoptees in the United States (and in many European countries), Korean adoptees are in a position to shape the future of transnational adoption not just for Korean adoption but for other transnational adoption as well.

Korean and other forms of transnational and transracial adoption are again (or maybe still) at a crossroads today: adoption policy and the experiences of those in adoption triads (adoptees, adoptive parents, and birth parents) are riddled with contradictions. Federal domestic adoption law forbids consideration of race in adoptive placement, but U.S. commitment to the Hague Adoption Convention includes giving consideration to adoptees' ethnic, religious, and cultural backgrounds in transnational adoption. Societal understandings of transnational adoption as child salvation still prevail, but adoption research increasingly emphasizes serious potential harms to adoptees as a direct result of their having been adopted.[2] Even though reports of scandalously corrupt or unethical practices within the transnational adoption industry are increasingly common in scholarly research and investigative journalism,[3] globalization of reproduction through "outsourcing,"[4] including transnational adoption, embryo adoption, and transnational commercial surrogacy appears to be a growth industry. As they develop, these practices will continue to be contentious—but they will continue.

Tobias Hübinette, a fellow adoption researcher who is, like myself, a Korean adoptee, is also heavily involved in his Korean adoptee community. He sometimes appears in the films of Jane Jin Kaisen, a Korean Danish adoptee artist. In one of these films, *Tracing Trades*,[5] Hübinette walks out alone into a bleak and snowy landscape. His voiceover narrates, "We are a one-generation immigrant group." This is a profound truth about transnational adoptees; the adoptee cultural and social production that is so important to so many adoptees cannot really be passed on to an adoptee's children. Since the defining characteristic of a transnational adoptee identity is having been adopted—having experienced the rupture caused by the loss of birth family and country and the absorption into another family and country—an adoptee identity cannot, by definition, be inherited, but only imposed. Further, because the lack of understanding and acknowledgment of issues surrounding adoption within the family is a core part of many adoptees' experiences, adoptee identity is not reproducible even by adoptees who choose to adopt children themselves. Thus, in American transnational adoption, the next generation of adoptee transmigrants is not the generation born to the first, as with other groups of migrants (e.g., first-, second-, and third-generation Korean Americans), but is instead the next group of new adoptees, born and relinquished in foreign countries and transported across borders for adoption in America. The next generation will be raised not by today's adoptees, but by the next younger generation of adoptive parents, who sometimes harshly judge the generation that preceded them as backward and uninformed.

Adoption demographer Peter Selman has documented the decline of transnational adoption generally, and overseas adoption from Korean specifically, over the past decade.[6] The end of Korean transnational adoption, which I think is inevitable considering the shame that transnational adoption evokes among an increasingly wealthy South Korean populace, looms equally large among both activists who support the practice and those who oppose it.[7] So far, neither group has succeeded in fully addressing the cultural or demographic consequences of this future for the worldwide population of Korean adoptees. For those proponents of adoption who maintain that transnational adoption is a win-win solution for parentless children and childless parents, the end of transnational adoption from any source is disastrous. However, even the staunchest supporters of adoption would be hard pressed to argue that adoption, and its effects in the family, are meant to be reproduced; by the time adoptees give birth to children of their own, no one would want them to reproduce themselves as transnational adoptees and give up their children to be parented by foreign strangers. For those who work to end transnational adoption, many of whom are adoptees, the disappearance of Korean adoptee communities is a necessary result of their activism. Although adoptee community and identity is of great value to many of these activists, they are also silent on this future they envision; realistically, anti-adoption activism works against the very existence of future Korean adoptees and of Korean adoptee communities.

Even if Korean adoption ends, it will likely not be as a reaction to problems within the practice, but because South Korea no longer wants to participate in a practice that is associated with poor and undeveloped nations. Since current practices of transnational adoption depend on economic inequity between sending and receiving nations, Korean adoption may even continue as transnational adoption *to* Korea. In any case, we will still be left with the legacy of over sixty years of Korean adoption: the well-funded infrastructure of the globalized adoption industry, fueled by demand from Western parents and working within neoliberal economies that accommodate Western labor needs by providing reproductive services on a free market. David Oh and Omotayo Banjo's criteria for neoliberal multiculturalism include "valorizing personal choice and freedom, minimize[ing] anti-imperialist discourses through narrative conventions that have audiences identify with the colonizer rather than the colonized . . . deny[ing] racism through its appeal to false universalism and . . . the representation of global capitalism as unproblematically benefitting [those] who are subject to it."[8] All of these elements are in place in the transnational adoption industry today.

It is within this complicated social and economic landscape that the paradox of human rights in the context of transnational adoption takes shape: if parenting is a right, is it a right for all, even those for whom reproduction is socially or biologically impossible? If we accept that parenting is a right for all, not just for the rich, transnational adoption as it is currently practiced is largely unethical, since most adoptable children are taken from women or couples involuntarily or relinquished by parents under social and economic duress. But if we accept parenting as a right for all, we must also ask how these rights inherently impinge on the rights of children. If, on the other hand, we accept that parenting is not a right—as it clearly is not today—then it becomes a privilege, for sale to the highest bidder.

Korean adoptees are increasingly visible in research and increasingly vocal in debates about adoption, but their voices and those of other minoritized peoples are still often drowned out in public discourses about race and adoption. During the drafting of the Hague Adoption Convention in 1993, adoptee concerns were largely overlooked because adoptees were not consulted. Today, because of adoptee participation in public discourses of transnational adoption, staff who administer the Hague Adoption Convention acknowledge the importance of including adoptee perspectives before considering future policy changes. At a 2014 academic and policy conference focusing on comparisons between transnational adoption and commercial global surrogacy, I was struck by parallels between the emerging surrogacy industry and the early transnational adoption industry. Although there were several adopted scholars participating, I noted a general lack of concern about the perspectives of surrogate children, not because no one cared, but simply because none were present. Minoritized populations, no matter how central they may be to discussions about their welfare, must be present to be heard. With this in mind, I have suggested fresh ways of looking at Korean and other transnational adoption. In my understanding of Korean adoption, positions within adoption social and cultural structures must be taken into account as a key influence on beliefs about how and if transnational adoption is working, and whom it benefits. In this work, through their stories, Korean adoptees emerge as subjects through whom American national, political, and racial beliefs and practices are most intimately played out.

NOTES

INTRODUCTION A HISTORY OF KOREAN AMERICAN ADOPTION IN PRINT

1. I focus here on newspaper accounts that match my Korean adoptee research populations in Minneapolis/St. Paul, Minnesota; Portland, Oregon; and Seattle, Washington. But this was a national news phenomenon, as documented by Catherine Ceniza Choy in *Global Families: A History of Asian International Adoption in America* (New York: New York University Press, 2013).
2. Verónica Anzil describes many similar characterizations of transnational adotpees assimilating into Spanish cultures in Spanish newspaper coverage of transnational adoption in "Adopting 'Imaginaries': International Adoption in the Spanish Press," *Adoption and Fostering* 37, no. 1 (2013): 71–82.
3. Laura Briggs, *Somebody's Children: The Politics of Transracial and Transnational Adoption* (Durham, NC: Duke University Press, 2012).
4. Eleana Kim, *Adopted Territory: Transnational Korean Adoptees and the Politics of Belonging* (Durham, NC: Duke University Press, 2010).
5. "Korean Child Welcomes Rescuer Here," *Seattle Times*, October 26, 1958.
6. Ibid.
7. Ibid.
8. "Adopted Koreans Fully 'Americanized,'" *Seattle Times*, August 10, 1975.
9. Ibid.
10. Don Stewart, "Interracial Adoption Could Enrich Lives, Suburb Women Told," *Minneapolis Star*, February 27, 1970
11. Ibid.
12. Ibid.
13. Ibid.
14. Erica Wood, "Native Instincts," *St. Paul Pioneer Press and Dispatch*, August 18, 1998.
15. Ibid.
16. Mark Jerng, *Claiming Others: Transracial Adoption and National Belonging* (Minneapolis: University of Minnesota Press, 2010), xxxv.
17. Choy, *Global Families*.
18. Mia Tuan and Jiannbin Lee Shiao, *Choosing Ethnicity, Negotiating Race: Korean Adoptees in America* (New York: Russell Sage Foundation, 2011), 48.
19. Kristi Brian, *Reframing Transnational Adoption: Adopted Koreans, White Parents, and the Politics of Kinship* (Philadelphia: Temple University Press, 2012).

CHAPTER 1 A KOREAN AMERICAN ADOPTION ETHNOGRAPHY: METHOD, THEORY, AND EXPERIENCE

1. Oral History 22. Oral histories in this publication are drawn from ethnographic materials collected by the author. When an oral history contributor is quoted, he or she is cited by his or her oral history number in order to protect his or her anonymity. These numbers roughly correspond to the order in which each Korean American adoptee contributed his or her story.
2. Martin F. Manalansan IV, "Introduction," in *Cultural Compass: Ethnographic Explorations of Asian America*, ed. Martin F. Manalansan IV (Philadelphia: Temple University Press, 2000), 1–13.
3. Jeffery W. Burroughs and Paul Spickard, "Ethnicity, Multiplicity, and Narrative: Problems and Possibilities," in *We Are a People: Narrative and Multiplicity in Constructing Ethnic Identity*, ed. Jeffery W. Burroughs and Paul Spickard (Philadelphia: Temple University Press, 2000), 244–253.
4. France Winddance Twine and Jonathan W. Warren, *Racing Research, Researching Race: Methodological Dilemmas in Critical Race Studies* (New York: New York University Press, 2000).
5. Manalansan, "Introduction."
6. Gary Y. Okihiro, "Oral History and the Writing of Ethnic History," in *Oral History: An Interdisciplinary Anthology*, ed. David K. Dunaway and Willa K. Baum (Walnut Creek, CA: AltaMira Press, 1996), 199–214.
7. Ann Oakley, "Interviewing Women: A Contradiction in Terms," in *Doing Feminist Research*, ed. H. Roberts (London: Routledge, 1981), 30–61; Shulamit Reinharz, *Feminist Methods in Social Research* (New York: Oxford University Press, 1992).
8. Marjorie L. DeVault, *Liberating Method: Feminism and Social Research* (Philadelphia: Temple University Press, 1999). Peter Friedlander, "Theory, Method, and Oral History," in *Oral History*, ed. Dunaway and Baum, 150–159.
9. Elizabeth Lapovsky Kennedy and Madeline Davis, "Constructing an Ethnohistory of the Buffalo Lesbian Community: Reflexivity, Dialogue, and Politics," in *Out in the Field: Reflections of Lesbian and Gay Anthropologists*, ed. Ellen Lewin and William Leap (Urbana: University of Illinois Press, 1996).
10. Shulamit Reinharz, *On Becoming a Social Scientist: From Survey Research and Participant Observation to Experiential Analysis* (New Brunswick, NJ: Transaction Publishers, 1988). Devault, *Liberating Method*. Norman K. Denzin, *Performance Ethnography: Critical Pedagogy and the Politics of Culture* (Thousand Oaks, CA: Sage, 2003). Susan Krieger, *Social Science and the Self: Personal Essays on an Art Form* (New Brunswick, NJ: Rutgers University Press, 1991), and *The Mirror Dance* (Philadelphia: Temple University Press, 1983).
11. Kim V. L. England, "Getting Personal: Reflexivity, Positionality, and Feminist Research," *Professional Geographer* 46, no. 1 (1994): 80–89.
12. Oral History 7.
13. Jeannie, Hong, ed. *International Korean Adoptee Resource Book*. Seoul, South Korea: Overseas Korean Foundation, 2006.
14. Andrea Fontana and James H. Frey, "The Interview: From Structured Questions to Negotiated Text," in *Collecting and Interpreting Qualitative Materials*, ed. Norman K. Denzin and Yvonna S. Lincoln (Thousand Oaks, CA: Sage, 2003), 645–672.
15. Linda Tuhiwai Smith, *Decolonizing Methodologies: Research and Indigenous Peoples* (London: Zed Books, 1999).

16. Norma Williams, *The Mexican American Family: Tradition and Change* (Walnut Creek, CA: AltaMira Press, 1990). See also Marie Smyth, "Insider-Outsider Issues in Researching Violently Divided Societies," in *Researching Conflict in Africa: Insights and Experiences*, ed. Gillian Robinson, Elisabeth Porter, Marie Smyth, Albrecht Schnabel, and Eghosa Osaghae (Santiago, Chile: United Nations University Press, 2005).
17. This response is much in the tradition of feminist studies scholar Susan Krieger, who acknowledges the necessity of emotionally processing, in the context of her research in *Social Science and the Self*.
18. Shahnaz Khan, "Reconfiguring the Native Informant: Positionality in the Global Age," *Signs* 30, no. 4 (2005): 2017–2035.
19. Norman K. Denzin, "Introduction: The Discipline and Practice of Qualitative Research," in *Handbook of Qualitative Research*, 2nd ed., ed. Norman K. Denzin and Yvonna S. Lincoln (Thousand Oaks, CA: Sage, 2000).
20. Khan, "Reconfiguring the Native Informant," 2025.
21. Eleana Kim, "Remembering Loss: The Cultural Politics of Overseas Adoption from South Korea" (PhD diss., New York University, 2007). Eleana Kim, *Adopted Territory: Transnational Korean Adoptees and the Politics of Belonging* (Durham, NC: Duke University Press, 2010).

CHAPTER 2 "ELIGIBLE ALIEN ORPHAN": THE COLD WAR KOREAN ADOPTEE

1. Oral History 21.
2. Alexandra Young, "Developments in Intercountry Adoption: From Humanitarian Aid to Market-Driven Policy and Beyond," *Adoption & Fostering* 36, no. 2 (2012): 67–78.
3. From demographic sources compiled by Tobias Hübinette for 1948–1978 in "Comforting an Orphaned Nation: Representations of International Adoption and Adopted Koreans in Korean Popular Culture" (PhD diss., Stockholm University, 2005), and from Richard H. Weil, "International Adoption: The Quiet Migration," *International Migration Review* 18, no. 2 (1984): 276–293.
4. For an excellent essay on the contemporary connections between love and violence in transnational adoption contexts, see Kit Myers, "'Real' Families: The Violence and Love in New Media Adoption Discourse," *Critical Discourse Studies* 11, no. 2 (2014): 175–193.
5. Ramsey Liem, "History, Trauma, and Identity: The Legacy of the Korean War for Korean Americans," *Amerasia Journal* 29, no. 3 (2004): 111–129.
6. William Stueck, *Rethinking the Korean War: A New Diplomatic and Strategic History* (Princeton, NJ: Princeton University Press, 2004), 216.
7. Ibid.
8. Ibid.
9. Steven Casey, *Selling the Korean War: Propaganda, Politics, and Public Opinion in the United States, 1950–1953* (New York: Oxford University Press, 2008).
10. Eleana Kim, "The Origins of Korean Adoption: Cold War Geopolitics and Intimate Diplomacy" (Working Paper for the U.S.-Korea Institute at the Paul H. Nitze School of Advanced International Studies, Johns Hopkins University, WPS 09-9, October, 2009), 6. Available from http://uskoreainstitute.org/wp-content/uploads/2010/02/USKI_WP0909_KimAdoptee.pdf.
11. Ibid., 8, from *Los Angeles Times*, January 17, 1956.

12. Laura Briggs, *Somebody's Children: The Politics of Transracial and Transnational Adoption* (Durham, NC: Duke University Press, 2012).
13. Bruce Cumings, *Korea's Place in the Sun: A Modern History*, updated ed. (New York: W. W. Norton, 2005), 303.
14. Casey, *Selling the Korean War*.
15. Christina Klein, *Cold War Orientalism: Asia in the Middlebrow Imagination, 1945–1961* (Berkeley: University of California Press, 2003).
16. Robert J. Lentz, *Korean War Filmography: 91 English Language Features through 2000* (Jefferson, NC: McFarland & Company, 2008).
17. Samuel Fuller (director), *The Steel Helmet* (Lippert Pictures, 1951). Martin Goldsmith, Jesse Lasky Jr., Eugene King, and Richard Tregaskis (story), Fred F. Sears (director), *Mission Over Korea* (1953). Vincent B. Evans and Charles Grayson, Douglas Sirk (director), *Battle Hymn* (1958).Stanford Whitmore, Denis Sanders (director), *War Hunt* (1962).Lay Beirne Jr. and Rondald Davidson, Francis D. Lyon (director), *The Young and the Brave* (1963).Milton Mann, Han-chul Yu, and Kook-jin Jang, Manli Lee and Milton Mann (directors), *Marine Battleground* (1966).
18. Stueck, *Rethinking the Korean War*.
19. Arissa Oh, "From War Waif to Ideal Immigrant: The Cold War Transformation of the Korean Orphan," *Journal of American Ethnic History* 31, no. 4 (2012): 34–55.
20. Liem, "History, Trauma, and Identity," 114.
21. Ibid., 126.
22. Oh, "From War Waif to Ideal Immigrant."
23. Catherine Ceniza Choy, *Global Families: A History of Asian International Adoption in America* (New York: New York University Press, 2013).
24. Hübinette, "Comforting an Orphaned Nation."
25. The United States also sends a small number of mostly African American children for adoption, so therefore is the "sending" country with the highest GNP. For more information, see Dana Naughton, "Exiting or Going Forth? An Overview of USA Outgoing Adoptions," in *Intercountry Adoption: Policies, Practices, and Outcomes*, ed. Judith L. Gibbons and Karen Smith Rotabi (Farnham: Ashgate, 2012).
26. Population data for Korean adoptees compiled by Hübinette in "Comforting an Orphaned Nation," as follows: 1948–1978: Weil, "International Adoption: The Quiet Migration"; 1979–1988: Francisco Pilotti, "Intercountry Adoption: Trends, Issues, and Policy Implications for the 1990s," *Childhood* 1 (1993): 165–177; 1989–2002: U.S. Department of State, Immigrant visas issued to orphans coming to the U.S.; 2003–2006: U.S. Department of State, Immigrant visas issued to orphans coming to the U.S.
27. Hübinette, "Comforting an Orphaned Nation." Hübinette references the South Korean Ministry of Health and Welfare in his compilation of these numbers.
28. Oral History 31.
29. Oral History 28.
30. Ibid.
31. Oral History 29.
32. Oral History 23.
33. Oral History 21.
34. Oral History 12
35. International Social Service, American Branch Papers, Box 10, "Children-Independent Adoption Schemes, Holt, Harry, Vol. I 1955–1958." Minneapolis: University of Minnesota Social Welfare History Archives.

36. Rebecca Burditt, "Seeing Is Believing: 1950s Popular Media Representations of Korean Adoption in the United States," in *Proceedings of the First International Korean Adoption Studies Research Symposium*, ed. Kim Park Nelson, Eleana Kim, and Lene Myoung Peterson. Paper presented at the First International Korean Adoption Studies Research Symposium, Seoul, South Korea, July 31, 2007.
37. U.S. Citizenship and Immigration Services, "Legislation from 1941–1960."
38. For a discussion of this appeal, see Klein, *Cold War Orientalism*.
39. Oh, "From War Waif to Ideal Immigrant," 42.
40. The Adoption History Project, "Proxy Adoptions," last updated Feb. 24, 2012, available from http://pages.uoregon.edu/adoption/topics/proxy.htm.
41. Arnold Lyslo, "A Few Impressions on Meeting the Harry Holt Plane, the 'Flying Tiger,' Which Arrived in Portland, Oregon, December 27, 1958," American Branch Papers International Social Service, Box 10, Folder: "Children-Independent Adoption Schemes, Holt, Harry, vol. II 1958–1959." Minneapolis: University of Minnesota Social Welfare History Archives, 1958–1958.
42. International Social Service, American Branch Papers, Box 10, "Children—Independent Adoption Schemes, Holt, Harry, vol. I 1955–1958." Minneapolis: University of Minnesota Social Welfare History Archives.
43. International Social Service, American Branch Papers, Box 10, Folder: "Proxy Adoptions." Minneapolis: University of Minnesota Social Welfare History Archives.
44. Oral History 21.
45. The need and use of special legislation is also documented by Choy in *Global Families*.
46. Oral History 10.
47. Ibid.
48. Oral History 12.
49. Oral History 41.
50. See also a discussion of the term "alien" used in self-reference among Korean adoptees, in Eleana Kim, *Adopted Territory: Transnational Korean Adoptees and the Politics of Belonging* (Durham, NC: Duke University Press, 2010).
51. Jodi Kim, *Ends of Empire: Asian American Critique and the Cold War* (Minneapolis: University of Minnesota Press, 2010).
52. Ibid.
53. Oral History 27.
54. Burditt, "Seeing Is Believing."
55. Kim, *Adopted Territory*.
56. Ibid., 64.
57. Ibid.
58. Oral History 10.
59. Oral History 24.
60. Oral History 26.
61. Oral History 24.
62. Oral History 28.
63. Oral History 21.
64. Oral History 25.
65. Oral History 55.
66. Oral History 25.
67. Oral History 12.
68. Oral History 29.

69. Sarah Potter, *Everybody Else: Adoption and the Politics of Domestic Diversity in Postwar America* (Athens: University of Georgia Press, 2014).
70. Oral History 22.
71. Oral History 28.
72. Oral History 41.
73. Oral History 28.
74. Oral History 28.
75. Oral History 25.
76. Oral History 28.
77. Oral History 25.
78. Oral History 22.
79. For a more in-depth discussion of these racial politics of Korean American adoption, see chapter 5, "'White' Koreans: Korean Adoptees, Racial Visibility, and the Politics of Passing."

CHAPTER 3 ADOPTION RESEARCH DISCOURSE AND THE RISE OF TRANSNATIONAL ADOPTION, 1974–1987

1. Rita J. Simon and Howard Altstein, *Adoption, Race, and Identity: From Infancy to Young Adulthood*, 2nd ed. (New Brunswick, NJ: Transaction Publishers, 2002).
2. "Children-Independent Adoption Schemes, Holt, Harry, Vol. I 1955–1958," International Social Service, American Branch Papers, Box 10, Social Welfare History Archives, Anderson Library, University of Minnesota, Minneapolis, Minnesota.
3. For an excellent meta-analytical summary of 270 international, empirical studies on transnational adoption, see Femmie Juffer and Marinus H. van Ijzendoorn, "Review of Meta-Analytical Studies on the Physical, Emotional, and Cognitive Outcomes of Intercountry Adoptees," in *Intercountry Adoption: Policies, Practices, and Outcomes*, ed. Judith Gibbons and Karen Smith Rotabi (Burlington, VT: Ashgate Publishing, 2012), 175–186.
4. Patricia Fronek and Denise Cuthbert, "The Future of Inter-Country Adoption: A Paradigm Shift for this Century," *International Journal of Social Welfare* 21 (2012): 215–224.
5. Jonathan Dickens, "Social Policy Approaches and Social Work Dilemmas in Intercountry Adoption," in *Intercountry Adoption*, ed. Gibbons and Rotabi, 43–54.
6. Jesús Palacios and David Brodzinsky, "Adoption Research: Trends, Topics, Outcomes," *International Journal of Behavioral Development* 34:3 (2010): 270–284.
7. Rita J. Simon and Howard Altstein, *Transracial Adoption* (New York: Wiley, 1977).
8. Ibid.
9. Rita J. Simon and Howard Altstein, *Transracial Adoptees and Their Families: A Study of Identity and Commitment* (New York: Praeger, 1987), 85.
10. Ibid.
11. Rita J. Simon, "Adoption of Black Children by White Parents in the USA," in *Adoption: Essays in Social Policy, Law, and Sociology*, ed. P. Bean (New York: Tavistock Publications, 1984), 229–242.
12. Ibid.
13. Charles Zastrow, *Outcome of Black Children–White Parents Transracial Adoptions* (Palo Alto, CA: R&E Research Associates, Inc., 1977).
14. Ibid.
15. Lela B. Costin and Shirley H. Wattenberg, "Identity in Transracial Adoption: A Study of Parental Dilemmas and Family Experiences," in *Race, Education, and Identity*, ed. Gajendra K. Verma and Christopher Bagley (New York: St. Martin's Press, 1979), 220–235.

16. Simon and Altstein, *Transracial Adoptees and Their Families*, 112.
17. Palacios and Brodzinsky, "Adoption Research."
18. Lucille Grow and Deborah Shapiro, *Black Children, White Parents: A Study of Transracial Adoption*, (Washington, DC: Child Welfare League of America Press, 1974), 233.
19. William Feigelman and Arnold R. Silverman, "The Long-Term Effects of Transracial Adoption," *Social Service Review* 58:4 (1984): 588–602.
20. Mark Jerng, *Claiming Others: Transracial Adoption and National Belonging* (Minneapolis: University of Minnesota Press, 2010), xxxiv.
21. Simon and Altstein, *Transracial Adoption*, 4.
22. Ibid., 98.
23. Ibid.
24. For a deeper discussion of the phenomenon of racial colorblindness as a strategy to remove race, see chapter 4.
25. Simon and Altstein, *Transracial Adoptees and Their Families*.
26. Dong Soo Kim, "Issues in Transracial and Transcultural Adoption," *Social Casework* 59:8 (1978): 477–486.
27. Ibid.
28. Kristi Brian, *Reframing Transnational Adoption: Adopted Koreans, White Parents, and the Politics of Kinship* (Philadelphia: Temple University Press, 2012).
29. Barbara Yngvesson, *Belonging in an Adopted World: Race Identity and Transnational Adoption* (Chicago: University of Chicago Press, 2010), 28.
30. S. P. Kim, S. Hong, and B. S. Kim, "Adoption of Korean Children by New York Area Couples: A Preliminary Study," *Child Welfare United States* 58:7 (1979): 419–428.
31. Rita J. Simon and Howard Altstein, *Transracial Adoption: A Follow-Up* (Lexington, MA: Lexington Books, D. C. Heath and Company, 1981).
32. Simon and Altstein, *Transracial Adoptees and Their Families*.
33. Owen Gill and Barbara Jackson, *Adoption and Race: Black, Asian, and Mixed Race Children in White Families* (New York: St. Martin's Press, 1983), 132.
34. Simon and Altstein, *Transracial Adoption*.
35. Ibid.
36. Ibid.
37. Ibid.
38. J. F. Shireman and P. R. Johnson, "A Longitudinal Study of Black Adoptions: Single Parent, Transracial, and Traditional," *Social Work* 31:3 (1986): 172–176.
39. Ibid.
40. Ibid.
41. Ruth G. McRoy and Louis A. Zurcher Jr., *Transracial and Inracial Adoptees: The Adolescent Years* (Springfield, IL: Charles C. Thomas, 1983), 16.
42. Ibid., 37.
43. Ibid., 139.
44. Ibid.
45. Ibid., 116.
46. Ibid., 136.
47. Simon and Altstein, *Transracial Adoption*.
48. Ibid., 49.
49. Ibid.
50. Implementation of the Interethnic Adoption Amendments Hearing before the Subcommittee on Human Resources of the Committee on Ways and Means, Sept. 15, 1998,

H.R. doc 105–111, 105th Cong. 1998 (Statement of Rita J. Simon). http://www.gpo.gov/fdsys/pkg/CHRG-105hhrg63768/html/CHRG-105hhrg63768.htm.

51. See Sara Dorow, *Transnational Adoption: A Cultural Economy of Race, Gender, and Kinship* (New York: New York University Press, 2006); Madeline H. Engel, Norma Kolko Phillips, and Frances A. DellaCava, "Cultural Differences and Adoption Policy in the United States: The Quest for Social Justice for Children," *International Journal of Children's Rights* 18 (2010): 291–308; Ravinder Barn, "'Doing the Right Thing': Transracial Adoption in the USA," *Ethnic and Racial Studies* 36:8 (2013): 1273–1291; Josie Crolley-Simic and M. Elizabeth Vonk, "White International Transracial Adoptive Mothers' Reflections on Race," *Child & Family Social Work* 2011:16 (2010): 169–178; Josie Crolley-Simic and M. Elizabeth Vonk, "Race and White Transracially Adoptive Mothers," *Journal of Ethnic and Cultural Diversity in Social Work* 21:4 (2012): 297–313; Miriam Klevan, "Resolving Race: How Adoptive Parents Discuss Choosing the Race of Their Child," *Adoption Quarterly* 15 (2012): 88–115.

52. Catherine Ceniza Choy, *Global Families: A History of Asian International Adoption in America* (New York: New York University Press, 2013).

CHAPTER 4   AN ADOPTEE FOR EVERY LAKE: MULTICULTURALISM, MINNESOTA, AND THE KOREAN TRANSRACIAL ADOPTEE

1. Oral History 45.
2. Tobias Hübinette, "Korean Adoption History," in *Guide to Korea for Overseas Adopted Koreans*, ed. E. Kim (Seoul: Overseas Koreans Foundation, 2004). "Transracial Adoptions," The Adoption History Project, last modified Feb. 24, 2012, http://pages.uoregon.edu/adoption/topics/transracialadoption.htm. "Indian Adoption Project," The Adoption History Project, last modified Feb. 24, 2012, http://pages.uoregon.edu/adoption/topics/IAP.html.
3. Rita J. Simon and Howard Altstein, *Adoption across Borders: Serving the Children in Transracial and Intercountry Adoptions* (Lanham, MD: Rowman & Littlefield, 2000).
4. Ibid.
5. Peter Selman, "The Global Decline of Intercountry Adoption: What Lies Ahead?" *Social Policy and Society* 11:3 (2012): 381–397.
6. Simon and Altstein, *Adoption across Borders*.
7. Richard H. Weil, "International Adoption: The Quiet Migration," *International Migration Review* 18:2 (1984): 276–293.
8. Simon and Altstein, *Adoption across Borders*.
9. Francisco Pilotti, "Intercountry Adoption: Trends, Issues, and Policy Implications for the 1990s," *Childhood* 1 (1993): 165–177.
10. Simon and Altstein, *Adoption across Borders*.
11. Constance Pohl and Kathy Harris, *Transracial Adoption: Children and Parents Speak* (New York: Franklin Watts, 1992).
12. Elaine Tyler May, *Barren in the Promised Land: Childless Americans and the Pursuit of Happiness* (Cambridge, MA: Harvard University Press, 1995).
13. Pohl and Harris, *Transracial Adoption*.
14. Ruth G. McRoy, "Attachment and Racial Identity Issues: Implications for Child Placement Decision Making," *Journal of Multicultural Social Work* 3:3 (1994): 59–74.
15. Simon and Altstein, *Transracial Adoption*, 34.
16. Dorothy Roberts, *Shattered Bonds: The Color of Child Welfare* (New York: Basic Civitas Books, 2002).

17. Here, both medical and social "advances" that enable parenting for infertile couples or individuals are understood as technologies, including both medical procedures and social changes. Through these technologies, cultural expectations of parenting in Western countries have transformed into rights, in that many adults now understand parenting to be an option even if they are unable or unwilling to conceive without medical or legal procedures.
18. Pamela Anne Quiroz, *Adoption in a Color-Blind Society* (Perspectives on a Multiracial America) (Lanham, MD: Rowman & Littlefield, 2007).
19. National Association of Black Social Workers, "Preserving Families of African Ancestry," Position Paper (1972), http://c.ymcdn.com/sites/nabsw.org/resource/collection/0D2D2404-77EB-49B5-962E-7E6FADBF3D0D/Preserving_Families_of_African_Ancestry.pdf.
20. Roberts, *Shattered Bonds*, 246.
21. Charles E. Jones and John F. Else, "Racial and Cultural Issues in Adoption," *Child Welfare* 58:6 (1979): 374.
22. E. Wayne Carp, "Introduction: A Historical Overview of American Adoption," *Adoption in America: Historical Perspectives*, ed. E. Wayne Carp (Ann Arbor: University of Michigan Press, 2004).
23. Jones and Else, "Racial and Cultural Issues in Adoption," 373–382.
24. Sara Dorow, *Transnational Adoption: A Cultural Economy of Race, Gender, and Kinship* (New York: New York University Press, 2006).
25. Asian American population in the United States was less than 1 percent in the 1970 census, and less than 0.5 percent in 1960. "Table 8, Race and Hispanic Origin of the Population by Nativity: 1850 to 1990, Historical Census, Statistics on the Foreign-Born Population of the Unites States: 1850 to 1990," U.S. Bureau of the Census.
26. Heather Jacobson, *Culture Keeping: White Mothers, International Adoption, and the Negotiation of Family Difference* (Nashville: Vanderbilt University Press, 2008).
27. There are some very limited exceptions; for example, one of the Korean/Korean American churches in Minnesota has taken an active role in reaching out to local Korean adoptees.
28. Carp, "Introduction: A Historical Overview of American Adoption."
29. Ibid., 20.
30. E. Wayne Carp, *Family Matters: Secrecy and Disclosure in the History of Adoption* (Cambridge, MA: Harvard University Press, 2000).
31. Jacobson, *Culture Keeping*.
32. David M. Smolin, "Child Laundering: How the Intercountry Adoption System Legitimizes and Incentivizes the Practices of Buying, Trafficking, Kidnapping, and Stealing Children," *Wayne Law Review* 52:1 (2006): 113–200.
33. Roberts, *Shattered Bonds*.
34. Ana Teresa and Ortiz Laura Briggs, "The Culture of Poverty, Crack Babies, and Welfare Cheats: The Making of the 'Healthy White Baby Crisis,'" *Social Text*, no. 3 (2003): 39–57.
35. Weil, "International Adoption," and Pilotti, "Intercountry Adoption."
36. David Oh and Omotayo Banjo, "Outsourcing Postracialism: Voicing Neoliberal Multiculturalism in *Outsourced*," *Communication Theory* 22 (2012): 449–470.
37. Christian Joppke and Steven Lukes, "Introduction: Multicultural Questions," in *Multicultural Questions*, ed. Christian Joppke and Steven Lukes (New York: Oxford University Press, 1999). Christopher Newfield and Avery F. Gordon, "Multiculturalism's Unfinished Business," in *Mapping Multiculturalism*, ed. Avery F. Gordon and Christopher Newfield (Minneapolis: University of Minnesota Press, 1996), 76–124.

38. Wen Jin, *Pluralist Universalism: An Asian Americanist Critique of U.S. and Chinese Multiculturalisms* (Columbus: Ohio State University Press, 2012).
39. Newfield and Gordon. "Multiculturalism's Unfinished Business."
40. Joppke and Lukes, "Multicultural Questions."
41. David R. Roediger, *How Race Survived US History: From the American Revolution to the Present* (New York: Verso, 2008).
42. Ayelet Shachar, "The Paradox of Multicultural Vulnerability: Individual Rights, Individual Groups, and the State," in *Multicultural Questions*, ed. Christian Joppke and Steven Lukes (New York: Oxford University Press, 1999).
43. Jin, *Pluralist Universalism*.
44. Newfield and Gordon, "Multiculturalism's Unfinished Business," 80–81.
45. John Willinsky, "What Was Multiculturalism?" in *Precarious International Multicultural Education Hegemony, Dissent, and Rising Alternatives*, ed. Handel Kashope Wright (Rotterdam: Sense Publishers, 2012), 15–39. Indeed, recent research has revealed that Whites tend to be disinvested in the promotion of diversity unless they see themselves as its major beneficiaries. See also Victoria Plaut, Flannery Garnett, Laura Buffardi, and Jeffery Sanchez-Burks, "'What About Me?' Perceptions of Exclusion and Whites' Reactions to Multiculturalism," *Journal of Personality and Social Psychology* 10:2 (2011): 337–353.
46. Olaf Kaltmeier, Josel Raab, and Sebastian Thies, "Multiculturalism and Beyond: The New Dynamics of Identity Politics in the Americas," *Latin American and Caribbean Ethnic Studies* 7:2 (2012): 103–104.
47. Kristi Brian, *Reframing Transnational Adoption: Adopted Koreans, White Parents, and the Politics of Kinship* (Philadelphia: Temple University Press, 2012).
48. Ibid.
49. Jacobson, *Culture Keeping*.
50. Barbara Yngvesson, *Belonging in an Adopted World: Race Identity and Transnational Adoption* (Chicago: University of Chicago Press, 2010), 100.
51. Oh Myo Kim, Reed Reichwald, and Richard Lee, "Cultural Socialization in Families with Adopted Adolescents: A Mixed Method, Multi-Informant Study," *Journal of Adolescent Research* 28:1 (2013): 69–95.
52. John E. Brandl, "Policy and Politics in Minnesota," *Daedalus: Journal of the American Academy of Arts and Sciences* 129:3 (2000): 191–220.
53. Ibid.
54. Michael O'Keefe, "Social Services: Minnesota as Innovator," *Daedalus: Journal of the American Academy of Arts and Sciences* 129:3 (2000): 247–267.
55. Ibid.
56. Personal communication, Lynne Haggar, Post-Adoption Services Coordinator, Lutheran Social Services, October 10, 2008.
57. The orphan train project operated between 1854 and 1929 under the belief that impoverished urban children (many of them Catholic and Jewish) would fare better in Midwestern rural settings; the orphan trains were filled with children traveling west to be raised on Protestant farms in the Midwest. Some were embraced as members of families, others essentially became child farm laborers.
58. Eleana Kim, *Adopted Territory: Transnational Korean Adoptees and the Politics of Belonging* (Durham, NC: Duke University Press, 2010).
59. Oral History 8.
60. Ibid.
61. Oral History 4.
62. Oral History 8.

63. Oral History 7.
64. Oral History 15.
65. Oral History 32.
66. Oral History 47.
67. Oral History 37.
68. Oral History 57.
69. Oral History 3.
70. Oral History 4.
71. Mia Tuan, *Forever Foreigners or Honorary Whites? The Asian Ethnic Experience Today* (New Brunswick, NJ: Rutgers University Press, 1998).
72. Oral History 32.
73. Oral History 6.
74. Experiences of racism among Korean American adoptees are also commonly reported in the sociological research of Tuan and Shiao; see Mia Tuan and Jiannbin Lee Shiao, *Choosing Ethnicity, Negotiating Race: Korean Adoptees in America* (New York: Russell Sage Foundation, 2011).
75. Brian, *Reframing Transnational Adoption*, 72.
76. Oral History 38.
77. Oral History 3.
78. Brian documents similar findings in *Reframing Transracial Adoption*.
79. Oral History 8.
80. Oral History 7.
81. Oral History 7.
82. Oral History 4.
83. Sara Docan-Morgan, "'They Don't Know What It Is Like to Be in My Shoes': Topic Avoidance about Race in Transracially Adoptive Families," *Journal of Social and Personal Relationships* 28:3 (2010): 336–355.
84. Oral History 37.
85. Oral History 15.
86. Oral History 32.
87. Oral History 6.
88. Oral History 15.
89. Oral History 47.
90. Oral History 4.
91. Oral History 57.
92. Oral History 54.
93. Oh and Banjo, "Outsourcing Postracialism," 453.

CHAPTER 5 ADOPTEES AS WHITE KOREANS: IDENTITY, RACIAL VISIBILITY, AND THE POLITICS OF PASSING AMONG KOREAN AMERICAN ADOPTEES

1. Oral History 12.
2. Daniel Bernardi, "Introduction: Race and the Hollywood Style," in *Classic Hollywood, Classic Whiteness*, ed. Daniel Bernardi (Minneapolis: University of Minnesota Press, 2001), xiii–xiii.
3. Miri Song, *Choosing Ethnic Identity* (Malden, MA: Polity Press, 2003).
4. James Weldon Johnson, *The Autobiography of an Ex-Colored Man* (Boston: Sherman French & Company, 1912).

5. Song, *Choosing Ethnic Identity*.
6. Neil Gotanda, "Multiculturalism and Racial Stratification," in *Mapping Multiculturalism*, ed. Avery F. Gordon and Christopher Newfield (Minneapolis: University of Minnesota Press, 1996), 238–252.
7. Christopher Newfield and Avery F. Gordon, "Multiculturalism's Unfinished Business," in *Mapping Multiculturalism*, ed. Gordon and Newfield, 76–124. Pamela Anne Quiroz, *Adoption in a Color-Blind Society* (Perspectives on a Multiracial America) (Lanham, MD: Rowman & Littlefield, 2007).
8. Quiroz, *Adoption in a Color-Blind Society*.
9. Eduardo Silva, *Racism Without Racists: Color-blind Racism and the Persistence of Racial Inequality in America*, 3rd ed. (Plymouth, UK: Rowman & Littlefield, 2014), 3.
10. Paul Gilroy, *Against Race: Imagining Political Culture beyond the Color Line* (Cambridge, MA: Belknap Press of Harvard University Press, 2000). Antonia Darder and Rodolfo D. Torres, *After Race: Racism after Multiculturalism* (New York: New York University Press, 2004).
11. Min Zhou and Jennifer Lee, "Introduction: The Making of Culture, Identity, and Ethnicity among Asian American Youth," in *Asian American Youth: Culture, Identity, and Ethnicity*, ed. Jennifer Lee and Min Zhou (New York: Routledge, 2004), 1–32.
12. C. M. Steele and J. Aronson, "Stereotype Threat and the Intellectual Test Performance of African Americans," *Journal of Personality and Social Psychology* 69:5 (1995): 797–811.
13. Quiroz, *Adoption in a Color-Blind Society*.
14. Dale Hudson, "Vampires of Color and the Performance of Multicultural Whiteness," in *The Persistence of Whiteness*, ed. Daniel Bernardi (New York: Routledge, 2007), 127–156.
15. Michael Omi and Howard Winant, *Racial Formation in the United States: From the 1960s to the 1980s, Critical Social Thought* (New York: Routledge & Kegan Paul, 1986).
16. Vincent J. Cheng, *Inauthentic: The Anxiety over Culture and Identity* (New Brunswick, NJ: Rutgers University Press, 2004), 27.
17. Mary C. Waters, *Ethnic Options: Choosing Identities in America* (Berkeley: University of California Press, 1990).
18. Ibid.
19. Song, *Choosing Ethnic Identity*, 1, 22.
20. Mia Tuan, *Forever Foreigners or Honorary Whites? The Asian Ethnic Experience Today* (New Brunswick, NJ: Rutgers University Press, 1998).
21. Mario Rios Perez and Sharon S. Lee, "Balancing Two Worlds: Asian American and Latina/o College Students' Life Stories," *Journal of American Ethnic History* 27:4 (2008): 107–113.
22. Matthew Frye Jacobson, *Whiteness of a Different Color: European Immigrants and the Alchemy of Race* (Cambridge, MA: Harvard University Press, 2008). James W. Loewen, *The Mississippi Chinese: Between Black and White* (Cambridge, MA: Harvard University Press, 1971). Aiwha Ong, *Flexible Citizenship: The Cultural Logics of Transnationality* (Durham, NC: Duke University Press, 1999) and *Buddha Is Hiding: Refugees, Citizenship, and the New America* (Berkeley: University of California Press, 2003).
23. Guofang Li and Lihshing Wang, "Introduction: The Old Myth in a New Time," in *Model Minority Myth Revisited: An Interdisciplinary Approach to Demystifying Asian American Educational Experiences* ed. Guofang Li and Lishing Wang (Greenwich, CT: Information Age Publishing, 2008).
24. Many Korean adoptees were not actually orphans because they had living parents at the time of relinquishment, but were designated as orphaned in order to comply with legal requirements of transnational adoption.

25. Ong, *Buddha Is Hiding*, 145.
26. Kit Myers, "'Real' Families: The Violence and Love in New Media Adoption Discourse," *Critical Discourse Studies* 11:2 (2014): 175–193.
27. Tuan, *Forever Foreigners*.
28. Min Zhou, "Are Asian Americans Becoming 'White'?" *Contexts* 3:1 (2004): 29–37.
29. Donna Jean Akiye Kato Ida, "Depression, Hopelessness, and Suicide Ideation among Asian-American Students" (PhD diss., University of Colorado at Boulder, 1989).
30. "United States Demographic and Housing Estimates: 2007," U.S. Census Bureau.
31. Dina C. Maramba, "Understanding Campus Climate through the Voices of Filipina/o American College Students," *College Student Journal*, 2008, available from http://findarticles.com/p/articles/mi_m0FCR/is_4_42/ai_n30911941/.
32. Perez and Lee, "College Students' Life Stories."
33. Khatharya Um, "A Dream Denied: Educational Experiences of Southeast Asian American Youth Issues and Recommendations, an Issue Paper Based on Findings from the First National Southeast Asian Youth Summit, University of California–Berkeley, December 9, 2000." Southeast Asia Resource Action Center, 2000, available from http://www.searac.org/ydfinal-2_03.pdf.
34. Perhaps this is another example of the "forever foreigner" stereotype through the misidentification of all Asian Americans as Asian nationals.
35. Institute of Education Sciences National Center for Education Statistics, "Employees in Degree-Granting Institutions, by Race/Ethnicity, Sex, Employment Status, Control and Type of Institution, and Primary Occupation: Fall 2007."
36. William Wei, *The Asian American Movement* (Philadelphia: Temple University Press, 1993).
37. Eugenia Escueta and Eileen O'Brien, "Asian Americans in Higher Education: Trends and Issues," in *The Asian American Educational Experience: A Sourcebook for Teachers and Students*, ed. Don T. Nakanishi and Tina Yamano Nishida (New York: Routledge: 1995), 259–272.
38. Institute of Education Sciences 2007.
39. Ibid.
40. Tuan, *Forever Foreigners*, 161.
41. Heather Jacobson, *Culture Keeping: White Mothers, International Adoption, and the Negotiation of Family Difference* (Nashville: Vanderbilt University Press, 2008).
42. Richard C. Tessler, Gail Gamache, and Liming Liu, *West Meets East: Americans Adopt Chinese Children* (Westport, CT: Bergin & Garvey, 1999), 20.
43. Sara Dorow, *Transnational Adoption: A Cultural Economy of Race, Gender, and Kinship* (New York: New York University Press, 2006); Jacobson, *Culture Keeping*; Kristi Brian, *Reframing Transnational Adoption: Adopted Koreans, White Parents, and the Politics of Kinship* (Philadelphia: Temple University Press, 2012).
44. "The Asian Population: 2010. 2010 Census Briefs." Bureau of the Census. March 2012. http://www.census.gov/prod/cen2010/briefs/c2010br-11.pdf
45. Zhou, "Are Asian Americans Becoming 'White'?"
46. Oh Myo Kim, Reed Reichwald, and Richard Lee, "Cultural Socialization in Families with Adopted Adolescents: A Mixed-Method, Multi-Informant Study," *Journal of Adolescent Research* 28:1 (2013): 69–95.
47. Henry Yu, *Thinking Orientals* (New York: Oxford University Press, 2002), 101, 109.
48. This is debatable in her example, since a number of her subjects were living with their non-White mothers.
49. France Winddance Twine, "Brown-Skinned White Girls," in *Displacing Whiteness: Essays in Social and Cultural Criticism*, ed. Ruth Frankenburg (Durham, NC: Duke University Press, 1997), 214–243.

50. Phrase borrowed from Twine, "Brown-Skinned White Girls," 218.
51. Hawley Fogg-Davis, *The Ethics of Transracial Adoption*,(Ithaca, NY: Cornell University Press, 2002).
52. Twila L. Perry, "The Transracial Adoption Controversy: An Analysis of Discourse and Subordination," *New York University Review of Law & Social Change*, 21:1 (1993–1994): 33–108.
53. Quiroz, *Adoption in a Color-Blind Society* and Jacobson, *Culture Keeping*.
54. Song, *Choosing Ethnic Identity*, 18. Song discusses the politically correct tendency to emphasize culture over race in contemporary British society, and I would argue that the substitution of culture for race operates similarly in American society.
55. Interestingly, the practice of colorblindness can also be individuated within adoptive families; in *Choosing Ethnicity, Negotiating Race*, Tuan and Shiao document White adoptive families who judge their Korean adopted children not to have color, while asserting highly racialized attitudes toward people of color outside the family.
56. Dorow, *Transnational Adoption*, 181.
57. Brian, *Reframing Transnational Adoption*.
58. Cheng, *Inauthentic*, 70.
59. Laura Briggs, "Making 'American' Families: Transracial Adoption and U.S. Latin America Policy," in *Haunted by Empire*, ed. Laura Ann Stoler (Durham, NC: Duke University Press, 2006), 606–645. Briggs describes the inheritance of adoptive parents' cultures by their adopted children.
60. Maria Root, "Rethinking Racial Identity Development," in *We Are a People: Narrative and Multiplicity in Constructing Ethnic Identity*, ed. Jeffery W. Burroughs and Paul Spickard (Philadelphia: Temple University Press, 2000), 205–20. Root advocates for this type of complicated and layered multiplicity for mixed-race individuals.
61. Jiannbin Lee Shiao and Mia Tuan, "'Some Asian Men are Attractive to Me, But for a Husband . . .' Korean Adoptees and the Salience of Race in Romance," *DuBois Review* 5:2 (2008): 259–285. Shiao and Tuan write extensively about race preferences in dating among Korean adoptees and the significance of adoptee choices of "natural partners."
62. Oral History 37.
63. Oral History 38.
64. Oral History 40.
65. Oral History 36.
66. Oral History 7.
67. Twine, "Brown-Skinned White Girls."
68. Richard Lee, Hyung Chol Yoo, and Sara Evans, "Coming of Age of Korean Adoptees: Ethnic Identity Development and Psychological Adjustment," in *Korean-Americans: Past, Present, and Future*, ed. Ilpyong J. Kim (Hollym International Corp., 2004), 203–224.
69. Oral History 11.
70. Ibid.
71. Richard M. Lee, "The Transracial Adoption Paradox: History, Research, and Counseling Implications of Cultural Socialization," *The Counseling Psychologist* 31:6 (2003): 711–744.
72. Oral History 4.
73. Sara Docan-Morgan, "Korean Adoptees' Retrospective Reports of Intrusive Interactions: Exploring Boundary Management in Adoptive Families," *Journal of Family Communications* 10 (2010): 137–157.
74. Christopher Bagley and Loretta Young. "The Identity, Adjustment and Achievement of Transracially Adopted Children: A Report and Empirical Report," in *Race, Education,*

and Identity, ed. Gajendra K. Verma and Christopher Bagley (New York: St. Martin's Press, 1979), 192–219. William Feigelman,"Adjustments of Transracially and Inracially Adopted Young Adults," *Child and Adolescent Social Work Journal* 17:3 (2000): 165–183. Madelyn Freundlich and Joy Kim Lieberthal, "The Gathering of the First Generation of Adult Korean Adoptees: Adoptees' Perceptions of International Adoption" (Adoption Institute, 2000), paper published online, available from http://www.adoptioninstitute.org/proed/korfindings.html. Leslie D. Hollingsworth, "Effect of Transracial/Transethnic Adoption on Children's Racial and Ethnic Identity and Self-Esteem: A Meta-Analytic Review," *Marriage & Family Review* 25:1–2 (1997): 99–130. H. J. M. Versluis-den Bieman and F. C. Verhulst, "Self-Reported and Parent Reported Problems in Adolescent International Adoptees," *Journal of Child Psychology & Psychiatry & Allied Disciplines* 36:8 (1995): 1411–1428.
75. Oral History 7.
76. Oral History 39.
77. Oral History 59.
78. Grace Kim, Karen L. Suyemoto, and Castellano B. Turner, "Sense of Belonging, Sense of Exclusion, and Racial Ethnic Identities in Korean Transracial Adoptees," *Cultural Diversity and Ethnic Minority Psychology* 16:2 (2010): 179–190.
79. Jiannbin Shiao and Mia Tuan, "A Sociological Approach to Race, Identity, and Asian Adoption," in *International Korean Adoption: A Fifty-Year History of Policy and Practice*, ed. M. Elizabeth Vonk, Kathleen Bergquist, Dong Soo Kim, and Marvin Feit (New York: Routledge, 2007), 155–170.
80. Dani I. Meier, "Loss and Reclaimed Lives: Cultural Identity and Place in Korean-American Intercountry Adoptees" (PhD diss., University of Minnesota, 1998).
81. Oral History 28.
82. Oral History 7.
83. Oral History 38.
84. Root, "Rethinking Racial Identity Development."
85. Cookie White Stephan and Walter G. Stephan, "What Are the Functions of Ethnic Identity?" in *We Are a People: Narrative and Multiplicity in Constructing Ethnic Identity*, ed. Jeffery W. Burroughs and Paul Spickard (Philadelphia: Temple University Press, 2000) 229–243.
86. Joy Hoffman and Edlun Vallejo Peña, "Too Korean to be White and Too White to Be Korean: Ethnic Identity Development among Transracial Korean Adoptees," *Journal of Student Affairs Research and Practice* 50:2 (2013): 152–170.
87. Oral History 8.
88. Oral History 11.
89. Ibid.
90. This strategy is also described as "practical identification" by Song in *Choosing Ethnic Identity*, though she claims this as a position between dominant culture and one's own community, suggesting this is a position of ambiguity between "real" and "convenient" identities.
91. Song, *Choosing Ethnic Identity*.
92. Lee, "The Transracial Adoption Paradox."
93. Adam Pertman, *Adoption Nation: How the Adoption Revolution Is Transforming America* (New York: Basic Books, 2000).
94. Omi and Winant, *Racial Formation in the United States*, 60.
95. Janis L. McDonald, "Looking in the Honest Mirror of Privilege: 'Polite White' Reflections." *Columbia Journal of Gender and Law* 12:3 (2003): 650–659.

96. Oral History 3.
97. Oral History 11.
98. Oral History 47.
99. Jenny Johnson, "Adoption in Korea." Distribution list e-mail message, 10 August 2006.
100. Kristi Brian also documents the disciplining of Korean adoptees by American adoption agencies to support the practice of Korean adoption in *Reframing Transnational Adoption*.
101. Twila Perry articulates a similar critique, focusing on the transfer from a devalued mother to a valued mother, and how children who experience this transfer are considered by society at large to be lucky, in "Transracial and International Adoption: Mothers, Hierarchy, and Feminist Legal Theory," *Yale Journal of Law and Feminism* 10 (1998): 101–164.

CHAPTER 6 *URI NARA*, OUR COUNTRY: KOREAN AMERICAN ADOPTEES IN THE GLOBAL AGE

1. Oral History 38.
2. Nina Glick Schiller, "Transmigrants and Nation-States: Something Old and Something New in U.S. Immigrant Experience," in *Handbook of International Migration: The American Experience*, ed. Josh DeWind, C. Hirschman, and P. Kasinitz (New York: Russell Sage, 1999), 94–119, quoted in Erika Lee and Naoko Shibusawa, "Guest Editors' Introduction: What Is Transnational Asian American Studies? Recent Trends and Challenges," *Journal of Asian American Studies* 8:3 (2005): vii–xvii.
3. Linda G. Basch, Nina Glick Schiller, and Cristina Blanc-Szanton, *Nations Unbound: Transnational Projects, Postcolonial Predicaments, and Deterritorialized Nation-States*, 4th ed. (New York: Gordon and Breach, 1998).
4. Wanni W. Anderson and Robert G. Lee, "Asian American Displacements," in *Displacements and Diasporas: Asians in the Americas*, ed. Wanni W. Anderson and Robert G. Lee (New Brunswick, NJ: Rutgers University Press, 2005).
5. Inderpal Grewal, *Transnational America: Feminisms, Diasporas, Neoliberalisms* (Durham, NC: Duke University Press, 2005).
6. Ibid., 7.
7. The South Korean adoptee support organization Global Overseas Adoptees' Link estimates the resident population of Korean adoptee returnees to number between two hundred and three hundred.
8. Peter Selman, "The Global Decline of Intercountry Adoption: What Lies Ahead?" *Social Policy and Society* 11:3 (2012): 381–397.
9. Jeannie Hong, *International Korean Adoptee Resource Book* (Seoul: Overseas Koreans Foundation, 2006).
10. Tobias Hübinette, "Comforting an Orphaned Nation: Representations of International Adoption and Adopted Koreans in Korean Popular Culture" (PhD diss., Stockholm University, 2005). David Kim, as cited in Elise Prébin's book *Meeting Once More: The Korean Side of Transnational Adoption* (New York: New York University Press, 2013), claims Holt began homeland tours in 1983.
11. Dani Meier discusses his encounters with Korean adoptees with similar responses to Korea as a place in his dissertation, "Loss and Reclaimed Lives: Cultural Identity and Place in Korean American Intercountry Adoptees" (PhD diss., University of Minnesota, 1998).
12. Oral History 6.
13. Oral History 29.

14. A sense of "homelessness" among Korean adoptees is also documented by Dani Meier in "Loss and Reclaimed Lives."
15. Hong, *International Korean Adoptee Resource Book*. This information is based on the search statistics of each agency that participated in overseas adoption: Social Welfare Society, Eastern Social Welfare Society, Korean Social Services, and Holt Children's Services. It is unknown how each agency counts a search attempt, and it is possible that an adoptee who visits or inquires more than once would also be counted more than once. There also seems to be some inconsistency in what each agency counts as a search, since Social Welfare Society had over 13,000 of the total 19,599 searches in this five-year period, even though it did not facilitate a proportionally higher number of overseas adoptions compared to the other agencies.
16. Ibid., 24.
17. Hosu Kim has written about these shows in her paper "Television Mothers: Korean Birthmothers Lost and Found in the Search-and-Reunion Narratives," *Cultural Studies Critical Methodologies* 12:5 (2012): 438–449, as has Prébin in *Meeting Once More*.
18. Hong, *International Korean Adoptee Resource Book*.
19. Oral History 36.
20. Oral History 27.
21. Oral History 4.
22. Oral History 54.
23. Kim Park Nelson, "'Loss is more than sadness': Reading Dissent in Transracial Adoption Melodrama in *The Language of Blood* and *First Person Plural*," *Adoption and Culture* 1:1 (2008): 101–128.
24. Prébin, *Meeting Once More*; Eleana Kim, *Adopted Territory: Transnational Korean Adoptees and the Politics of Belonging* (Durham, NC: Duke University Press, 2010). Hübinette, "Comforting an Orphaned Nation."
25. In-Jin Yoon, "A Comparison of South and North Korean Policy for Overseas Koreans," paper presented at the International Conference on the Korean Diaspora and Strategies of Global Korean Network, Seoul, South Korea, October 11, 2002.
26. Nicole Sheppard, Vice Secretary General, Global Overseas Adoptees' Link. Personal Communication, August 20, 2007.
27. Oral History 51.
28. Jeanyoung Lee, "Korea's Policy for Ethnic Koreans Overseas," *Korea Focus* 11:4 (2003): 108–132, available at http://www.koreafocus.or.kr/essays/view.asp?volume_id=29&content_id=411&category=G.
29. Jaeho Jeon, "Changes in the Korean Identity in the Globalization Era," *New Asia Research Institute Quarterly* 12:1 (2005)
30. Jane Jeong Trenka, "Adoption Is a Feminist Issue: Towards an Imaginative Feminism," paper presented at the Conference of the Korean Association for Feminist Studies in English Literature, Seoul, South Korea, June 9, 2007.
31. South Korean nationality law accorded South Korean citizenship only to children born to South Korean fathers, until 1997. After 1997, children with a South Korean father or mother were considered South Korean. From the formation of the South Korean state in 1948 until 1997, children of South Korean mothers and foreign fathers would not have been considered South Korean nationals.
32. Diana Marre, "'We Do Not Have Immigrant Children at This School, We Just Have Children Adopted from Abroad': Flexible Understandings of Children's 'Origins,'" in *International Adoption: Global Inequalities and the Circulation of Children*, ed. Diana Marre and Laura Briggs (New York: New York University Press, 2009), 226–243.

33. Formerly Immigration and Naturalization Services (INS).
34. Erika Lee, *At America's Gates: Chinese Immigration during the Exclusion Era, 1882–1943* (Chapel Hill: University of North Carolina Press, 2003).
35. "The Child Citizenship Act of 2000," U.S. Citizenship and Immigration Services.
36. "Fact Sheet: Child Citizenship Act of 2000," U.S. Department of State; the act went into force on February 27, 2001.
37. Heather Jacobson, *Culture Keeping: White Mothers, International Adoption, and the Negotiation of Family Difference* (Nashville: Vanderbilt University Press, 2008).
38. Ken Maguire, "Law Makes Foreign Adoptees Citizens," Associated Press, available from http://www.holtintl.org/infoupdates/pdfs/aparticle.pdf.
39. Patricia M. Urban, "International Adoption: U.S. Proof of Citizenship." What You Need to Know about Adoption, accessed April 30, 2003, http://adoption.about.com/library/weekly/aa090202a.htm.
40. Tram Nguyen, *We Are All Suspects Now: Untold Stories from Immigrant America after 9/11* (Boston: Beacon Press, 2005).
41. "Our Role," Intercountry Adoption Office Of Children's Issues, U.S. Department Of State, 2009. Available from adoption.state.gov/meet/role.html.
42. Bill Ong Hing, "Beyond the Rhetoric of Assimilation and Cultural Pluralism: Addressing the Tension of Separatism and Conflict in an Immigration-Driven Multiracial Society," *California Law Review* 81:4 (1993): 863–925.
43. Noah Pickus, "To Make Natural: Creating Citizens for the Twenty-First Century," in *Immigration and Citizenship in the Twenty-First Century*, ed. Noah Pickus (New York: Century Rowman & Littlefield, 1998), 107–140, 133.
44. Alejandro Portes and Rubén G. Rumbaut, *Legacies: The Story of the Immigrant Second Generation* (Berkeley: University of California Press, 2001), 117.
45. I use the term *pre-assimilation* to denote the general lack of choice in engaging in assimilative processes for most transnational and transracial adoptees; although assimilation is certainly a survival mechanism for adoptees of color in the America, it is not, I argue, generally chosen, but is (perhaps inadvertently, but still powerfully and predominantly) assigned by the White families and communities of many adoptees. See the conclusion for a more thorough investigation of this phenomenon and the Whiteness of Korean adoptees.
46. Oral History 49.
47. Oral History 48.
48. Oral History 57.
49. Joseph Collentine and Barbara F. Freed, "Learning Context and Its Effects on Second Language Acquisition, an Introduction," *Studies in Second Language Acquisition* 26 (2004): 153–171.
50. Oral History 57.
51. Andrea Louie, *Chineseness across Borders: Renegotiating Chinese Identities in China and the United States* (Durham, NC: Duke University Press, 2004).
52. Oral History 64.
53. Oral History 54.
54. Oral History 49.
55. Ibid.
56. Oral History 62.
57. Oral History 54.
58. Donna R. Gabaccia, *We Are What We Eat: Ethnic Food and the Making of Americans* (Cambridge, MA: Harvard University Press, 2000).

59. Hasia R. Diner, *Hungering for America: Italian, Irish, and Jewish Foodways in the Age of Migration* (Cambridge, MA: Harvard University Press, 2001), 4.
60. Oral History 62.
61. *Kimchi* is a generic term for the preserved side dishes, most commonly cabbage or Korean radish, without which no Korean meal is considered complete.
62. Oral History 63.
63. Ibid.
64. Oral History 59.
65. Oral History 51.
66. Oral History 62.
67. Prébin, *Meeting Once More*.
68. Oral History 49.
69. Diner, *Hungering for America*, 4.
70. Jiannbin Lee Shiao and Mia Tuan, "Korean Adoptees and the Salience of Race in Romance," paper presented at the American Sociological Association, Montréal, Canada, August 11–14, 2006.
71. Oral History 63.
72. Oral History 49.
73. Oral History 62.
74. Oral History 58.
75. Oral History 49.
76. Oral History 32.
77. Oral History 63.
78. Oral History 64.
79. Oral History 57.
80. Anderson and Lee, "Asian American Displacements," 9.

CONCLUSION: THE ENDS OF KOREAN ADOPTION

1. Maggie Jones, "Why a Generation of Adoptees Is Returning to South Korea," *New York Times Magazine*, January 14, 2015, http://www.nytimes.com/2015/01/18/magazine/why-a-generation-of-adoptees-is-returning-to-south-korea.html?_r=0.
2. Some recent adoption research is concerned with abuses in the adoption systems, or, like this research, examines social or cultural harms to transnational adoptees and their families, but a few studies have documented adoption as a risk factor in adoptee social or mental health. These reports began with the Swedish 2002 cohort study by Anders Hjern, Frank Lindblad and Bo Vinnerljung published in *The Lancet*, which found increased risk of social and psychological problems among Swedish transnational adoptees. A recent American study, "Risk of Suicide Attempt in Adopted and Nonadopted Offspring," by Margaret A. Keyes, Stephen M. Malone, Anu Sharma, William G. Iacono, and Matt McGue, also found a heightened risk of suicide or suicide attempt among American adoptees, most of whom were Korean adoptees. See *Pediatrics* 132:4 (2013): 1–8. doi: 10.1542/peds.2012-3251.
3. Examples include the work of legal scholar David Smolin and of investigative reporters Kathryn Joyce, E. J. Graff, and the Reuters investigative team led by Megan Twohey.
4. Laura Briggs and Diana Marre point out international histories of political and class war that led to "outsourcing" as less expensive labor overseas is increasingly utilized for reproductive functions. See the Introduction to *International Adoption: Global*

    Inequities and the Circulation of Children, ed. Laura Briggs and Diana Marre (New York: New York University Press, 2009).
5. Jane Jin Kaisin (film director), *Tracing Trades*. In *Rethinking Nordic Colonialism: A Five Act Interdisciplinary Art Project*, The Faeroe Islands Art Museum, Torshavn, Faroe Islands, 2006.
6. Peter Selman, "The Global Decline of Intercountry Adoption: What Lies Ahead?" *Social Policy and Society* 11:3 (2012): 381–397.
7. An article by Onishi Norimitsu in the October 9, 2008, issue of the *New York Times* headlined "Korea Aims to End Stigma of Adoption and Stop 'Exporting' Babies" reported that South Korea plans to phase out international adoption completely by 2012. To date, no such prohibition has been enacted, though the numbers of overseas adoptions from Korea has dropped to a few hundred annually in recent years. Although South Korea has announced plans to end out-of-country placements in the past, the increase in the domestic Korean population's willingness to adopt (which the article also reports) may eventually enable the South Korean government to follow through with plans to end international adoption from Korea for good. For more on how shame motivates sending countries to curtail overseas adoption, see Jeremy Youde's "Shame, Ontological Insecurity and Intercountry Adoption," *Cambridge Review of International Affairs* 27:3 (2014): 424–441.
8. David Oh and Omotayo Banjo, "Outsourcing Postracialsm: Voicing Neoliberal Multiculturalism in *Outsourced*," *Communication Theory* 22 (2012): 449–470.

BIBLIOGRAPHY

Anderson, Wanni W., and Robert G. Lee. "Asian American Displacements." In *Displacements and Diasporas: Asians in the Americas*, edited by Wanni W. Anderson and Robert G. Lee, 3–21. New Brunswick, NJ: Rutgers University Press, 2005.

Anzil, Verónica. "Adopting 'Imaginaries': International Adoption in the Spanish Press." *Adoption & Fostering* 37:1 (2013): 71–82.

Bagley, Christopher, and Loretta Young. "The Identity, Adjustment, and Achievement of Transracially Adopted Children: A Review and Empirical Report." In *Race, Education, and Identity*, edited by Gajendra K. Verma and Christopher Bagley, 192–219. New York: St. Martin's Press, 1979.

Barn, Ravinder. "'Doing the Right Thing': Transracial Adoption in the USA." *Ethnic and Racial Studies* 36:8 (2013): 1273–1291.

Basch, Linda G., Nina Glick Schiller, and Cristina Blanc-Szanton. *Nations Unbound: Transnational Projects, Postcolonial Predicaments, and Deterritorialized Nation-States*. 4th ed. New York: Gordon and Breach, 1998.

Bernardi, Daniel. "Introduction: Race and the Hollywood Style." In *Classic Hollywood, Classic Whiteness*, edited by Daniel Bernardi, xiii–xxvi. Minneapolis: University of Minnesota Press, 2001.

Brandl, John E. "Policy and Politics in Minnesota." *Dædalus: Journal of the American Academy of Arts and Sciences* 129:3 (2000): 191–220.

Brian, Kristi. *Reframing Transracial Adoption: Adopted Koreans, White Parents, and the Politics of Kinship*. Philadelphia: Temple University Press, 2012.

Briggs, Laura. "Making 'American' Families: Transracial Adoption and U.S. Latin America Policy." In *Haunted by Empire*, edited by Laura Ann Stoler, 606–645. Durham, NC: Duke University Press, 2006.

———. *Somebody's Children: The Politics of Transracial and Transnational Adoption*. Durham, NC: Duke University Press, 2012.

Briggs, Laura, and Diana Marre. "Introduction." In *International Adoption: Global Inequalities and the Circulation of Children*, edited by Diana Marre and Laura Briggs, 1–28. New York: New York University Press, 2009.

Burditt, Rebecca. "Seeing Is Believing: 1950s Popular Media Representations of Korean Adoption in the United States." In *Proceedings of the First Korean Adoption Studies Research Symposium*, edited by Kim Park Nelson, Eleana Kim, and Lene Myoung Peterson. Seoul, South Korea: IKAA, 2007.

Burroughs, Jeffery W., and Paul Spickard. "Ethnicity, Multiplicity, and Narrative: Problems and Possibilities." In *We Are a People: Narrative and Multiplicity in Constructing Ethnic Identity*, edited by Jeffery W. Burroughs and Paul Spickard, 244–253. Philadelphia: Temple University Press, 2000.

Carp, E. Wayne. *Adoption in America: Historical Perspectives.* Ann Arbor: University of Michigan Press, 2002.

———. *Family Matters: Secrecy and Disclosure in the History of Adoption.* Cambridge, MA: Harvard University Press, 2000.

Casey, Steven. *Selling the Korean War: Propaganda, Politics, and Public Opinion in the United States, 1950–1953.* New York: Oxford University Press, 2008.

Cheng, Vincent J. *Inauthentic: The Anxiety over Culture and Identity.* New Brunswick, NJ: Rutgers University Press, 2004.

"The Child Citizenship Act of 2000." U.S. Citizenship and Immigration Services, 2000. http://uscis.gov/graphics/publicaffairs/factsheets/adopted.htm.

Choy, Catherine Ceniza. *Global Families: A History of Asian International Adoption in America.* New York: New York University Press, 2013.

Collentine, Joseph, and Barbara F. Freed. "Learning Context and Its Effects on Second Language Acquisition, an Introduction." *Studies in Second Language Acquisition* 26 (2004): 153–171.

Costin, Lela B., and Shirley H. Wattenberg. "Identity in Transracial Adoption: A Study of Parental Dilemmas and Family Experiences." In *Race, Education, and Identity,* edited by Gajendra K. Verma and Christopher Bagley. New York: St. Martin's Press, 1979.

Crolley-Simic, Josie, and M. Elizabeth Vonk. "Race and White Transracially Adoptive Mothers." *Journal of Ethnic and Cultural Diversity in Social Work* 21:4 (2012): 297–313.

———. "White International Transracial Adoptive Mothers' Reflections on Race." *Child & Family Social Work* 16 (2011): 169–178.

Cumings, Bruce. *Korea's Place in the Sun: A Modern History.* Updated ed. New York: W. W. Norton, 2005.

Darder, Antonia, and Rodolfo D. Torres. *After Race: Racism after Multiculturalism.* New York: New York University Press, 2004.

Denzin, Norman K. "Introduction: The Discipline and Practice of Qualitative Research." In *Handbook of Qualitative Research,* 2nd ed., edited by Norman K. Denzin and Yvonna S. Lincoln. Thousand Oaks, CA: Sage Publications, 2000.

———. *Performance Ethnography: Critical Pedagogy and the Politics of Culture.* Thousand Oaks, CA: Sage Publications, 2003.

DeVault, Marjorie L. *Liberating Method: Feminism and Social Research.* Philadelphia: Temple University Press, 1999.

Dickens, Jonathan. "Social Policy Approaches and Social Work Dilemmas in Intercountry Adoption." In *Intercountry Adoption: Policies, Practices, and Outcomes,* edited by Judith L. Gibbons and Karen Rotabi. Burlington, VT: Ashgate, 2012.

Diner, Hasia R. *Hungering for America: Italian, Irish, and Jewish Foodways in the Age of Migration.* Cambridge, MA: Harvard University Press, 2001.

Docan-Morgan, Sara. "Korean Adoptees' Retrospective Reports of Intrusive Interactions: Exploring Boundary Management in Adoptive Families." *Journal of Family Communications* 10 (2010): 137–157.

———. "'They Don't Know What It Is Like to Be in My Shoes': Topic Avoidance about Race in Transracially Adoptive Families." *Journal of Social and Personal Relationships* 28:3 (2010): 336–355.

Dorow, Sara. *Transnational Adoption: A Cultural Economy of Race, Gender, and Kinship.* New York: New York University Press, 2006.

Engel, Madeline H., Norma Kolko Phillips, and Frances A. DellaCava. "Cultural Differences and Adoption Policy in the United States: The Quest for Social Justice for Children." *International Journal of Children's Rights* 18 (2010): 291–308.

England, Kim V. L. "Getting Personal: Reflexivity, Positionality, and Feminist Research." *Professional Geographer* 46:1 (1994): 80–89.

Escueta, Eugenia, and Eileen O'Brien. "Asian Americans in Higher Education: Trends and Issues." In *The Asian American Educational Experience: A Sourcebook for Teachers and Students*, edited by Don T. Nakanishi and Tina Yamano Nishida, 259–272. New York: Routledge, 1995.

"Fact Sheet: Child Citizenship Act of 2000." U.S. Department of State. http://www.uscis.gov/sites/default/files/files/pressrelease/CCA_102504.pdf.

Feigelman, William. "Adjustments of Transracially and Inracially Adopted Young Adults." *Child and Adolescent Social Work Journal* 17:3 (2000): 165–183.

Feigelman, William, and Arnold R. Silverman. *Chosen Children: New Patterns of Adoptive Relationships*. New York: Praeger Publishers, 1983.

———. "The Long-Term Effects of Transracial Adoption." *Social Service Review* 58:4 (1984): 588–602.

Fogg-Davis, Hawley. *The Ethics of Transracial Adoption*. Ithaca, NY: Cornell University Press, 2002.

Fontana, Andrea, and James H. Frey. "The Interview: From Structured Questions to Negotiated Text." In *Collecting and Interpreting Qualitative Materials*, edited by Norman K. Denzin and Yvonna S. Lincoln, 645–672. Thousand Oaks, CA: Sage Publications, 2003.

Freundlich, Madelyn, and Joy Kim Lieberthal. "The Gathering of the First Generation of Adult Korean Adoptees: Adoptees' Perceptions of International Adoption." www.adoptioninstitute.org/proed/korfindings.html.

Friedlander, Peter. "Theory, Method, and Oral History." In *Oral History: An Interdisciplinary Anthology*, edited by David K. Dunaway and Willa K. Baum, 150–159. Walnut Creek, CA: AltaMira Press, 1996.

Fronek, Patricia, and Denise Cuthbert. "The Future of Inter-Country Adoption: A Paradigm Shift for This Century." *International Journal of Social Welfare* 21 (2012): 215–224.

Gabaccia, Donna R. *We Are What We Eat: Ethnic Food and the Making of Americans*. Cambridge, MA: Harvard University Press, 2000.

Gill, Owen, and Barbara Jackson. *Adoption and Race: Black, Asian, and Mixed Race Children in White Families*. New York: St. Martin's Press, 1983.

Gilroy, Paul. *Imagining Political Culture beyond the Color Line*. Cambridge, MA: Belknap Press of Harvard University Press, 2000.

Glick Schiller, Nina. "Transmigrants and Nation-States: Something Old and Something New in U.S. Immigrant Experience." In *Handbook of International Migration: The American Experience*, edited by J. DeWind, C. Hirschman, and P. Kasinitz, 94–119. New York: Russell Sage, 1999.

Gotanda, Neil. "Multiculturalism and Racial Stratification." In *Mapping Multiculturalism*, edited by Avery F. Gordon and Christopher Newfield, 238–252. Minneapolis: University of Minnesota Press, 1996.

Grewal, Inderpal. *Transnational America: Feminisms, Diasporas, Neoliberalisms*. Durham, NC: Duke University Press, 2005.

Grow, Lucielle J. Grow and Deborah Shapiro. *Black Children–White Parents: A Study of Transracial Adoption*. Washington, DC: Child Welfare League of America Press, 1974.

Hing, Bill Ong. "Beyond the Rhetoric of Assimilation and Cultural Pluralism: Addressing the Tension of Separatism and Conflict in an Immigration-Driven Multiracial Society." *California Law Review* 81:4 (1993): 863–925.

Hoffman, Joy, and Edlun Vallejo Peña. "Too Korean to Be White and Too White to Be Korean: Ethnic Identity Development among Transracial Korean Adoptees." *Journal of Student Affairs Research and Practice* 50:2 (2013): 152–170.

Hollingsworth, Leslie D. "Effect of Transracial/Transethnic Adoption on Children's Racial and Ethnic Identity and Self-Esteem: A Meta-Analytic Review." *Marriage & Family Review* 25:1–2 (1997): 99–130.

Hong, Jeannie, ed. *International Korean Adoptee Resource Book*. Seoul, South Korea: Overseas Koreans Foundation, 2006.

Hübinette, Tobias. "Comforting an Orphaned Nation: Representations of International Adoption and Adopted Koreans in Korean Popular Culture." Ph.D. diss., Stockholm University, 2005.

Hudson, Dale. "Vampires of Color and the Performance of Multicultural Whiteness." In *The Persistence of Whiteness*, edited by Daniel Bernardi, 127–156. New York: Routledge, 2007.

Ida, Donna Jean Akiye Kato. "Depression, Hopelessness, and Suicide Ideation among Asian-American Students." Ph.D. diss., University of Colorado at Boulder, 1989.

Implementation of the Interethnic Adoption Amendments. Hearing before the Subcommittee on Human Resources of the Committee on Ways and Means, House of Representatives. 105th Congress, 2nd Session. Statement of Rita J. Simon. September 15, 1998. http://www.gpo.gov/fdsys/pkg/CHRG-105hhrg63768/html/CHRG-105hhrg63768.htm.

"Indian Adoption Project," The Adoption History Project. Last modified Feb. 24, 2012. http://pages.uoregon.edu/adoption/topics/IAP.html.

Institute of Education Sciences National Center for Education Statistics. "Employees in Degree-Granting Institutions, by Race/Ethnicity, Sex, Employment Status, Control and Type of Institution, and Primary Occupation: Fall 2007." Digest of Education Statistics, 2007. http://nces.ed.gov/programs/digest/d08/tables/ dt08_246.asp.

International Social Service, American Branch Papers, Box 10. "Children-Independent Adoption Schemes, Holt, Harry, Vol. I 1955–1958." Minneapolis: University of Minnesota Social Welfare History Archives.

International Social Service, American Branch Papers, Box 10. "Proxy Adoptions." Minneapolis: University of Minnesota Social Welfare History Archives.

Jacobson, Heather. *Culture Keeping: White Mothers, International Adoption, and the Negotiation of Family Difference*. Nashville: Vanderbilt University Press, 2008.

Jacobson, Matthew Frye. *Whiteness of a Different Color: European Immigrants and the Alchemy of Race*. Cambridge, MA: Harvard University Press, 1998.

Jeon, Jaeho. "Changes in the Korean Identity in the Globalization Era." *New Asia Research Institute Quarterly* 12:1 (2005).

Jerng, Mark C. *Claiming Others: Transracial Adoption and National Belonging*. Minneapolis: University of Minnesota Press, 2010.

Jin, Wen. *Pluralist Universalism: An Asian Americanist Critique of U.S. and Chinese Multiculturalisms*. Columbus: Ohio State University Press, 2012.

Johnson, James Weldon. *The Autobiography of an Ex-Colored Man*. Boston: Sherman French & Company, 1912.

Jones, Charles E., and John F. Else. "Racial and Cultural Issues in Adoption." *Child Welfare United States* 58:6 (1979): 373–382.

Joppke, Christian, and Steven Lukes. "Introduction: Multicultural Questions." In *Multicultural Questions*, edited by Christian Joppke and Steven Lukes, 1–24. New York: Oxford University Press, 1999.

Kaltmeier, Olaf, Josel Raab, and Sebastian Thies. "Multiculturalism and Beyond: The New Dynamics of Identity Politics in the Americas." *Latin American and Caribbean Ethnic Studies* 7:2 (2012): 103–104.

Keyes, Margaret A., Stephen M. Malone, Anu Sharma, William G. Iacono, and Matt McGue. "Risk of Suicide Attempt in Adopted and Nonadopted Offspring." *Pediatrics* 132:4 (2013): 1–8. doi: 10:1542/peds.2012–3251.

Khan, Shahnaz. "Reconfiguring the Native Informant: Positionality in the Global Age." *Signs: Journal of Women in Culture and Society* 30:4 (2005): 2017–2035.
Kim, Dong Soo. "Issues in Transracial and Transcultural Adoption." *Social Casework* 59:8 (1978): 477–486.
Kim, Eleana. *Adopted Territory: Transnational Korean Adoptees and the Politics of Belonging*. Durham, NC: Duke University Press, 2010.
———. "*The Origins of Korean Adoption: Cold War Geopolitics and Intimate Diplomacy*." WPS 09–9 of the Working Paper Series for the U.S.-Korea Institute at the Paul H. Nitze School of Advanced International Studies, Johns Hopkins University. October 2009. http://uskoreainstitute.org/wp-content/uploads/2010/02/USKI_WP0909_KimAdoptee.pdf.
———. "Remembering Loss: The Cultural Politics of Overseas Adoption from South Korea." Ph.D. diss., New York University, 2007.
Kim, Grace, Karen L. Suyemoto, and Castellano B. Turner. "Sense of Belonging, Sense of Exclusion, and Racial Ethnic Identities in Korean Transracial Adoptees." *Cultural Diversity and Ethnic Minority Psychology* 16:2 (2010): 179–190.
Kim, Jodi. *Ends of Empire: Asian American Critique and the Cold War*. Minneapolis: University of Minnesota Press, 2010.
Kim, Oh Myo, Reed Reichwald, and Richard Lee. "Cultural Socialization in Families with Adopted Adolescents: A Mixed Method, Multi-Informant Study." *Journal of Adolescent Research* 28:1 (2013): 69–95.
Kim, S. P., S. Hong, and B. S. Kim. "Adoption of Korean Children by New York Area Couples: A Preliminary Study." *Child Welfare United States* 58:7 (1979): 419–427.
Klein, Christina. *Cold War Orientalism: Asia in the Middlebrow Imagination, 1945–1961*. Berkeley: University of California Press, 2003.
Klevan, Miriam. "Resolving Race: How Adoptive Parents Discuss Choosing the Race of Their Child." *Adoption Quarterly* 15 (2012): 88–115.
Krieger, Susan. *The Mirror Dance*. Philadelphia: Temple University Press, 1983.
———. *Social Science and the Self: Personal Essays on an Art Form*. New Brunswick, NJ: Rutgers University Press, 1991.
Lapovsky Kennedy, Elizabeth, and Madeline Davis. "Constructing an Ethnohistory of the Buffalo Lesbian Community: Reflexivity, Dialogue, and Politics." In *Out in the Field: Reflections of Lesbian and Gay Anthropologists*, edited by Ellen Lewin and William Leap. Urbana: University of Illinois Press, 1996.
Lee, Erika. *At America's Gates: Chinese Immigration during the Exclusion Era, 1882–1943*. Chapel Hill: University of North Carolina Press, 2003.
Lee, Erika, and Naoko Shibusawa. "Guest Editors' Introduction: What Is Transnational Asian American Studies? Recent Trends and Challenges." *Journal of Asian American Studies* 8:3 (2005): vii–xvii.
Lee, Jeanyoung. "Korea's Policy for Ethnic Koreans Overseas." *Korea Focus* 11:4 (2003): 108–132.
Lee, Richard M. "The Transracial Adoption Paradox: History, Research, and Counseling Implications of Cultural Socialization." *The Counseling Psychologist* 31:6 (2003): 711–744.
Lee, Richard M., Hyung Chol Yoo, and Sara Roberts. "The Coming of Age of Korean Adoptees: Ethnic Identity Development and Psychological Adjustment." In *Korean-Americans: Past, Present, and Future*, edited by Ilpyong J. Kim, 203–224. Hollym International, 2004.
Lentz, Robert J. *Korean War Filmography: 91 English Language Features through 2000*. Jefferson, NC: McFarland & Company, 2008.
Li, Guofang, and Lihshing Wang. "Introduction: The Old Myth in a New Time." In *Model Minority Myth Revisited: An Interdisciplinary Approach to Demystifying Asian American*

Educational Experiences, edited by Guofang Li and Lihshing Wang, 1–18. Greenwich, CT: Information Age Publishing, 2008.

Liem, Ramsey. "History, Trauma, and Identity: The Legacy of the Korean War for Korean Americans." *Amerasia Journal* 29:3 (2004): 111–129.

Louie, Andrea. *Chineseness across Borders: Renegotiating Chinese Identities in China and the United States.* Durham, NC: Duke University Press, 2004.

Maguire, Ken. "Law Makes Foreign Adoptees Citizens." Associated Press, 2001. http://www.holtintl.org/aparticle.pdf.

Manalansan, Martin F. "Introduction." In *Cultural Compass: Ethnographic Explorations of Asian America*, edited by Martin F. Manalansan, 1–13. Philadelphia: Temple University Press, 2000.

Maramba, Dina C. "Understanding Campus Climate through the Voices of Filipina/o American College Students." *College Student Journal*, 2008. Marre, Diana. "'We Do Not Have Immigrant Children at This School, We Just Have Children Adopted from Abroad': Flexible Understandings of Children's 'Origins.'" In *International Adoption: Global Inequalities and the Circulation of Children*, edited by Diana Marre and Laura Briggs, 226–243. New York: New York University Press, 2009.

May, Elaine Tyler. *Barren in the Promised Land: Childless Americans and the Pursuit of Happiness.* Cambridge, MA: Harvard University Press, 1995.

McDonald, Janis L. "Looking in the Honest Mirror of Privilege: 'Polite White' Reflections." *Columbia Journal of Gender and Law* 12:3 (2003): 650–659.

McRoy, Ruth G. "Attachment and Racial Identity Issues: Implications for Child Placement Decision Making." *Journal of Multicultural Social Work* 3:3 (1994): 59–74.

McRoy, Ruth G., and Louis Zurcher Jr. *Transracial and Inracial Adoptees: The Adolescent Years.* Springfield, IL: Charles C. Thomas, 1983.

Meier, Dani I. "Loss and Reclaimed Lives: Cultural Identity and Place in Korean-American Intercountry Adoptees." Ph.D. diss., University of Minnesota, 1998.

Multiethnic Placement Act of 1994 (MEPA), Pub. L. 103–382, 108 Stat. 4056, as amended by Pub. L. 104–88, 110 Stat. 1903, 42 U.S.C. §§622, 671, and 1996a.

Myers, Kit. "'Real' Families: The Violence and Love in New Media Adoption Discourse." *Critical Discourse Studies* 11:2 (2014): 175–193.

Newfield, Christopher, and Avery F. Gordon. "Multiculturalism's Unfinished Business." In *Mapping Multiculturalism*, edited by Avery F. Gordon and Christopher Newfield, 76–124. Minneapolis: University of Minnesota Press, 1996.

Nguyen, Tram. *We Are All Suspects Now: Untold Stories from Immigrant America after 9/11.* Boston: Beacon Press, 2005.

Oakley, Ann. "Interviewing Women: A Contradiction in Terms." In *Doing Feminist Research*, edited by H. Roberts, 30–61. London: Routledge, 1981.

Oh, Arissa. "From War Waif to Ideal Immigrant: The Cold War Transformation of the Korean Orphan." *Journal of American Ethnic History* 31:4 (2012): 34–55.

Oh, David, and Omotayo Banjo. "Outsourcing Postracialism: Voicing Neoliberal Multiculturalism in *Outsourced*." *Communication Theory* 22 (2012): 449–470.

O'Keefe, Michael. "Social Services: Minnesota as Innovator." *Dædalus: Journal of the American Academy of Arts and Sciences*, Special Issue: "Minnesota: A Different America?" 129:3 (2000): 247–267.

Okihiro, Gary Y. "Oral History and the Writing of Ethnic History." In *Oral History: An Interdisciplinary Anthology*, edited by David K. Dunaway and Willa K. Baum, 199–214. Walnut Creek, CA: AltaMira Press, 1996.

Omi, Michael, and Howard Winant. *Racial Formation in the United States: From the 1960s to the 1980s, Critical Social Thought.* New York: Routledge & Kegan Paul, 1986.

Ong, Aihwa. *Buddha Is Hiding: Refugees, Citizenship, and the New America.* Berkeley: University of California Press, 2003.

———. *Flexible Citizenship: The Cultural Logics of Transnationality.* Durham, NC: Duke University Press, 1999.

Ortiz, Ana Teresa, and Laura Briggs. "The Culture of Poverty, Crack Babies, and Welfare Cheats: The Making of the 'Healthy White Baby Crisis.'" *Social Text* 21:3 (2003): 39–57.

Palacios, Jesús, and David Brodzinsky. "Adoption Research: Trends, Topics, Outcomes." *International Journal of Behavioral Development* 34:3 (2010): 270–284.

Park Nelson, Kim. *The Adult Korean American Adoptee Oral History Project: A Collection of 66 Life Course Histories.* 2/19/2003–1/13/2007.

———. "'Loss is more than sadness': Reading Dissent in Transracial Adoption Melodrama in *The Language of Blood* and *First Person Plural*." In *Adoption and Culture: The Journal of the Alliance for the Study of Adoption, Identity, and Kinship* 1:1 (2008): 101–128

Perez, Mario Rios, and Sharon S. Lee. "Asian American and Latina/o College Students' Life Stories." *Journal of American Ethnic History* 27:4 (2008): 107–113.

Perry, Twila L. "The Transracial Adoption Controversy: An Analysis of Discourse and Subordination." *New York University Review of Law & Social Change* 21:1 (1994): 33–108.

Pickus, Noah. "To Make Natural: Creating Citizens for the Twenty-First Century." In *Immigration and Citizenship in the Twenty-First Century,* edited by Noah Pickus, 107–140. New York: Century Rowman & Littlefield Publishing, 1998.

Pilotti, Francisco. "Intercountry Adoption: Trends, Issues, and Policy Implications for the 1990s." *Childhood* 1 (1993): 165–177.

Pohl, Kathy Harris, and Constance. *Transracial Adoption: Children and Parents Speak.* New York: Franklin Watts, 1992.

Portes, Alejandro, and Rubén G. Rumbaut. *Legacies: The Story of the Immigrant Second Generation.* Berkeley: University of California Press, 2001.

Potter, Sarah. *Everybody Else: Adoption and the Politics of Domestic Diversity in Postwar America.* Athens: University of Georgia Press, 2014.

Prébin, Elise. *Meeting Once More: The Korean Side of Transnational Adoption.* New York: New York University Press, 2013.

Quiroz, Pamela Anne. *Adoption in a Color-Blind Society: Perspectives on a Multiracial America.* Lanham, MD: Rowman & Littlefield, 2007.

Reinharz, Shulamit. *On Becoming a Social Scientist: From Survey Research and Participant Observation to Experiential Analysis.* New Brunswick, NJ: Transaction Publishers, 1988.

Roberts, Dorothy. *Shattered Bonds: The Color of Child Welfare.* New York: Basic Civitas Books, 2002.

Roediger, David R. *How Race Survived US History: From the American Revolution to the Present.* New York: Verso, 2008.

Root, Maria. "Rethinking Racial Identity Development." In *We Are a People: Narrative and Multiplicity in Constructing Ethnic Identity,* edited by Jeffery W. Burroughs and Paul Spickard, 205–220. Philadelphia: Temple University Press, 2000.

Selman, Peter. "The Global Decline of Intercountry Adoption: What Lies Ahead?" *Social Policy and Society* 11:3 (2012): 381–397.

Shachar, Ayelet. "The Paradox of Multicultural Vulnerability: Individual Rights, Individual Groups, and the State." In *Multicultural Questions,* edited by Christian Joppke and Steven Lukes, 87–111. New York: Oxford University Press, 1999.

Shiao, Jiannbin, and Mia Tuan. "A Sociological Approach to Race, Identity, and Asian Adoption." In *International Korean Adoption: A Fifty-Year History of Policy and Practice*, edited by M. Elizabeth Vonk, Kathleen Bergquist, Dong Soo Kim, and Marvin Feit, 155–170. New York: Routledge, 2007.

———. "'Some Asian Men are Attractive to Me, But for a Husband . . .': Korean Adoptees and the Salience of Race in Romance." *DuBois Review* 5:2 (2008): 259–285.

Shireman, J. F., and P. R. Johnson. "A Longitudinal Study of Black Adoptions: Single Parent Transracial, and Traditional." *Social Work* 31:3 (1986): 171–176.

Silva, Eduardo. *Racism Without Racists: Color-Blind Racism and the Persistence of Racial Inequality in America*. 4th ed. Plymouth, UK: Rowman & Littlefield, 2014.

Simon, Rita. J. "Adoption of Black Children by White Parents in the USA." In *Adoption: Essays in Social Policy, Law, and Sociology*, edited by P. Bean, 229–242. New York: Tavistock Publications, 1984.

Simon, Rita J., and Howard Altstein. *Adoption, Race, and Identity: From Infancy to Young Adulthood*. New Brunswick, NJ: Transaction Publishers, 2002.

———. *Transracial Adoptees and Their Families: A Study of Identity and Commitment*. New York: Praeger, 1987.

———. *Transracial Adoption*. New York: Wiley, 1977.

———. *Transracial Adoption: A Follow-Up*. Lexington, MA: Lexington Books, D. C. Heath and Company, 1981.

Smith, Linda Tuhiwai. *Decolonizing Methodologies: Research and Indigenous Peoples*. London: Zed Books, 1999.

Smolin, David M. "Child Laundering: How the Intercountry Adoption System Legitimizes and Incentivizes the Practices of Buying, Trafficking, Kidnapping, and Stealing Children." *Wayne Law Review* 52:1 (2006): 113–200.

Smyth, Marie. "Insider-Outsider Issues in Researching Violently Divided Societies." In *Researching Conflict in Africa: Insights and Experiences*, edited by Gillian Robinson Elisabeth Porter, Marie Smyth, Albrecht Schnabel, and Eghosa Osaghae. Santiago, Chile: United Nations University Press, 2005.

Song, Miri. *Choosing Ethnic Identity*. Malden, MA: Polity Press, 2003.

Steele, Claude M., and Joshua Aronson. "Stereotype Threat and the Intellectual Test Performance of African Americans." *Journal of Personality and Social Psychology* 69:5 (1995): 797–811.

Stueck, William. *Rethinking the Korean War: A New Diplomatic and Strategic History*. Princeton NJ: Princeton University Press, 2004.

Tessler, Richard C., Gail Gamache, and Liming Liu. *West Meets East: Americans Adopt Chinese Children*. Westport, CT: Bergin & Garvey, 1999.

Trenka, Jane Jeong. "Adoption Is a Feminist Issue: Towards an Imaginative Feminism." Paper presented at the Conference of the Korean Association for Feminist Studies in English Literature, Seoul, South Korea, June 9, 2007.

Tuan, Mia. *Forever Foreigners or Honorary Whites? The Asian Ethnic Experience Today*. New Brunswick, NJ: Rutgers University Press, 1998.

Tuan, Mia, and Jiannbin Lee Shiao. *Choosing Ethnicity, Negotiating Race: Korean Adoptees in America*. New York: Russell Sage Foundation, 2011.

Twine, France Winddance. "Brown-Skinned White Girls: Class, Culture, and the Construction of White Identity in Suburban Communities." In *Displacing Whiteness*, edited by Ruth Frankenburg, 214–243. Durham, NC: Duke University Press, 1997.

Twine, Frances Winddance, and Jonathan W. Warren. *Racing Research, Researching Race: Methodological Dilemmas in Critical Race Studies*. New York: New York University Press, 2000.

Um, Khatharya. "A Dream Denied: Educational Experiences of Southeast Asian American Youth Issues and Recommendations, an Issue Paper Based on Findings from the First National Southeast Asian Youth Summit, University of California-Berkeley, December 9, 2000." Southeast Asia Resource Action Center, 2000. http://www.searac.org/ydfinal-2_03.pdf.

Versluis-den Bieman, H. J. M., and F. C. Verhulst. "Self-Reported and Parent Reported Problems in Adolescent International Adoptees." *Journal of Child Psychology & Psychiatry & Allied Disciplines* 36:8 (1995): 1411–1428.

Waters, Mary C. *Ethnic Options: Choosing Identities in America.* Berkeley: University of California Press, 1990.

Wei, William. *The Asian American Movement.* Philadelphia: Temple University Press, 1993.

Weil, Richard H. "International Adoption: The Quiet Migration." *International Migration Review* 18:2 (1984): 276–293.

White Stephan, Cookie, and Walter G. Stephan. "What Are the Functions of Ethnic Identity?" In *We Are a People: Narrative and Multiplicity in Constructing Ethnic Identity*, edited by Jeffery W. Burroughs and Paul Spickard, 229–243. Philadelphia: Temple University Press, 2000.

Williams, Norma. *The Mexican American Family: Tradition and Change.* Reynolds Series in Sociology. Walnut Creek, CA: AltaMira Press, 1990.

Willinsky, John. "What Was Multiculturalism?" In *Precarious International Multicultural Education: Hegemony, Dissent, and Rising Alternatives*, edited by Handel Kashope Wright, 15–39. Rotterdam: Sense Publishers, 2012.

Yngvesson, Barbara. *Belonging in an Adopted World: Race, Identity, and Transnational Adoption.* Chicago: University of Chicago Press, 2010.

Yoon, In-Jin. "A Comparison of South and North Korean Policy for Overseas Koreans." Paper presented at the International Conference on the Korean Diaspora and Strategies of Global Korean Network, Seoul, South Korea, October 11, 2002.

Youde, Jeremy. "Shame, Ontological Insecurity, and Intercountry Adoption." *Cambridge Review of International Affairs* 27:3 (2014): 424–441.

Young, Alexandra. "Developments in Intercountry Adoption: From Humanitarian to Market-Driven Policy and Beyond." *Adoption & Fostering* 36:2 (2012): 67–78.

Yu, Henry. *Thinking Orientals.* New York: Oxford University Press, 2002.

Zastrow, Charles. *Outcome of Black Children–White Parents Transracial Adoptions.* Palo Alto, CA: R&E Research Associates, 1977.

Zhou, Min. "Are Asian Americans Becoming 'White'?" *Contexts* 3:1 (2004): 29–37.

Zhou, Min, and Jennifer Lee. "Introduction: The Making of Culture, Identity, and Ethnicity among Asian American Youth." In *Asian American Youth: Culture, Identity, and Ethnicity*, edited by Jennifer Lee and Min Zhou, 1–32. New York: Routledge, 2004.

INDEX

Act on the Immigration and Legal Status of Overseas Koreans (1999), 162
adjustment, 13, 75, 79–82
adoptee communities, 28, 30, 57, 146, 191–192
adoptee conferences, 37–38, 156
adoptee organizations, 9, 12, 18, 22, 23–25, 30, 31, 37–38, 101, 103, 141
adoptees: attitudes about race, 46; interactions with non-adopted Asian Americans, 64, 70; relationships with non-adopted Asians, 84
adoption agencies: and adoption research, 31, 35–36, 89, 155; and birth parents, 97; corruption and, 190; Holt International, 58; in Minnesota, 18, 102–103; and immigration law, 52; information given to adoptive parents by, 50; policies for adoptive placement, 93–94, 99; promotion of Korean adoption, 103, 147–148; proxy adoption, 53; record keeping, 163; role in birth search, 157–160; transracial adoption policies, 15
adoption demographics, 9, 18, 45–47, 73, 93, 130, 154, 170, 191
adoption history, 13, 31, 36, 41–46, 65, 72–91, 92–97, 101–103, 165–170
adoption laws, 154
adoption research. *See* research
adoption triad, 36
adoptive families: acculturation and, 22–23; and birth search, 159–160; conflicts with birth families, 96–97, 189; cultural enrichment by adoption, 4; eligibility requirements, 93; enrichment by adoption, 78; and formation of adoptee racial identity, 86–87; influence on immigration policy, 52–53, 55–56, 165–169; influence on transnational adoption practice, 47, 147–148; information given to adopted children, 49–50; journalistic accounts of, 59, 65, 71; and multiculturalism, 99–100; parents' role in adoption research, 13, 13, 18, 33, 72, 75–80, 84, 89–91, 100; proxy adoption, 53–54; racial difference in, 3; racial differences, 81–83; racial etiquette, 135–137, 144–146; racial preferences of, 130; racism in, 9, 112–113, 169; response to racism against adoptees, 66, 86, 111–114;

valorization of, 4–7, 14–15, 65, 88; and White acculturation of transracial adoptees, 131–133
African American transracial adoption: history, 92–97, 92, 102; journalistic accounts of, 15; opposition to, 74; research on, 77–80, 85–88
AK Connection (adoptee organization), 22, 23–24, 37–38, 103
Altstein, Howard, 72, 74, 75, 77–80, 82–89
American Indian transracial adoption. *See* Native American transracial adoption
Anderson, Wanni, 152, 187
anticommunism, 42–44. *See also* Cold War
antimiscegenation laws, 102
art and cultural production, 19, 36
Asian American communities: immigration and, 187; interaction with transracial adoptees, 10, 62, 70–71, 84, 101, 106–110, 118, 134, 169; low incidence of adoption in, 96; mental health issues, 128; and model minority stereotype, 127–130, 144; population size, 116–117, 129; racialization, 126–132; racism in, 138; relative size of adoptee population in, 130; social roles of, 130; transnationality of, 152
Asian American Studies, research on transracial adoption, 10, 19, 35
Asian diasporas, 96, 151, 186–187
Asian exclusion, 1, 41, 45, 52–53, 65, 154, 165–166. *See also* immigration
assimilation: as aspect of racial exceptionalism, 13, 42; and common perceptions of Korean adoptees, 148; comparisons among immigrant groups, 153; expectations of adoptive families and communities, 46, 53, 61–65, 70, 130, 135; identity formation and, 131–133, 143; as indicator of successful adoption, 1, 3–5, 15, 18, 75, 79–83, 90–91; in Korean society, 184; in multiculturalism, 99–100, 119–120; negative consequences of, 122; in U.S. naturalization law, 168–169
authenticity: adoptees' feelings of racial inauthenticity, 64, 139–140, 143; in Chinese American identity, 174; as factor in racial identity, 121–125; problematized by intercultural adoption, 132, 149

225

The Autobiography of an Ex-Colored Man (J. W. Johnson), 122

Bagley, Christopher, 75
Banjo, Otomayo, 98, 119, 192
Basch, Linda, 152
Battle Hymn (film), 44, 59
Bean, P., 75
behavior problems, 84
Bernardi, Daniel, 121–122
biracial adoptees. *See* mixed-race adoptees
birth families: activism of, 96; adoptees' memories of, 47–49, 133; child custody conflicts with, 189; circumstances of relinquishing children, 49–51, 57–58, 63, conflicts with adoptive families, 96–97; disempowerment of, 17, 76, 90–91; family registry (*hojeok*), 163–164; losses experienced by, 76; search for, 7–9, 51, 57–58, 157–164, 175, 184
birth records, 20
birth search, 7–9, 51, 57–58, 157–164, 175, 184
Black transracial adoption. *See* African American transracial adoption
Blanc-Szanton, Christina, 152
blogs: *See* Internet
Bonilla-Silva, Eduardo, 123
Boyd, Cynthia, 15
Brian, Kristi, 9, 83, 99, 111, 130
Brodzinsky, David, 77
Brown, Dusten, 189
Burditt, Rebecca, 51, 59
Burroughs, Jeffrey, 19

Carp, Wayne, 96
celebrity adoptions, 90
census categories, 127
Chappell, Crystal Lee Hyun, 7
Cheng, Vincent, 125, 132
Chicago School (of sociology), 131
Child Citizenship Act (2000), 166–167, 168
child removal, 97
Children's Home Society, 102
child salvation, 1, 3, 5–6, 11, 41, 43–45, 51–53, 57–65, 67, 71, 76, 128, 190
China: adoption from, 73, 130; ethnic Koreans in, 163; non-adopted return migrants, 174
Choy, Catherine Ceniza, 9, 90
Christianity, 43–44, 53, 60, 65, 77, 88
citizenship: adoptees' access to, 1, 55–57, 154, 162–168, 183; and family relationships, 11; global, 14; and multiculturalism, 99; and racialization, 127
Citizens League, 101
civil rights movements, 28–29, 47, 74, 91, 93, 95, 98, 123, 125
Clark Doll Racial Preference Selection Test, 86
Clearwater, Boyd, 2
Cold War, 2, 4, 11–13, 41–71, 53, 60, 65, 154
college, Asian and Asian American faculty, 129, 106–110, 111, 135–136, 142, 185

Colombia, adoption from, 80
colonialism, 18, 76, 99, 130, 177, 192
colorblindness: in adoption policy, 78; in adoptive families, 4, 6, 10–11, 14, 81–83, 87, 98, 111–113, 130–133; critiques of, 119–120; as tenet of multiculturalism, 91–92, 121–123, 125, 144–145, 148
communism. *See* anticommunism; Cold War
compassion fatigue, 27
consumerism, 98, 125
Costin, Lela, 75, 79
Crisis of Representation (Denzin), 34
critical race studies, 73, 89
culture camps, 36, 103, 106, 147
Cummings, Bruce, 43
Cuthbert, Denise, 76

Darder, Antonia, 123
dating, 68–69, 82, 86, 118, 133, 135, 145, 181–183
Davis, Madeline, 27
Denzin, Norman, 27, 33, 34
deportation, 167
depression, 32, 128, 136–137, 140, 161
DeVault, Marjorie, 25, 27
Dickens, Jonathan, 76
Diff'rent Strokes (television program), 99
Diner, Hasia, 178, 181
disability, 61, 84
Docan-Morgan, Sara, 113, 137
domestic transracial adoption, 92–97
Dorow, Sara, 130, 132

Eastern Bloc nations, adoption from, 93
education, 106–108
Eisenhower, Dwight, 55
Else, John, 75
England, Kim, 28
English language: proficiency required for U.S. immigration, 168; teaching in Korea, 171, 173–178, 182, 186
Escueta, Eugenia, 129
ethnic studies, 34
ethnographic method, 9, 11–14, 17–40. *See also* oral histories; research methodology
Europe: adoption from, 41, 53, 154; immigration from, 124; Korean adoption in, 102, 171, 190
evangelism. *See* Christianity
exceptionalism. *See* racial exceptionalism
Exchange Visitor Program, 166

F-4 visa, 162, 180, 187
Fair Share Refugee Act (1961), 52
families. *See* adoptive families; birth families
family registry. *See* hojeok
Feigelman, William, 75, 80
feminism, 20, 25, 34–35
fertility. *See* infertility; reproductive technologies
films, 36, 43–44, 59, 70, 72, 74, 158, 191
Fontana, Andrea, 30
food, 113, 172, 178–181

Frey, James, 30
Friedlander, Peter, 25
Fronek, Patricia, 76

Gamache, Gail, 130
Gatherings, the. *See* IKAA Gatherings
gender/sexuality studies, 34
Germany, cultural values favoring adoption, 102
Gill, Owen, 75, 84
Gilroy, Paul, 123
Glick Schiller, Nina, 152
globalization, 1, 11, 14, 98, 175, 180, 190, 192–193
Global Overseas Adoptees' Link (GOAL), 170
gratitude, 67, 148–149
Greece, adoption from, 53
Grewal, Inderpal, 153
Grow, Lucille, 74, 80

H-1 visa, 153, 166
Hague Adoption Convention, 190, 192
hagwons (cram schools), 175
Haiti, 189
Harvey, Kay, 4
He, Anna Mae, 189
Hess, Dean, 59
Hing, Bill Ong, 168
history of transracial adoption, 92–97, 102–103
Hmong, 168
Hoffman, Joy, 142
hojeok (family registry), 163–164
Hollingsworth, Leslie, 80
Holt, Harry, 53, 58
Holt Children's Services, 155
Holt International, 49, 51, 54, 58, 60
Hong, S., 75, 83
Hübinette, Tobias, 155, 191
Hudson, Dale, 124
humanitarianism: military engagements as humanitarian acts, 3; as motivation for adoption, 41, 43, 53, 59–60, 74, 88
hybridity. *See* racial identity

identity formation: as adoptee, 30, 38, 61–62, 62, 71, 103–110, 140, 152; Asian American, 17, 22; of author, 23; and civil rights activism, 125; effects of multiculturalism on, 99–100; hybridity, 130; in Korea, 150–157, 164, 171–188; multiple facets of, 8; national, 22; naturalization of, 164–170; previous research on, 74–83, 85–87, 90; racial, 10, 11, 14, 20, 22, 62–65, 68, 71, 105–119, 121–126; sexual, 108; transnationality, 81, 104, 151, 159, 183–186. *See also* racial identity
"I Have a Dream" speech (King), 123
IKAA Gatherings, 37–38
immigration: adoptees as child migrants, 166; adoptees insulated from other immigrant communities, 169; adoption as form of, 1, 11, 152–154, 168–169; Asian exclusion, 1, 45; encounters with Asian immigrants, 109; of non-adopted Koreans, 44; policies favoring transnational adoption, 45–46, 52–57, 70, 153–154, 164–166, 187–188; and racialization of immigrant groups, 127; and rejection of immigrant identity, 168; restrictions after September 11, 2001, 166–167; Scandinavian and German ethnic, 101; Vietnamese, 134–135, 168. *See also* naturalization
Immigration and Nationality Act (1961), 52
Immigration and Nationality Act (1965), 52–53
Indian Child Welfare Act (1978), 80, 95, 189
Indian Ocean tsunami (2004), 189
Indian transracial adoption. *See* Native American transracial adoption
individualism, 132
infantilization, 4, 103
infertility, 94
International Korean Adoptee Associations (IKAA) Gatherings of Korean Adoptees: *See* IKAA Gatherings
International Social Service, 53–54, 73
Internet, 22, 31, 36
invisibility. *See* racial invisibility
isolation. *See* racial isolation

Jackson, Barbara, 75, 84
Jackson, Henry, 55
Jacobson, Heather, 100, 130
Jacobson, Matthew Frye, 127
Japan: adoption from, 53; ethnic Koreans in, 163, 107
Japanese Americans, 142
Jerng, Mark, 9, 81
Jim Crow laws, 123
Jin, Wen, 98
Johnson, James Weldon, 122
Johnson, P. R., 75, 86
Jones, Charles, 75
Jones, Maggie, 189
journalism, 1–9, 14, 36, 41, 43, 54, 58–60, 71, 74, 99, 189

Kaisen, Jane Jin, 191
Kennedy, Elizabeth Lapovsky, 27
Khan, Shahnaz, 34
Khmer, 127
Kim, B. S., 75, 83
Kim, Dong Soo, 74, 82, 83
Kim, Eleana, 37, 43, 59
Kim, Grace, 140
Kim, Oh Myo, 100
Kim, S. P., 75, 83
King, Dr. Martin Luther, 123
Korea: and adoptee identity formation, 150–157, 164, 171–188; adoptees' memories of, 47–51, 179; adoptees returning to, 8, 12, 14, 30, 155–190; attitudes toward adoptees, 185–186; class distinctions in, 176; dual citizenship, 162–163; family registry (*hojeok*), 163–164;

Korea (continued)
  government role in transnational adoption, 45; IKAA Gatherings, 37–38; legislative proposal to end foreign adoption, 147; limits on adoption, 190; as model of transnational adoption practice, 45; nationalism, 177; news coverage of, 1–11; oral histories collected in, 25, 47, 101, 150; relationship with United States, 11, 44–45; social changes following Korean War, 45; visas available to adoptees, 162–164; visits by adoptees, 30, 155, 100
Korean American communities, 101, 179
Korean language, 147, 150–151, 156, 171–178, 186
Korean War: children orphaned by, 1–11; in context of Cold War, 42; and origins of Korean adoption, 42–46; refugees, 44, 12, 41, 59, 102
Krieger, Susan, 27

Lee, Erika, 152, 165–166
Lee, Richard, 83, 100, 135, 144
Lee, Robert, 152, 187
legislators. *See* U.S. Congress
Li, Guofang, 128
Liem, Ramsay, 42
Life (magazine), 59
literature. *See* art and cultural production
Loewen, James, 127
Long Yang Club, 108
loss, 7, 9, 81, 84–85, 90–91
Lutheran Social Services, 102
Lynn, Joy (Chun Cha), 2

Manalansan, Martin, 19
Marine Battleground (film), 44
marketing of international adoption, 99
Marre, Diana, 165
marriage, 47, 181–183
McCall's (magazine), 59
McDonald, Janis, 145
McRoy, Ruth, 75, 86–87, 89
Meier, Dani, 140
mental health, 32, 128, 136–137, 140, 161
methodology. *See* ethnographic method; oral histories; research
military. *See* Korean War; U.S. military
Minnesota, 4, 10, 24, 46–47, 92, 101–104, 116, 143
Minnesota Adopted Koreans (adoptee organization), 103
Mission over Korea (film), 44
mixed-race adoptees, 10, 15, 43–45, 48–51, 56, 61–63
model minority image, 127–131, 144
Morris, Wayne, 54
motherland tours, 155
multiculturalism: and adoptee identity, 64, 100, 104; and adoption policy and practice, 6, 14–15, 92, 98–99; in adoptive families, 132; in American and Korean societies, 157; in American immigration, 153; critiques of, 13, 99, 119–120, 123, 125; and experiences of racism, 111, 116; forms of, 98–99; history of, 97–100; mainstream embrace of, 10; neoliberal conception of, 192; transracial adoption in, 14–15; versions of, 97–100, 123
Multiethnic Placement Act (1994), 96
Myers, Kit, 128

National Association for Korean Schools, 96
National Association of Black Social Workers, 80, 82, 88, 94
Native American transracial adoption, 74, 77, 85–86, 88, 93–95, 189
native informant, 33
naturalization, 52–53, 56, 108, 166–169, 187
newspapers. *See* journalism
North American Council on Adoptable Children, 94

O'Brien, Eileen, 129
Office of Children's Issues, 167
Ogan, Sergeant, 3
Oh, Arissa, 44
Oh, David, 98, 119, 192
Okihiro, Gary, 20
one-drop rule, 127
Ong, Aiwha, 127–128
Operation Babylift, 3
opposition to transracial adoption, 95–96
oral histories: on birth search, 157–162; on dating and sexuality, 181–183; on encounters with Asian Americans, 107–110; of "first-generation" adoptees, 46–71; on identity formation, 104–107, 133–134; in Korea, 150–188; methodology, 11–12, 17–40; in Minnesota, 101–119; of non-adopted Korean Americans, 44; in Pacific Northwest, 25, 46–71
Oregon. *See* Pacific Northwest
orphan trains, 102
orphanages, 2, 48–50, 54, 59
orphans, 1, 2, 43, 44, 44
Overseas Koreans Foundation, 155, 157–158

Pacific Northwest, oral histories collected in, 25, 46–71
Palacios, Jesús, 77
parenting by adoptees, 47, 64
parents. *See* adoptive families; birth families
passing. *See* racial passing
patriotism, 51, 53, 125
performing arts, racism in casting, 115
Perry, Twila, 132
Pickus, Noah, 168
Pierce, Bob, 43
Portes, Alejandro, 168
postcolonial theory, 73, 89
postmodernism, 34
postracialism, 98–99, 119–120
Potter, Sarah, 65
Prébin, Elise, 180

prostitution, 48, 61, 66, 90
proxy adoption, 53–54, 100

racelessness, 10, 82
racial etiquette, 120, 135–137, 144–148
racial exceptionalism: transracial adoptees as exceptional subjects, 6, 13, 42, 65–71; in U.S. immigration, 45, 53–54, 154
racial hierarchies, 46, 126–130, 133–140, 148, 152, 175
racial identity: activist movements, 125; adoptee self-perception, 10, 70, 119, 134; adoptees as "White" Koreans, 121–149; Asian American racialization, 127–131; changes in, 136, 138, 140, 142; and dating, 68; as distinct from cultural identity, 18, 140; enforcement of, 123; experiences influencing identity formation, 105–120; flexibility of, 133–145; hybridity, 122, 124, 126, 140–149, 183; and lack of personal knowledge, 61; methods of defining, 125; multiple ethnic or racial identities, 19, 22; parental perceptions of, 78–79; popular perceptions of Korean adoptees, 7, 46; in previous adoption research, 78–83, 85–87, 90, 100; social enforcement of, 121–123, 143. *See also* identity formation; racial invisibility; racism
racial isolation, 14, 55, 58–65, 70, 84, 92, 102, 104–105, 116–119, 141, 153
racialization: of African Americans, 122; of Asian Americans, 127, 132, 181; in contemporary multiculturalism, 99, 148; gender as factor in, 181; influence of immigration statuson, 166; of transracial adoptees, 67, 104–107, 111–116, 121–145, 166; in transracial adoption, 9–10, 85
racial passing: in Korea, 174; by Korean adoptees, 121–126; legal structures encouraging, 122.
racial stereotypes: of Asian Americans, 14, 109, 115, 127–129; coping strategies, 121; held by transracially adopted children, 86–87; model minority, 95, 128, 130, 144; and racial visibility, 123–125; stereotype threat, 10, 70, 124
racial visibility/invisibility, 121–133, 136, 145, 155
racism: adoption as antiracism, 6, 9, 83, 85; adoptive parents' responses to, 94, 113; anti-immigrant sentiment, 169; by Asian Americans, 138; experienced by adoptees, 14–15, 28–29, 65–70, 85–87, 104, 106–107, 111–120, 134, 138–139; in adoption policy, 95–99; in adoptive families, 9, 28–29, 112, 169; influence on identity formation, 103; institutional, 6, 98, 123, 177; internalized, 134–135, 169, 177; Jim Crow laws, 123; in Korea, 139, 175–177, 186; in neoliberalism, 98–100, 192; not addressed by multiculturalism, 90, 92, 94, 100, 119–120, 121–124, 132; in performing arts, 115
"rainbow family," 99

rape, 50, 61
Refugee-Escapee Act (1957), 52
Refugee Relief Act (1955), 52
Reichwald, Reed, 100
Reinharz, Shulamit, 27
reproductive surrogacy, 190, 193
reproductive technologies, 93–94
research: ethnographic, 9, 11–14, 17–40; methodological issues, 17–40, 76; native informants, 33; social work, 3, 20, 42, 71, 72–92. *See also* oral histories
Rhee, Syngman, 59
Ri, Kang Koo, 59
Roberts, Dorothy, 94
Root, Maria, 142
Rumbaut, Ruben, 168
Russia, ethnic Koreans in, 163

Scandinavia, cultural values favoring adoption, 100–102
schools, 86, 105, 106, 113–120, 134
Second World War: origins of proxy adoption in, 53, 66, 93; as precursor to Cold War, 42
self-esteem, 81
Selman, Peter, 73, 191
Seoul, South Korea, 25, 139, 150, 170, 171
sexuality, 18, 108, 181–183
Shapiro, Deborah, 74, 80
Shiao, Jiannbin, 9, 140, 181
Shibusawa, Naoko, 152
Shireman, J. F., 75, 86
Silverman, Arnold, 75, 80
Simon, Rita, 72, 74, 75, 77–80, 82–89
Skreen, Chet, 3
Smith, Linda Tuhiwai, 31
social work: debate about transracial adoption, 95; race matching in adoption, 65; research, 13, 20, 42, 71, 72–92
Song, Miri, 126–127, 143
South Korea. *See* Korea
Spain, 165
Spickard, Paul, 19
Steele, Claude, 124
The Steel Helmet (film), 44
Stephan, Walter, 142
stereotype threat, 124
Stueck, William, 42
substance abuse: by adoptees, 84, 157; as reason for child removal, 97, 140–141
success of adoptions, 7, 13, 15, 18, 31, 71, 75, 79–81, 83, 87, 90
surrogacy. *See* reproductive surrogacy
Suyemoto, Karen, 140
Sweden, 100–102

Tessler, Richard, 130
Tokyo Rose, 66
Torres, Rodolfo, 123
transnationalism, 151–154, 183–186
transparency, in research, 17
transracial adoption paradox, 135, 144
Tuan, Mia, 9, 127–129, 140, 181

Turner, Castellano, 140
Twine, France Winddance, 19, 131–132, 135

United Nations: Hague Adoption Convention, 190, 192; role in Korean War, 42
U.S. Citizenship and Immigration Services, 165, 167, 169
U.S. Congress, 52, 54–55, 89
U.S. Indian Adoption Project, 93
U.S. military: as child rescuers, 2, 3, 4, 6; as fathers of mixed-race children, 45, 48, 50–51, 56; Korean adoptees serving in, 170; Korean children as mascots for, 2, 44, 59

Vallejo Peña, Edlun, 142
Verma, Gajendra, 75
Vietnam War, 3
Vietnamese immigrants, 134–135, 168
visibility. *See* racial invisibility

Wang, Lishing, 128
War Hunt (film), 44
Washington State. *See* Pacific Northwest
Waters, Mary, 126
Watson, K. W., 75, 86
Wattenberg, Shirley, 75, 79
Web. *See* Internet

Webster (television program), 99
Wei, William, 129
Whiteness: of adoption industry, 76; of adoptive parents, 76, 89, 119, 133; advantages of, 124; analogous to Americanness, 130; as dominant discourse, 123; and ethnic choices, 126; goal of assimilationism, 18; as performance, 122–123; in transracial adoptee identity, 10, 14, 106, 119, 131–146, 177
White privilege, 4, 79, 87, 123, 131, 135, 143–144
White Stephan, Cookie, 142
Williams, Norma, 31
Willinsky, John, 99
women's studies, 34
Woods, Tiger, 122
World Vision International, 43, 49
World War II. *See* Second World War

Yngvesson, Barbara, 83, 100
Young, Loretta, 75
The Young and the Brave (film), 44
Yu, Henry, 130

Zastrow, Charles, 74, 77–80
Zurcher, Louis, 75, 86–87

ABOUT THE AUTHOR

KIM PARK NELSON is an associate professor of American Multicultural Studies at Minnesota State University at Moorhead. She is a scholar and educator of Korean adoption, Asian American studies, American race relations, and American studies. Park Nelson was the three-time lead organizer for the International Symposia on Korean Adoption Studies, which took place in Seoul in 2007, 2010, and 2013.

CPSIA information can be obtained
at www.ICGtesting.com
Printed in the USA
LVOW05s1330250118
563986LV00033B/579/P